The Writings of Kōda Aya

A STUDY OF THE EAST ASIAN INSTITUTE

Studies of the East Asian Institute, Columbia University
The East Asian Institute is Columbia University's center for research, publication, and teaching on modern East Asia. The Studies of the East Asian Institute were inaugurated in 1962 to bring to a wider public the results of significant new research on modern and contemporary East Asia.

THE WRITINGS OF

Kōda Aya

A JAPANESE

LITERARY

DAUGHTER

ALAN M. TANSMAN

YALE UNIVERSITY PRESS

NEW HAVEN & LONDON

Translations of the following works by Kōda
Aya appear here courtesy of Tama Aoki:
"Hina" © 1955, "Kami" © 1951, "Kunshō" ©
1949, "Kuroi suso" © 1955, *Nagareru*
(extracts) © 1956, and *Tō* (extracts) © 1965.

Designed by Nancy Ovedovitz and set in
Galliard type by Keystone Typesetting, Inc.
Printed in the United States of America by
Edwards Brothers, Ann Arbor, Michigan.

*Library of Congress Cataloging-in-Publication
Data*

Tansman, Alan M., 1960–
    The writings of Kōda Aya, a Japanese
    literary daughter / Alan M. Tansman.
    p.   cm. — (Study of the East Asian
    Institute)
    Includes translation of A. Kōda's works.
    Includes bibliographical references and
    index.
    ISBN 0-300-05724-5
    1. Kōda, Aya, 1904–   —Criticism and
interpretation.   I. Kōda Aya, 1904–   —
Selections.   English.   1993.   II. Title.
III. Series: Studies of the East Asian Institute.
PL832.O33z85   1993
895.6′444—dc20   92-33630
                                             CIP
A catalogue record for this book is available
from the British Library.

The paper in this book meets the guidelines
for permanence and durability of the
Committee on Production Guidelines for
Book Longevity of the Council on Library
Resources.

10   9   8   7   6   5   4   3   2   1

To the memory of my father

Contents

ACKNOWLEDGMENTS ix

1 CREATING A PERSONA 1

2 MASTERING THE PAST 16

3 LESSONS OF THE FATHER 43

4 WAR AND RECOVERY 57

5 A WORLD OF OBJECTS 70

6 *FLOWING* 102

7 RETURN TO THE FATHER 136

APPENDIX: FOUR STORIES 153

NOTES 193

INDEX 211

Acknowledgments

Many individuals have helped in the writing of this book. For incisive readings of the manuscript at various stages I thank Robert Danly, Kenneth Haltman, Edward Kamens, Laura Katzman, Louisa Rubinfien, Ann Sherif, Dennis Washburn, and Elizabeth Wolstein. For their detailed comments and valuable advice on the manuscript I especially thank Ken Ito and Paul Anderer. For her meticulous and patient editing I thank Mary Pasti of Yale University Press. For her intellectual encouragement and guidance over many years I thank Carol Gluck. For their administrative and personal support at Dartmouth College I thank the Asian Studies Program faculty and staff, especially Shalom Goldman and Pat Henricks.

I began this book as a dissertation at Yale University, where I was supported by Sumitomo and Yale Prize fellowships. A Japan Foundation Fellowship allowed me a year in Japan, where I had the privilege of working with Eto Jun, to whom I am deeply indebted for his unstinting commitment of time and learning.

I owe my most profound gratitude to Edwin McClellan, who taught me how to read Japanese literature.

Note: Japanese names appear in Japanese style, family name first. In Japan writers are often referred to by their given name, as is the case with Aya.

CHAPTER 1

Creating

a Persona

Living a life that spanned the twentieth century in Japan—as Kōda Aya (1904–1990) did—meant being exposed to a whirlwind of economic and social change. As a woman, Aya must have experienced shifts in social life that rocked her understanding of personal and social identity. That she was an artist as well—separated from her traditional female role by her choice of profession—would have made her more keenly aware of the increasing distance between personal desire and societal expectation.

Kōda Aya struggled with the personal and social restrictions placed upon her as a woman and as a writer in modern Japan. As the daughter of the literary giant Kōda Rohan, Aya was educated in seemingly opposed ways: to be a proper housewife and mother and to possess a sharp literary vision. Inevitably, she experienced life with her father as a burden but also as a source of sustenance. Out of this dual inheritance Aya created a literature that allowed her to accommodate her desires to the demands of society as her father imparted them. She found a space of verbal and imaginative freedom by creating personae and domestic metaphors that both endorsed her given roles and distanced her from them.

But what can we make of the fact that the demands of society seem largely absent in Aya's writing, that she was a woman writer who was apparently uninterested in the social, economic, and literary battles raging about her, especially those over the question of the modern woman in a new Japan? Could she so successfully shield herself from the outside world that society remained largely irrelevant? Where did her private life intersect the world outside? In what clear or refracted way did her contacts with public life appear in her writing? How can Aya's personal drama illuminate the difficult interaction between individual identity and changing social roles that so marks Japan's twentieth century?

In the case of Kōda Aya, the most sequestered of lives intersected with the most public and explosive of issues, the problem of gender in the modern world. The discourse of modernity in Japanese intellectual life employs the language of gender: that which resists the modern—the anti-rational, non-Western, native core of Japanese culture—has figured in the culture as feminine, and femininity has been the trope used to evoke the authentic, unsullied native genius. "Feminine" literature—where *feminine* implies subtle gradations of psychological states and evocations of "Japanese" beauty within a confined sphere—has been invoked as an alternative to the baleful effects of a Western, male, overly intellectual, and unrooted modern sensibility.

Although the link between modernity and gender is not unique to Japan, it takes a distinct shape there. If almost all Japanese intellectual life in the twentieth century has been a defense and a critique of modernity, the scripting of femininity as premodern, and non-Western, suggests that women may be more central to this discourse in Japan than in other countries. During the mid-1950s in Japan—a period of social transformation and cultural retrenchment, of rapid change and increasing cultural nostalgia—Kōda Aya's writing was a touchstone for culture critics searching for the "premodern," "feminine," quintessentially "Japanese" qualities of their culture. Aya's writing thus elicits broad questions about modernity and gender in modern Japanese intellectual life, illuminating their interaction at a specific moment in postwar Japan.

Aya's career also exemplifies how literary and social values play off one another, at times in mutual support, at times in apparent contradiction. How does a woman's social status relate to her literary status as a woman writer? If femininity as an aesthetic attribute was a term of high praise for a writer like Aya, femininity as a cultural attribute involved coping with restrictions that might have prevented a woman from writing. Aya lived in a culture—and in a household—that valorized her literary sensibilities while it threatened to squelch her artistic impulses. Her career shows the tension between feminine social and literary status and the possibilities for literary creation, given that status.

Aya tried to leave the shadow thrown by her father, the literary giant

Kōda Rohan, in order to create a personal literary voice, to transform her allotted social space and language.[1] The notion of transformation is an important key to understanding Aya's career and to examining the question of personal and social identity. It also allows us to see Aya as engaged in her time, not just her private battles. Her writing involved a transformation of identity, but it also shows how one writer picked up the pieces left by the Pacific War (1931–1945) and turned them into sources of creativity. Many of her literary obsessions rest on the notion of transformation: she was obsessed with material objects and the literary attempt to instill them with meaning; with the transformation of objects into living forces and the evolution of living forces into disembodied things; with the dislocations caused by tragic events and the world of memory into which these events threw their participants. These obsessions may not have been created by the war or even by the death of Aya's father, but they were certainly fostered by these experiences.

The war and its aftermath exerted a powerful influence on Aya's imagination. The greater societal experience was echoed in her father's death and thus resonated all the more powerfully; the coincidence of personal and public trauma determined the shape her narratives took. Death and destruction formed Aya's career as a writer and remained at the core of her imagination.

The experiences and events that filled Aya's life until her emergence as a writer at age forty-three do not make for dramatic biography, nor do they make it easy to refute the image of her as a passive, domestic woman. She lived a private life, her passions were personal, her interests confined to the narrow world of her family and home. She spent her energy in the domestic sphere, rarely reaching out for ways to channel her intelligence and creativity. She was born, married, and divorced; she graduated from a women's college, attended sewing school, and ran a small sake shop. We gather from her memoirs that she mostly spent her years cleaning, serving, and nurturing. She tended to the personal needs of her father, who had been famous since the final decades of the nineteenth century, and acted as hostess to the literary types who flowed endlessly in and out of his house.

Her transformation of those years of domestic service into a beautiful and philosophically attentive literature, her phoenixlike change from little woman in the kitchen to independent and authoritative literary stylist, all of this must be discussed to understand her career, which sparked out of obscurity in 1947 and in a span of ten years brought a shower of praise that turned her into a publicly and critically recognized writer. In 1949 she published articles in various journals and began a daily newspaper column; by 1958 she had won two literary awards (she would win more), had seen a novel made into an award-winning film, and, with the publication of her collected works, had secured a position in the literary world as well as in the culture at large.[2]

It would be difficult to find signs of a language being shaped or a literature being formed in Aya's first four decades. Her career as a writer began late in life, and as she would insist throughout her career with almost perverse humility, her first published pieces—remembrances of her famous father commissioned by high-brow literary journals such as *Chūō kōron*—were neither the ripened words of a longtime literary apprentice nor the works of an aspiring writer taking a new direction. Aya, it would seem, made her debut in the public world of letters fully formed (springing, some said, full-clad from her father's head). Her career was not marked by public acts nor by an attempt to present herself as a public figure; even after she became nationally recognized, she maintained her privacy and kept her distance from the literary world. She seldom, if ever, explicitly discussed literature except to insist that her writing grew, willy-nilly, out of inexperience and ineptitude.

Aya incorporated the rhetoric of personal inadequacy into her literary persona by using the language of her environment, the language of restrictive and confining domesticity. She created a self-identity that made the act of writing tenable: if she was to speak at all, it would be as a passive woman. She did not risk open rebellion against her father or the social strictures of her world. She described her writings as "the grumbling of a woman blinded by the light of death" and insisted to her readers that "even in a house of learning the blind are born."[3] She established her own identity by self-denial; she asserted herself while hiding from self-assertion. As with Emily Dickinson, "her ostensible passivity . . . created and defended a safe place within which her mind could be active and free."[4]

Women writing in and against a patriarchal culture are not the only ones to cloak themselves in a less intellectual or less socially elevated persona as a literary strategy. The creation of a Jewish literature in nineteenth-century Europe depended on the finesse of educated, Europeanized intellectuals in disguising themselves as ignorant, uneducated shtetl Jews, as narrators as well as authors. In the persona of a tailor, say, a narrator could comment on questions of literary form or cultural crisis analogically in a discussion of the tailoring of a length of fabric, much as Aya raised similar questions by writing about the preparation of food or the proper way to clean a house.[5]

In Aya's short story "Kitchen Sounds" ("Daidokoro no oto," 1962), for example, judgments of a woman's quality are made according to the sounds she generates in the preparation of food. Sankichi, the aging and ill owner of a small dining establishment, listens from his bed to his wife's slicing and chopping. In each swish and thunk he interprets her emotional state and assesses her as a cook and as a woman.

Married twice before, Sankichi dismissed each wife after learning her particular personality flaw. One ate too much and moved about the kitchen too sluggishly, one was too exuberant and had no patience for proper kitchen work; each earned his final disdain through the irritating or unpleasant sounds she made in the kitchen. Aki, his present wife, suffers under the weight of her husband's constant minute observation. She is aware of her husband's belief that even women trained to work in a proper or refined way will one day be undermined by their natural slovenliness. When the inevitable occurs, he tells her, "The parent who worked so hard to educate his child winds up a failure, and the child, too, loses out."[6]

Aya wrote "Kitchen Sounds" fifteen years after her debut as a writer. Over those years she created a language of domestic metaphor culled from her personal history and drawn from within the boundaries of her life as a woman. With this language she engaged various literary, intellectual, and existential themes; in "Kitchen Sounds" she deals with perhaps the most obsessive theme of her writing, the possibility of finding a place—away from the scrutiny of authority—that allows for imaginative freedom. The kitchen is one such place, but the constant gaze of the husband exemplifies the anxiety Aya always felt about her own independence as a writer.

In virtually all her work Aya writes about the home or similarly confined spaces, depicting domestic life and describing women who function as dutiful daughters, housewives, maids, or nurses. Yet Aya rarely expresses overt hostility toward the society that placed women in these subservient, nurturing roles. In fact, she endorsed traditional female roles, although her own struggle to become a writer belies her full acceptance. The respect she gave these women—she likened a maid to a doctor of philosophy (*KAZ* 4: 242)—and the complexity she lent to their straitened domestic lives derived from conflicting impulses: she condoned their assigned social status but desired to expand it in creative ways.

Japanese society offered Aya a set of values and expectations by which to live her life, a social script that she accepted as her guide.[7] But Aya used the inherited sense of who she was and how she should act—as daughter, wife, and mother—to sustain a creative identity that she chose for herself. She accommodated the powerful set of societal expectations to her own creative impulses. Like African American artists who wore the mask of the minstrel and expressed their creative impulses from behind it, Aya used limiting circumstances to achieve creative freedom.[8]

In the potentially grim and claustrophobic confines of the home, Aya found a world replete with opportunities for artistic expression and human endeavor. In the image she created of herself as a writer, in the scenes she chose to depict, and in the stories she chose to tell, Aya posed as deprived, passive, inadequate, and innocent—outwardly corresponding to the expectations held of her as a woman. She wrote about a social space closed off from the public, male world. She used her sense of herself as an unworthy child, quaking before a looming father, to develop the silently observant and seemingly passive literary personae of her fiction, who often seem to narrate scenes as if peering around corners.

Aya waged a war with her environment, using words as her weapons. She was provided with the weapons by her father, who also taught her the Neo-Confucian precept that to perceive the essence of everyday things led to mastery over them. Her philosophical training made her writing an act of "symbolic inversion," a term alien to Aya herself but which Barbara Babcock defines as "any act of expressive behavior which converts, contradicts, abrogates, or in some fashion presents an alternative to commonly held cultural codes, values, and norms."[9] Aya's works can be seen as a symbolic attempt to overcome the contradiction between her social parameters and her personal desires. She overcame it not by rejecting either aspect of her life but by joining them, by rewriting her domestic sphere into an aesthetically and existentially enriching world.

The notion of inversion described here is neither new to critical discourse nor peculiar to Japanese women writers. But Aya's apparent compliance with social convention was so extreme that the strategies employed to convert convention acquired subtle shadings. Aya is of particular interest for another reason: she wrote in a culture in which the valorization of feminine aesthetic values invited an adoption of oppressive social norms. In Aya's writing a thin line separates capitulation to the language of convention from manipulation of that language in subjectively expansive ways.

Perhaps this thin line has led Aya's readers to ignore the transformational quality of her work. Some critics have lamented the constricted lives that Japanese women writers have been forced to lead, but more often this restriction is read as a blessing, a necessary and not unfortunate circumstance that has given rise to a feminine literary aesthetic, legitimized by the writings of the tenth- and eleventh-century Heian court. Aya's stories have been seen as an antidote to the overintellectuality of male writers, as the preservation of a literary aesthetic expressing the essence of the Japanese spirit (canonized as feminine since at least the time of the eighteenth-century philologist Motoori Norinaga); and although her work has been faulted for lacking intellectual rigor, narrative structure, and objective character development, she has been lauded for her ability to write from the recesses of her body, instead of her mind, to know with her skin and feel with her entire being, to figuratively write herself onto the page.[10]

This elevation, by male critics, of the feminine values of restraint and beauty has not been limited to aesthetic matters; it has spilled over into social life and has been evoked by critics of modernity to affirm and dignify traditional values and to ensure an acceptance of conventional gender arrangements. Aya's memoirs and fiction have been applauded for their eloquent expression of the "Japanese spirit" and for their preservation of traditional values, both aesthetic and social, at a time—the 1950s—when those values were thought to be eroding. The praise has come in part because Aya writes almost exclusively about women who accept their roles as dutiful daughters, housewives, and maids and reveals in her memoirs a persona similarly accepting of a confined and passive status.

Praise for Aya also refers to her language, which, according to conservative male critics, has rejuvenated traditional, "feminine" notions of beauty. At one end of the spectrum is the critic Akiyama Shun, whose praise of Aya epitomizes the intersection of femininity and modernity: "Women's literature has continually clarified for us that certain something about our traditional Japanese disposition that is being undermined by radical modernization."[11] Akiyama looks to women's writing for salvation, for an alternative to a "modern" literature that emphasizes intellectual questions of self, society, and politics, for the salvaging of the ineffable, essential core of Japanese literature. Akiyama considers that literature written by men has been adolescent, obsessed with youthful questions of intellectual identity, and that women's literature has been adult, concerned with questions of literary style and linguistic nuance.

Akiyama is quick to point out, however, that women's writing does not lack intellectual depth; rather, the authors' intellectual energy is expended on aesthetic matters. Because women have avoided asking overtly political, "male" questions, they have likewise avoided a foreign conceptual vocabulary and been able to express the essence of Japaneseness, of "life" and "reality" untouched by artificial intellectual systems. The association of women's writing with what is natural and native receives even greater emphasis in Okuno Takeo's analysis; he argues that literature by women goes deeper than the typical male explorations of politics, morals, and philosophy and possesses a more profound "sensibility of naturalness and physicality."[12]

Critics like Okuno locate the naturalness and physicality of Aya's writing in her plentiful use of onomatopoetic and mimetic words. Such words are examples, in Okuno's view, of Aya's ability to transform perceptions into language unadulterated by intellectual machinations, and of her refusal (or inability) to write narration that describes and analyzes motivation and action with detachment and precision. Rather, the voice of Aya's narrator melds with the voice of each and every character; the narrator's perceptions merge with others'. According to another critic, "It is natural that Aya's point of departure as a prose stylist was her intrinsic feminine attitude . . . of sensuality."[13]

The style that pleased certain male critics frustrated some women writers. There is, for example, the criticism leveled by the politically oriented novelist Hirabayashi Taiko, one of a number of political women novelists who wrote before and after the Pacific War about the conflict between a woman and society, the dissatisfaction in women's lives, and the struggle for identity in a repressive society. Hirabayashi was disturbed that Aya was proffered awards at the same time that Nogami Yaeko was hailed for her overtly political work. Aya, claims Hirabayashi, deals only with description and explanation, never with ideas or solutions. Because Aya does not challenge the accepted notions of women's place, she has nothing to teach other women; no wonder most of her supporters are men. Aya's lack of political engagement, argues Hirabayashi, accounts for the praise lavished on her. Her prose is beautiful and nuanced, and her depiction of the worlds of women emotionally evocative, but her writings lack intellectual challenge. Little about her directly threatens stereotypes of women's proper place, their acceptance of that place, or their essentially emotional and unintellectual reaction to the world around them. Aya, in other words, confirms what men think—and hope—women are.[14]

That critics as disparate in their ethical concerns and aesthetic sensibilities as Hirabayashi Taiko and Akiyama Shun have appreciated only one aspect of Aya's literary strategy—each has, in his or her way, pigeonholed her as a feminine writer—says as much about their own ideological blinders as it does about the subtlety of Aya's writing. Critics have failed to notice her translation of restrictive and traditionally feminine spaces into a literature that subverts pat conceptions of gender and simplistic notions of narrowness and preciosity. Neither critical camp has been able to see the aspects of her writing that challenge the hallowed categories of tradition and femininity.

This critical blindness results in part from the peculiar place "women's literature" (*joryū bungaku*) occupies in the Japanese literary tradition. The most prestigious works in Japanese prose fiction are those of the Heian court women of the tenth and eleventh centuries. Although women themselves were more restricted in their literary pursuits after the eclipse of the court in the twelfth century and did not begin to write again in significant numbers until the twentieth century, the works of these Heian women has always occupied a central place in Japanese letters. Japanese literary history thus offers the interesting case of a female canon embedded in a male literary culture.[15] Even though social and economic pressures have prevented many women from writing, even into the middle of the twentieth century, for women to write has not been as daring an act in Japan as in the West. As Catharine Stimpson has observed: "Because the West has so masculinized the creation of public culture, for a woman to write at all seriously has been, in some degree, an act of defiance."[16] Without disregarding the quality of defiance that does exist in much Japanese women's writing, it can be said that literary pursuits have been more open to women in Japan. Their writing has been marginalized, but they have still been able to fit into a respected literary category and claim authorship of a prestigious portion of public culture.

By enshrining women's writing, critics have sequestered it, as the critical blindness to Aya's works demonstrates. Although the literary productions of the Heian court have been a major touchstone in matters of literary criticism, women's writing has been a genre peripheral to mainstream Japanese literature. In modern criticism, writing by women is praised in the exact terms used to condemn mainstream Japanese fiction—as narrow in scope, obsessively cloistered in its descriptions of psychological interiority, and unable to transcend emotion and thus adequately transmit the texture of social and political life.

Aya's writing has been cited as evidence for the existence of feminine literary qualities, but a close reading of her works finds that she actually confounds conventional notions of women's literary and social status, resisting the oppositions between men's and women's writing so often formulated by critics with regard to her work. Her use of literary inversion further complicates the relation of her writing to her social and literary status as a "woman writer."

Aya generally shied away from the expansive to embrace the intimate. In modern Japanese literature as a whole, which is not known for spectacular flights of the imagination (Christ descending from the sky or lone heroes battling great whales), Aya's narrowness is not anomalous or noteworthy. But her work lacks even the limited expansiveness to be found in some Japanese writers: she presents no ships sailing for America, as Arishima Takeo does, no men seeking existential solace high in the mountains, as

Shiga Naoya does. Her range is more reminiscent of the canonical works of the Heian writers, who almost willfully avoided writing of the life outside their own apartments—life over which they had no control—in order to focus on a world in which they felt sure of their judgments and perceptions. Like these women—and like the nineteenth-century American writer Sarah Orne Jewett—Aya suspended "the discourses of the great and busy world" by constructing a verbal "hermitage" and "scripting a private prayer."[17]

In a study of nineteenth-century British and American women's writings, Sandra Gilbert and Susan Gubar examine the dissatisfaction many women writers have felt within the tight spaces allotted to them. The imagery of enclosure, they say, "reflects the woman writer's own discomfort, her sense of powerlessness, her fear that she inhabits alien and incomprehensible places." Mary Mason, too, has found a quality of psychological suffocation in American women's autobiographies, which she calls "grim tale[s] of woman's claustrophobia when she cannot get out of the prison of the self." Certain American women writers have found the domestic sphere a place of suffocation and anger. The poet Anne Stevenson writes, "The mood of efficiency, of checking things off the list as you tear through a day's shopping, washing, cleaning, mending and so forth, is totally destructive of the slightly bored melancholy which nurtures my imagination. . . . I dread, and have always dreaded, that marriage, a home and family, would sap my creative energies, that they would devour my time and my personality, that they would, in a venomous way I can't explain, use me up."[18]

Aya's tale is neither grim nor claustrophobic, even though she, too, had an inadequate outlet for her creative energies. She chose to use the parameters drawn around her, if only imaginatively. She felt, like Edith Wharton, that "the creative mind thrives on a reduced diet."[19]

Trained by her father from an early age in the domestic arts and removed until late in life from the literary world and the trials of becoming a writer, Aya relied less on writing to establish her identity than did some of her contemporaries. For the novelist Sata Ineko, for example, the conflict between the desire to be a writer and the pressure to be a wife was never fully resolved. Aya was not haunted, like Sata, with the fear of losing her femininity in the struggle to be an artist. She did not have to choose between her socially defined self and her artistic self because she found a way of combining the two in her art.

For many women writers of Aya's generation, the baptism into the world of letters, unlike her own, was political. Hirabayashi Taiko, Hayashi Fumiko, Nogami Yaeko, Tsuboi Sakae, Miyamoto Yuriko, and Sata Ineko—who constitute the first wave of women writers to appear since the eleventh century—were all nurtured in the proletarian literary movement of the 1920s. For them, writing was a political act, an assessment of their role in society, an attempt to forge a new identity, and the presentation of an exemplary life to readers. Questions of love, marriage, career, and political involvement were urgent, and many of their novels—such as Miyamoto's *Nobuko* (1924–1926) and Nogami's *Machiko* (1928–1930)— were semiautobiographical accounts of the difficulties involved in being a woman and becoming a writer. In a novel like Sata's *Crimson* (*Kurenai*, 1936), these problems are never reduced to simple equations of class or gender, although the contradictions—between one's identity as a mother and one's identity as a writer, between the desire to love and be loved by a man and the need to be independent—are at the core of Sata's fiction. We even sense that these contradictions were created by Sata and may never be fully resolved because the story springs from their tension. Sata's novel implies that without the impossibility of having both love and career, there is no battle between individual and society, no proper material for the writer.[20]

Aya can hardly be called a feminist. She rarely gives overt expression to such conflicts as engaged these other women writers, because her concept of herself as a woman and as a writer adhered to the social self supplied by her culture. This overlap of personal and social identities raises doubts about the element of subversion in Aya's writing. Her acceptance of her role can seem to be capitulation, and her accommodation to the language of her father can seem to be complete acceptance of it. Aya's ability to accept inherited notions of herself while continuing to use them as instruments of subjective expression must be questioned.[21] Her memoirs and shorter fictions are open to examination, but it is her masterpiece, *Flowing* (*Nagare-ru*, 1955), and shorter stories written around the same time that offer the most lucid insights into these suspicions. A discussion of these works will show that the strict dichotomy between the social and the personal cannot be upheld and in fact occludes more than it illuminates.

The dichotomy is refuted by a basic assumption guiding this study. While individuals are to a great degree shaped by social norms and pressures, a part of each individual resists invasion from the outside and represents a "residual area of inner freedom."[22] The self is never fully exhausted by socially defined roles; and literature, as an act of power, allows individuals to explore the ways they have been socially constructed and to discover an inner, private zone. In Victor Turner's anthropological formulation, writing can be a "cultural performance" in which writers become aware of the "nature, texture, style, and given meaning of their own lives as members of a sociocultural community." Writing fosters a "reflexive consciousness" of one's social conditioning and allows for not only the discovery but the very creation of a self.[23]

Such ideas may seem old-fashioned in light of structuralist and post-structuralist attacks on the concept of a self existing outside the framework of society or language. Underlying the premise of this study, however, is the assumption that Kōda Aya brought a creative intelligence to her writing, that she grappled with socially imposed values and structures and attempted to write within social and literary categories without being swallowed by them. The word *self,* then, designates the writer's imagination as it works to write itself onto the complex social and linguistic map of its time, where it continues to perform. In Aya's case, this self is no more or less than the persona she created, which moved between social imposition and individual impulse. This persona allowed Aya to stand both inside and apart from her socially created identity, to drape herself in socially approved garments with a touch of personal style.

Yet in Aya's writing, the negotiation between society and self can be so subtle that it becomes obscure. The great similarity between Aya's literary persona and the biographical Aya that we know from other sources has led critics in Japan to ignore the literary invention in her work. They have assumed that the Aya of the memoirs is Aya herself and that her fictional creations are the real Aya in slightly veiled form. Her public personality—as daughter of Kōda Rohan and later author in her own right—might also help explain the critics' habit of finding the real person in the written work. Even though the persona and the person do overlap, no absolute correlation exists between them. All self-presentation involves picking what to say and choosing how to say it and can never exactly coincide with who one is or thinks oneself to be.

This confusion of person and persona can be witnessed in Aya's prose, where the voice of the narrator often flows into the voice of the main character, and the eye surveying the scene from outside merges with the eye of a character observing the scene from within. In the opening of *Flowing,* the recorded perceptions seem to be those of the maid Rika. No personal pronouns are used in the original (in my somewhat literal translation I have kept them to a minimum), and only at the end, when the new maid's reactions are unambiguously transcribed, can we be sure who is speaking.

This was certainly the house, but there was no kitchen door. Where was the entrance?
　　The road was narrow, and people were constantly streaming across it, so that

I felt pressured each time, as if challenged. But I could do nothing about it, so I went and stood in the granite-paved entranceway set deep into the house. A room was right there. A fight didn't seem to be going on, but tinkling, strained voices came drifting out. I waited, but they went on. Careful not to look in too abruptly, I stood off at an angle and slid the lattice door open slightly. Everything inside became absolutely still. A water flea in a gutter came to mind. I quaked and turned into a water flea, when an innocent, lisping voice addressed me.

"Who's there?"

I replied, giving the name of my introducer and explaining that I was a maid there on trial. I cast a glance inside and thought, My, how filthy! So this is the entranceway of a geisha house!

When Rika is referred to in the third person for the first time quite a few pages later, the distance between the narrator and the maid grows; but the reference is abandoned as easily and as suddenly as it appeared, and the distance between Aya's omniscient narrator and the character collapses, leaving us again behind the maid's eyes. This modulation between first and third person continues throughout the novel; two voices mingle and diverge. A shift in voice may occur within a page, a paragraph, even a sentence, with a suddenness that is easily missed.

As one might expect, I am tired. Too tired. Although my lids are heavy, my eyes stay open. Although I am thoroughly exhausted, my nose is wide awake. The unaccustomed smell of cat is disgusting. I try not to listen, but my ears are alert. The broken watch is like a marching army. Why do I want to stay in such an unpleasant house? I turn over in bed, and the newspapers rustle. They're just scraps of paper. How horrible that furnace is. The stars—do I remember them twinkling high in the sky, seen through an opening the size of a tatami mat? The sky lay within the overhanging eaves, which pressed in from every side. Yes, she thought, that's right. It's mysterious, but my place is between these eaves and those eaves. Though unsure why, she felt that the space between the narrow eaves was the freest and most secure and that there was something comforting in being able to face the sky and reach up.[24]

The phrase that changes the passage from a first-person account into a third-person account is *no yō ni omou*, meaning "she thought it was as if," translated here as "she thought." Aya regularly uses this phrase and others like it—"she felt," "she considered," "she sympathized"—at the end of passages detailing Rika's first-person perceptions, thus stepping away from that character to speak again as a narrator outside the scene. Such pivotal phrases help create a style that is partly first person, partly third, flowing in and out of the minds of both character and narrator. Aya allows the language to flow in the stream of Rika's mind, then retreats as if to indicate that the distance between her and her creation is very short but not absolute. Immersion and distancing also characterize Rika's relation to her new world, into which she plunges and in which she desires to be submerged but from which she always maintains her distance.

The linguistic basis of the blending of voices and perspectives in Japanese narrative has been analyzed in general terms by Edward Fowler, who claims that "represented thought cannot be distinguished from direct utterance," that there is no way in Japanese prose fiction to create fictional beings who exist completely independent of a narrator's own thoughts, feelings, and perceptions. No omniscient narrator can aspire to a "universal brokerage of consciousness"; no representation can be made of the inner workings of numerous characters in a fictional world.[25]

Fowler articulates the relationship between narrator and protagonist that is found in *Flowing*; they couple and separate with such frequency and ease that any attempt to distinguish them is futile. But Fowler's claim is too far-reaching to adequately describe Aya's writing, or Japanese literature in general, for the conflation of identities occurs only with the narrator and Rika; and Rika, we come to feel, is like other characters in Aya's stories in being a surrogate for the narrator and, in turn, for Aya herself. In the rest of *Flowing,* the narrative voice allows individual characters—and there are many, including a dog and a cat—to reveal themselves from within. Rika and the narrator observe, describe, and judge, but here, too, the narrator often seems to disappear, leaving behind only Rika and her inner self.

Such narrative movement shows greater complexity than Fowler allows for. It also has a long pedigree, reaching back at least to the eleventh century and Lady Murasaki's *Tale of Genji*. The narrative voice or voices in that great novel allow for the emergence of individual characters and the revelation of how they think as only an omniscient narrator existing outside the fictional world, able to see into all minds, can allow. At the same time, the narrator seems a part of that fictional world, embedded in it and attuned to its workings. The narrator seems, paradoxically, both inside and outside at once. In *Flowing,* as in *Genji,* this narrative trick is accomplished by creating a character through whom the entire sensual world of the fiction flows but whose role in that world is slight enough to allow for her frequent and temporary disappearances from the scene. In *Genji* this character is a lady-in-waiting (*nyōbo*), a woman privy to the details of court life. Aya, too, relies on characters like ladies-in-waiting, though with more conspicuous parts; the maid is an example. The world of *Flowing* comes to us through Rika's eyes, our assessments of it from her mind, but at the turn of a phrase she can slip away to become the object of narration, the vision of another eye. The narrative voice, here as in *Genji,* can be both omniscient and embedded.[26] While such narrative movement reflects the linguistic possibilities and limitations of Japanese prose narrative, it also represents the persona created by Aya in her writing—an obsequious, passive, servile woman who assumes others' problems as her own and allows other voices to mingle with hers.

The difficulty of distinguishing the real Aya from the written Aya is compounded by two extraliterary facts. Because her first writings were autobiographical, by the time she began to write more fictionalized stories, she had a public persona that readers expected to see in her fictional creations; and because she acquiesced so convincingly to societal norms in her writing, because she had so little critical distance from her socialization, she could seem—and does seem to most readers—to be transcribing, not inventing, a life. In truth, however, the mask and its wearer never became one.

CHAPTER 2

Mastering

the Past

Aya's career as a writer began with the death of her father, and much of her creative energy in that career was spent grappling with her position as his daughter. Although her father's influence on her grew weaker as she developed as a writer, it remained the central obsession of her life and a motivation for her writing. In her attempts to record memories of him, then in more rigorously autobiographical pieces, and finally in the stories that fictionalized and generalized her past, Aya claimed more and more independence from her father. Yet she repeatedly came back to his death—the powerful event that unleashed her creativity; she wrote about it directly and indirectly, with great passion and with disciplined calm. As Walter Benjamin has said, "Death is the sanction of everything that the storyteller can tell."[1] Aya borrowed her authority from death. More than that, in writing about her father's death she wrote about her life with him, and in this re-creation of their shared past, she developed the literary persona of her fictional works.

Kōda Rohan was born in 1867. His career as a writer spanned sixty years and included the publication of more than forty volumes of writings. Tsubouchi Shōyō, one of the progenitors of modern Japanese literature, likened him to Leonardo da Vinci in the breadth of his interests and the depth of his scholarship; indeed, Rohan had a range of intellectual pursuits virtually unparalleled in the history of modern Japanese letters.[2] His career has commanded respect bordering on awe. Rohan, like Henry James, is regarded by intellectuals and scholars as a writer's writer: in 1937 he was the first to be awarded the most prestigious national literary award in Japan, the Medal of Culture, and in 1969 a poll of critics and professors placed him behind only Natsume Sōseki (1867–1916) and Mori Ōgai (1862– 1922) in importance as a literary figure. A passage describing a storm in his novel *The Five-Storied Pagoda (Gojū no to,* 1891) is taught to every Japanese student as an example of stylistic genius, and he is anthologized in virtually all collections of Japanese literature. But he is too difficult a stylist and too abstruse a thinker to enjoy a general readership; his arcane interests and pursuits have lent credence to his image as an erudite but pedantic scholar.[3]

Although he claimed that his major influences were Shakespeare, Milton, Goethe, the Chinese historian Ssu-ma Ch'ien, and the poet Tu Fu, Rohan is remembered for resisting the influences of Western literature and the contemporary attempt to modernize and simplify written Japanese; he wanted instead to preserve the beauties of the language and the traditions of his own country. He was largely responsible for the revival of classical literature in the 1890s and often wrote in a neoclassical style that eschewed the clarity and plainness of standard colloquial writing, which came to predominate letters in his lifetime—though he could write colloquially when he chose. In a number of ways he seemed out of his time and apart from his peers. The critic Masamune Hakuchō likened his prose to an old samurai wearing bulky armor—heavy on stylistic flourishes and requiring slow, careful treatment.[4] Rohan rejected the popular contemporary notion of writers as outlaws, who stand outside society and focus on their own small world. He was rare among Japanese novelists in possessing an epic literary vision, which encompassed fairy tales, history, metaphysics, and ethics; he did not merely describe the mental state of disgruntled and alienated intellectuals but wrote edifying fiction. His heroes were men with strong wills and sure ideals who learned to master their fate through ethical principles or art.

In his scholarly pursuits, too, Rohan was misplaced in time, closer to the Confucian scholar-gentleman than to the modern artist. At age thirty-eight he gave up writing fiction and spent most of the next four decades on scholarship. He wrote treatises on mathematics, business practice and ethics, and urban planning; he delved into Neo-Taoist alchemy, Buddhist metaphysics, and Confucian ethics; he wrote about fishing, food, and chess; he compiled dictionaries of flower names, cloud names, and words about seas and rivers; he devoted volumes to studies of historical personages and events; and he spent his last thirty years completing an exhaustive commentary on the work of the seventeenth-century poet Bashō.

His accomplishments and reputation weighed heavily on Aya, and the burden must have been increased by Rohan's attitude toward his role as a man of letters. He felt morally compelled to teach about and criticize his culture, to maintain ideals and principles and inculcate them in his readers.[5] As a child, he was strictly schooled in the classical texts of Confucian ethics, and he spent his life not only researching Confucianism and infusing his works with its ideals but living according to its standards of conduct. No doubt his sense of responsibility to society encompassed his family as well. In Aya's memoirs we can sense that every action he took and every word he spoke was intended to impart a lesson. In the smallest details of domestic life he was a teacher, strict though constantly concerned. The insecurities that gnawed at Aya throughout her career derived from the doubt that she could live up to her father's standard.

Like Alice James, the nineteenth-century American diarist, Aya was subjected to the intellectual and moral impositions of an exacting and scholarly father, and like James, she was an only daughter who had to sit in the shadow of a brilliantly successful family. A long lineage of mathematicians, musicians, Confucian scholars, and government officials preceded Aya's entry into the Kōda family. Her paternal grandmother, Kōda Yū, was the daughter of a shogunate official who was responsible for ceremony, protocol, and scheduling audiences at the imperial court; her paternal grandfather, Shigenobu, was an official of lower rank who married into the Kōda family. At the time of Rohan's birth the Kōda family was wealthy, possessing a mansion and secondary homes, and although it fell into poverty after the overthrow of the Tokugawa government in 1868, it did not fall into moral collapse, as so many other stipendiary samurai families did, but managed to maintain its strict standards of conduct and propriety. Rohan's mother made her son observe religious rituals, and with a firm, even frightening hand she trained him in the performance of household tasks; afraid of her scolding, Rohan learned to hide his pain when the work grew too demanding.[6]

Judging by the children she produced, Yū must have been a remarkable woman. Among her other sons was Shigetada (1860–1924), a naval officer turned national hero and symbol by his military exploits in the 1890s; and Shigetomo (1873–1954), a newspaper editor, professor, and translator of Tolstoy. But more impressive and more important to Aya than her uncles were her aunts. Nobuko (1870–1946) studied music in Vienna and Boston and was hailed by Mori Ōgai as the first authentic transmitter of Western music to Japan. In 1936 she was elected, along with Rohan, to the Imperial Academy of the Arts. Ando Koko (1878–1963), Nobuko's younger sister, studied music in Berlin and became an accomplished violinist, professor at Ueno Music School, and tutor to the crown princess.[7]

Though similar to Alice James in her exposure to familial success, Aya was less victimized by moral and social structures that might have denied her, as a woman, adequate outlets for her creative energies. And unlike James, Aya was provided with female role models—her aunts and her Heian predecessors—on whom to base a career as a writer. James produced a diary, which came to be considered an American classic after her death, but she spent most of her days as an invalid with various nervous diseases.[8] Aya was more fortunate: she grew up in a different era, when the idea of a woman venturing out into public was less uncommon—though public appearances were still rather restricted in Japan. Both writers possessed a personal heritage that offered them an opportunity, however risky and equivocal, to engage in intellectual and creative endeavors. Each heritage was also a burden, and only Aya seems to have borne hers without being crushed.

But it was only Rohan's death, and the interest shown by publishers in Aya's remembrances of him, that provided Aya access to a life of letters. Had it not been for his passing and his fame, she might have lived in anonymity. For the fifteen years after her first commission in 1947, Aya cast into prose the moments of family life and death that she had observed in silence for so long. The vividness and power of her writing, which she began so late in life and developed so quickly and assuredly, must be seen as an imaginative explosion of emotional energies and perceptions that had been held in abeyance for many years. When Aya finally opened up, years of astute observations poured forth with a precision and force that seem almost uncanny for someone not explicitly trained as a writer or expecting to write some day. Her creative energies matured over the course of decades, awaiting an appropriate moment and a suitable form in which to emerge.

The grief—and relief—that Aya experienced at her father's death unleashed emotions that demanded imaginative clarification. The request by various publishers to describe his last days gave Aya the opportunity to examine the values and meanings contained in the many incidents, images, and emotions she had been storing in her memory and assimilating into her personality for over forty years. Death was the moment in which the knowledge, wisdom, and experience contained in Rohan's life and work and passed on to Aya first assumed "transmissible form."[9] Aya expressed feelings whose force she might harness but whose power would never diminish. She dispensed with certain memories easily, in a deft description or two; but other scenes from her past gripped her so that she had to return to them again and again to master their influence on her. From the basic emotion of loss and separation she would never be released.

In writing about Rohan, Aya struggled to create a literary identity for herself, initially by confronting his influence on her, then by distancing herself from that influence. We can see in her first published memoirs the battle of a child against a parent who seems to engulf everyone and everything, whose sheer presence threatens the self-identity that a little girl— serving him in silence, fear, awe, and affection—strives to create for herself. The image Aya often evokes of her father is that of an absolute and unimpeachable moral force whose slightest criticism makes her want to roll into a little ball and disappear from the face of the earth. She tried to understand what it meant to be the daughter of a man whose reputation was well established by the time of her birth, at its peak as she entered adolescence, and almost legendary in the years before he died.

When Aya began writing, she embroiled herself in a contest with Rohan that involved more intense insecurities and more strident efforts at establishing her self-identity than if she had confined her struggle to the more typical parameters of parent-child conflict. Her struggle to emerge from her father's shadow, in other words, was intensified by her struggle to become a writer. She displayed the combined anger and affection, dependence and rebellion, common to all children growing up. Her emotions were those of a child coming to terms with the recent death of a parent. Because Aya was a fledgling writer, developing an idiosyncratic style to distance her writing from her father's, the depth and range of her emotions were even greater, spanning resentment, rage, frustration, and inadequacy, as well as tenderness, love, and an almost desperate need for approval. Her father was the primary source of turmoil, but he was also the source of sustaining strength. He stimulated her sense of defeat as well as her sense of fruitful striving. When writing about him and about her own past, more than history seems to be at stake: something invigorates her but fills her with uneasiness; she seems to be competing for a prize.

Their final days together provided Aya with the subject matter for her first prose pieces. She had access to private moments that the reading public longed to share. She served them up in her 1947 pieces "Miscellaneous Notes" ("Zakki"), "Last Moments" ("Shūen"), and "Funeral Diary" ("Sōsō no ki"). But her attempt to render a respectful and truthful image of her father quickly evolved into a depiction and analysis of her relationship to him. Though constrained by the task of describing him, she could not do so without writing about herself. Here she floundered. Her first pieces were met with critical acclaim; her prose was praised for its great evocative powers, her insights for their acumen. Critics were amazed by this amateur's manifest skills and often resorted to hyperbole to register their appreciation. Her prose was "unbearably perfect," according to one re-spected critic, and according to others, it represented the crumbs of genius left to her by her father. In the years ahead, this praise would haunt Aya. In an interesting reversal of sexual imagery, Rohan would be depicted in one cartoon as the well of ink and Aya as the pen dipping in.[10]

The indirectness of her autobiographical itinerary—acknowledging the presence of a larger figure before examining her own identity, discovering her own self through writing about another—indicates Aya's passivity toward the act of writing. Overtly she seemed to be writing about some-body else, but underneath she was disclosing much about herself.[11] The main interest of Aya's memoirs, then, does not lie in what they say about her father but in what they reveal about her own self-discovery. We see her as a suffering individual, always present behind the writing; as a writer, constantly struggling to express herself; and as a self-styled, self-invented literary persona, insistently projected from the page.

Aya did care about the veracity of the memories she chose to re-create. She approached the task of recording the past and evoking the image of her father with trepidation, precisely because she felt a responsibility toward the truth. Her respect for the sanctity of the past and her desire to create a present self-identity make the determination of the "truth" in Aya's mem-oirs exceedingly problematic. Because the impulse to record was at odds with the impulse to create, the final product became a combination of the two, a bending of truth to the needs of a creative imagination.

Given her initial status as a writer of memoirs, Aya has not received proper attention as a self-conscious literary artist. The critics have read her memoirs as literal records of her life with her father and have mined them for clues to his career and, secondarily, for clues to Aya's own. But they have failed to notice their formal literary qualities and the ways in which Aya used her writing to create a literary persona. And even though her literary beginnings derived from an impulse to remember, she quickly tired of writing solely about her father and her life with him. What remained of her biographical impulse in her later writings was less the content of her memories than the form in which she continued to unfold her narratives.

Aya often returns to the poignant moment of her father's death to locate her own birth as a writer. In "Funeral Diary" she writes of this moment in figurative language, focusing on her bond with her father and implicitly referring to the question of writing itself: "Our parting was a joining together of life and death. To the end of my father's life his power held me and refused to set me free. I was roped in by this power but little by little was able to rid myself of my attachment to him. Our parting breathed life into me and cut the cords of longing that linked us together."[12]

We would not be wrong to doubt the sincerity of Aya's emotion; although the severance of the bond was necessary for her emergence as a writer, the attachment and the way that Aya viewed it continued to be the single most important emotion fueling her writing. The cords were never really cut. In her first pieces she made careful but somewhat random observations of her father as he approached death: the atmosphere of the sick room, rain dripping from the ceiling, holes in the tatami mats; his facial expressions when falling asleep and when waking; his vomiting, his bleeding mouth, his trembling lips; the scars on his face and the way his dead face changed in the broiling heat of the summer with no dry ice to keep it fresh. Writing with the objectivity of a trained nurse taught Aya to take on the role of observer—a role that the narrators of her later fiction also assumed. She trained herself to look and to transmit what she saw in words. She also took on the role of preserver of memories (*KAZ* 1: 353).

In each of her memoirs we find Aya casting herself in the role of the disparaged daughter who struggles to grasp the meaning of her bond with her father, and at the same time we see Aya the writer training her eye to bring the scene before her into focus. This combination of emotional involvement and dispassionate observation lends tension and power to her writing. In the following passage she describes a fight with her father. The scene is his deathbed.

> His words flew at me like arrows. "You fool! What are you doing in here? Didn't I tell you to get out?"
>
> The tension that had been holding me up collapsed. "How can I leave you like this? I'm not going anywhere. I don't want to."
>
> I felt something inside me sink. Father replied, "I'm not talking about what you want. I'm telling you to get out."
>
> "I won't."
>
> "You pigheaded little . . . What use are you anyway?"
>
> "I don't care. If you're going to die, I want to die with you. It's natural for a child to wish to be with her parent."
>
> "Absolutely not. I will not let this go on. We are not one person. I will not allow this impudence."
>
> "I'm sorry, but it's important that I stay."
>
> "That's where you are wrong. Once I die, you're to think of me as dead and gone. It will be all over."
>
> "No. I can't do that."
>
> "Nevertheless, you must."
>
> "Could you watch me die?"

Father's partially visible face crumpled at my question. "That I could not bear." (*KAZ* 1: 28)

Aya continues to fight with her father to draw some word from him that will soothe her fear and sense of impending loss. In Rohan's voice we hear the recognition that the child must break away, even though she resists separation. At his death Aya rejects the possibility of ever separating from her father.

> Father lay on his back. Placing his left palm on his forehead and his right hand on my bare arm, he said, "Are you ready?" His hand was cold. I sat in silence, not understanding.
> "Yes, I am ready," I replied. I think at that moment a part of father entered me and formed an internal support. I understood now what he meant, and I was prepared for his death.
> He nodded, his hand on my face. His face was expressionless, his eyes gentle. "Then I am ready to die."
> Like him, I felt no particular emotion, nor did I shed any tears. I knew this was the end. "I understand," was all I said. Our parting had come. (*KAZ* 1: 32)

Aya's attempt to treat the scene of her father's death in a literary way—as unfolding gradually through dramatic tension and dialogue—is even more forceful in "Funeral Diary," where she gains aesthetic distance by describing her father as an object: "The father before me was an empty shell, a thing, a thing belonging to me, an important, irreplaceable thing. Perhaps I should think of it as a jewel. The more precious a thing, the more important it is, the more painful a slight flaw would seem to those beholding it, and the deeper the impression it would make on the beholders" (*KAZ* 1: 339). In lucid and emotionally distanced terms Aya continues to ponder the meaning of the thing before her. To lend vividness to her description, she writes in the present tense.

> This empty shell is my father, and I am its daughter. Filial emotions press on me. Those hands and feet—I know what it means to have tended that body day and night. I combed its hair; I wiped its chest. How dear I thought the living flesh. Since dismissing the help last year, I have always been nervous when facing my father. He was a great man, but there was something of the typical grandpa about him. His child was not too bright, but she had feelings, after all. We lived together selfishly, with no regard for society. Although I tended and nursed him, it never seemed that he, asleep, was the one being nursed and I, awake, was the nurse. There was only mutuality. In times of trouble, I cared for his living body, and he, for his part, consoled me when he saw my worried brow. He grieved for me; sometimes he even despaired of me. (*KAZ* 1: 340)

Father and daughter seem to wind their lives down together; he descends toward his death and she dwindles into a wisp of herself. Aya feels as close to him as a mother to a child and feels bound to him even after he dies: "In days gone past, Father's body belonged to me, and now death had emptied it out and given it to me. . . . It was an empty shell, but I still wanted to protect it" (*KAZ* 1: 341).

Aya continues with a minute description of her father's funeral, then gives the details of his cremation: the smoke rising from the crematorium chimney, the sifting for his bones by family and friends, the urn holding his ashes.

> Father gave off a mild warmth on my lap. I moved my face closer, and even the white cotton knot of the cloth wrapped around the urn emitted a breath of warm air. As I stepped out of the car, sunlight struck the shoulders of my black kimono, and my skin, slack with fatigue and lack of sleep, was dripping with sweat. The wind sent a cold shudder through me. Kobayashi approached. "Aya-*san,* I didn't realize. You look exhausted. Let me take that." Obediently, I passed my father to him. I felt faint. My daughter called to me and grabbed my arm. The myriad flowering plants along the road were thin and weak, and the dewy grass we had seen that morning had lost all its color. I was unable to contain myself, and a tear dropped from my eye. (*KAZ* 1: 347)

All the feelings that Aya stored over the years while at her father's side and all the strength of their bond seem to radiate from his ashes, whose warmth triggers memories of him and forces her to confront yet again the nature of their relationship and to attempt yet again to define her own identity. She comments after the preceding scene, "I don't read books. I don't mix with people. I feel most secure alone inside my kitchen" (*KAZ* 1: 350).

Aya wants to retreat into the secure and contained world that she imagines existed in her past, in the private world of the kitchen, where she prepared food for her father, peacefully unaware of his well-wishers, unaware of the confusion of the outside world and and even of her own task of writing. She was sincerely anxious about becoming a writer and about doing justice to her father; in her memoirs she undoubtedly tried to present something of the truth about herself and her feelings for him. Nevertheless, we cannot ignore the literary and dramatic nature of her self-presentation, her conscious creation of a literary persona who is a meek, self-sacrificing daughter devoted to the care of her father, who is ignorant of her father's larger sphere and uninterested in and unable to enter the world of letters. Aya later used this persona to create her own extended fictions. That Rohan's death released a flood of emotions in Aya is perfectly natural; that she channeled these emotions into her writing in creative, dramatic ways points to her literary talent.

Not until she had sufficiently (though never completely) purged herself of the memories of her father's death and gained the confidence that comes with venturing out into public and receiving critical approval did Aya begin to write more conventional autobiographical pieces. After completing her first memoirs, she was at a loss as to how to proceed and was told by her publishers to continue writing about Rohan by writing about herself. The fruits of this experiment, "Miso Dregs" ("Misokkasu," 1949) and "Flowering Plants" ("Kusa no hana," 1951), were praised for their subtlety of perception and sensitive use of language, but like her first pieces, they were faulted for lacking a formal, logical structure and were discussed in a slightly patronizing tone as a random collection of memories.

The criticism has some validity: Aya does not tell the story of a fully understood self, proceeding from a precise starting point through a tightly linked series of events to a logical conclusion. Her story of her life is less a chronology of facts than a tracing of her thoughts and feelings as her mind ranges over the past. She presents herself at pivotal junctures—birth, the death of relatives, school, sexual awakening—but she slips back and forth through time, from the present scene of her writing to the scene being described, to a more distant past, then forward again to the moment of writing. Her life does not so much unfold before readers as recur as a set of important scenes and emotions, which she circles in on again and again.

Aya accepted the criticism directed at her and in typical self-deprecating fashion claimed, almost too insistently, that writing was beyond her meager powers. Instead, she endorsed the image of herself as a mere "seller of memories." But she can be read with greater sympathy. As a seller of memories, she placed more importance on shuttling between present and past than on traveling a straight line from the past to the present. Because she began writing at a moment of great personal and historical loss, she became concerned with the effect that the past would have on her present; because she, the daughter of a famous writer, was concerned with forming an identity as a writer, she wanted to clarify the influences and forces that had brought her to write.

Born in the immediate aftermath of profound personal and national loss, Aya's writing moves to the past to salvage mementos for the present. Two images resonate through her memoirs and fiction, that of a bereaved daughter sifting through her father's ashes for bones and that of a young woman searching through the remains of her father's home, which was destroyed in a wartime conflagration. In "Fragment" ("Kakera," 1948) she finds a piece of a tray that her father had loved for over forty years, since the days when his first wife was alive. The fragment draws Aya back into her past, and the narrative presents childhood memories associated with the tray. As the story closes, Aya recalls her divorce and her father's death and decides to leave the bit of pottery on a heap of rubble: "Last summer Father journeyed across the boundary of this world. Chased by memories I do not wish other eyes to see, I crushed the fragment of beautiful blue and white porcelain that came from the frost, and I returned it to the earth again" (*KAZ* 1: 48). The past survives in the present in material embodiment, but Aya's attitude toward it is not simply nostalgic: though salvageable in some form, the past is also painfully irretrievable and easily desecrated by others' eyes.

If much of Aya's writing is shaped by the image of a past that impinges on the present, it can also be viewed as a continuing drama of self-definition and self-creation in which she projects her present concerns into the past. She revives past scenes that help her form a present self-identity. What she describes is neither past nor present alone but a union of the two. She constantly glances back, yet her nostalgia is anchored in her current concerns. She draws from the past what she needs to understand who she is and to give her current status as a writer the authority of development and influence. In other words, she creates from memory a personal myth by which to live and write. Because her impetus for writing was the loss of her father, she returns to him for subject matter. Because her immediate concern was with establishing herself as a writer, she depicts former scenes that allude to her future career.

To describe what Aya remembers of her own past would be difficult without discussing how she shapes her memories, how she gives form to her writing. She tried to capture in prose thoughts that she felt were uncapturable. In the afterword to "Miso Dregs," she wrote, "Thoughts are like dew and the pencil like the sun" (*KAZ* 2: 151). In a more developed metaphor, she describes how hard it is to write about her father and his friend the novelist Shimazaki Tōson (whom she calls *sensei*, or teacher), whom she has just met.

> Tonight the beetles or something like them are crying out. . . . I have been seated for some time gazing at the Gifu lantern that hangs from the eaves. Because of the season, a small electric bulb has been placed inside it. The autumn grasses drawn on the light blue shade seem to float. Sometimes the lantern sways left or right. The bulb inside is hanging from another string, so it doesn't move very much, but it, too, sways with the lantern. When the lantern sways, the light blue gently flows to one side and that side darkens. When it sways again, the color abruptly darkens on the other side. As I stare at the lantern, I seem more and

more to see a shifting water mark inside. From one side to the other the light blue smoothly flows, darkening in layers, but when it passes before the bulb, for a moment the light blue is translucent, without color. When this translucence purls into the distance and floats up in a dark layer, the depths are blue-green. I wonder how something translucent forms layers and darkens. The hair bristles on my arms, which rest on the rattan chair. A breeze passes over my skin; it seems to give warning: "I'm passing through!" I am perspiring, and the breeze again blows warmly over my arms. Precisely when I think it will surely come again, it disappears, just like that. I have countless memories of the sensei and my father, but the memories are, after all, like the water in the lantern. When I try to write them down, they become translucent. (*KAZ* 4: 179)

Aya worried about doing an injustice to her memories, yet she managed to commit them to paper. In "Miso Dregs" she writes, "It takes a great deal of resolution to sit here like this, surrounded by these memories. It is a struggle to compose myself and not throw away my pencil and walk away. The pressure of the scenes and emotions that well up in me is unendurable. The passage of thirty or forty years hasn't turned me into an adult at all. The indescribable pain of childhood is with me today as it was then, and it forces my eyes and mouth shut. I feel irritated and angry. It is impossible for me to write about my past. It's not that I don't want to or can't—I just have no words. I ask your forgiveness. I cannot cope with the image of my father, with the image of my mother, with my own inner heart" (*KAZ* 2: 86).

Memories force on Aya an attachment to and a longing for the past so intense that any attempt to order them in written form threatens to desecrate them. At times her memories seem to bubble up uncontrolled, but this quality of her style is less immaturity and lack of rigor than an attempt to do justice to her memories. She allows her memories to resound with some of the original power that she attaches to them, and does not always modify them in hindsight. Aya allows us to witness how her mind recalls the past; she transcribes the process of remembering. Often she lingers over an object from the past and lets it guide her deeper into her memories and then back out again. In the following passage she remembers an autumn night in her childhood when she sat alone at her study desk listening to the sound of a fulling stone.

Connections are interesting things. For some time I listened to the sound of the fulling stone coming from the dyer's house. Although the dyer lived close by for a long time and I came to know the sound well, I never actually saw the stone. This troubled me at first, and one day as I passed the dyer's house I peeked in the window, hoping to get a look at it. Inside, everything was neatly arranged, as always, but there were only stone platforms and nothing resembling a fulling stone. If I had really wanted to know what one looked like, I could easily have looked in a dictionary or, even more easily, asked my father, but realizing that I could find out, I became lazy and never bothered. After we moved to the center of town, I stopped hearing the sound. But for some reason I would hear the rap-rap-rapping of the stone inside me, and I no longer felt like asking my father or having the dyer show me what it looked like. The fulling stone with only a sound and no form filled me with a satisfying nostalgia. I heard the sound of the stone through the image in my imagination. (*KAZ* 2: 256)

Alluding to both the form of her writing and the aesthetic it serves, Aya shows her imagination responding to a vague, formless, but evocative, image from the past that derives its power from her memory of it. She allows the image to take her mind where it will. From inside her dark room she hears a sound outside the window; she allows it to sink into her and then takes off on a flight back to the source of the sound. Her mind is like a calm pool excited by a rock thrown in its center.

From this gleaming black desk in the study I trace the line of sound through the sliding door, past the sitting room, into the entranceway. It is dark outside. A bell rings when I open the small gate. There are no signs of life along the narrow gravel path. I go past the first house, past the second, the door of each shut tight. Perhaps it is the tenth house down. I cross a river on a small stone bridge to the first house on the other side. There is the fulling stone, the source of the rap-rap-rapping I listened to in nights past, the sound that came from the darkness. Now that I was there I didn't want to see what it looked like; I didn't want to understand everything there was to understand about it. I felt a sweet yearning in leaving it unknown. Sound has no form, and the fulling stone has always been known for the sound it makes.

Perhaps listening to it in the darkness allowed me to feel its essence; perhaps that made me happy. If I had wished to know everything about it, I could have asked my father or consulted a dictionary. But I no longer wanted to do this. There are faces that one glimpses briefly yet that remain forever in the heart because one hasn't fixed their identity. Connections can be very sad indeed. (*KAZ* 2: 257)

The passage leaves us unsure whether Aya went to see the fulling stone or whether she merely allowed her imagination to float beyond the walls of her house. In highly figurative and indirect language she accomplishes a number of things: she situates herself as a writer, inside a room, cut off from the world, with a free imagination; she shows the way in which her sense of loss—for her father, for her past—informs her aesthetic sensibilities; and she expresses how difficult it is to preserve connections, between people, between mental associations, and, by implication, between herself and her father. She writes, then, not in the methodical, strict fashion associated with the dictionary or with her father's own work but in a way that is associated with the elusive, evocative sound of the fulling stone. This is the only way she can legitimately write.

Because Aya stresses the integrity of her memories, the images of her early years and the emotional accents on those scenes often seem to contradict one another. Two broad types of emotion—the peaceful and the traumatic—appear, and these emotions often battle it out in her writing. Her mind can shift from feelings of insecurity, anomie, and conflict to feelings of security, warmth, and stability. Aya's presentation of her childhood thus changes according to the emotional light she chooses to cast on her memories. In an early essay in which she describes wandering from house to house during the bombing of Tokyo, she remembers her childhood home as imbued with peace and tranquillity:

> My father used to live near Hundred Flowers Park in Mukōjima; there I was born and lived until the age of twenty. At that time Mukōjima was quickly being turned into a factory area, but one could still see peaceful expanses of rice paddies and tilled fields. There were small homes along the narrow, meandering paths. At the farthest corner of the neighborhood, squeezing its way into the great river, was a small stream with water parsley and mustard and here and there a thicket, tangled during the summer with gourds and vines. There were large farmhouses, persimmon trees alongside wells, poorer farms, and terraces of pears. . . . The trees and plants visible under the passing sky were all the more brilliant for being seen through a fugitive lens, and they were all the more poignant for offering nothing to transient human feelings. How often I felt my heart quiver when that feeling of transience brought to mind things connected with my place of birth. (*KAZ* 1: 33)

A sense of loss figures in this passage, but the memory of what was lost is infused with feelings of peace and security. In another essay Aya remembers that same place possessing more active and uncontrolled energies.

> Mukōjima brings cherry trees, sea gulls, and the Tamanoi district to mind, but for those who have lived there, the memory of summer mosquitoes and autumn floods is equally strong. Until the flood-control channels were completed, residents always had to be concerned about the floods that came with the autumn equinox. The wealthier homes had emergency boats, and humbler places had rafts made of planks, logs, nails, and rope. Even children knew that in case of an emergency, window shutters could be used as rafts. All children my age shook with fear every moment—fear of the wind, the rain, the fire alarms, of the river's bursting its banks, of not surviving. And after the floods subsided, filth, poverty, and disease were everywhere. (*KAZ* 1: 116)

In writing of her birth Aya lights again and again on the day of her birth, the 210th day of 1904, the first day of autumn by the lunar calendar, the day of storms.

> The period between late August and early September is difficult. It is already autumn, according to the calendar, but there is none of the freshness of autumn. Summer has bleached itself out and drips sluggishly by. Everyone searches for signs that the new season is beginning, but any indications are obscured by the end of the old.
>
> People say that summers are sharp and clear, but the final days seem to me to linger irresolutely. Autumn begins with the sprouting of the delicate pampa grasses and the blooming of the ginkgoes—no wonder the signs of its arrival are faint. Perhaps the gods of nature placed the storms of early September between the two seasons to draw them together. They have done a fine job. But every year they seem to go a bit far. This year the 210th day landed on September 1.
>
> I was born on this day and have been reminded over and over again that I came into the world during a storm. Since early childhood I have had complicated feelings about the 210th day. I cannot deny that the coincidence sometimes fills me with pleasure, but when I am faced with real troubles, I have a shameful sense of fear and a bitter loneliness. (*KAZ* 1: 115)

Aya does seem to have entered the world as storms broke the suffocating heat of a Tokyo summer. Her father was at the height of his literary and mental powers, and as if to augur his later physical decline and the sapping of his energies by this new child, he noticed that he was going bald. Aya's description thus pinpoints a real moment in time, but what is important is that she describes herself as born in the midst of tension, though in a specified moment in the seasonal cycle—at a secure place in time. The image of the storm crystallizes her image of herself: as struggling against a battering wind but needing an anchor. The description of the storm is at odds with the gentle evocation of her birthplace in the earlier passage; but each memory records different moments of Aya's childhood, so the contrast seems unimportant, although it does represent her conflicting emotions. She continues the description of the storm in this way. "Why, as a child, does one never note the moment that floods or storms occur? How strange that what remains in the memory is what happens after the event. Children remember the details of their parents' fights, but they seem insensitive to natural disasters, which should elicit more instinctual fears. As long as everyone is safe at home and there is a roof to keep out the rain and a door to keep out the wind, a child remains untouched by the violence raging outside, no matter how severe it may be" (*KAZ* 1: 117).

A recurring theme in Aya's writing is the search for shelter inside warm, enclosed places. Her characters ache for the security of a defined domestic role among a network of people who accept their nurturing impulses. They are maids, nurses, and mothers, all needing to serve others. But they are never free from the raging of the outside world; the urgency behind their impulse to hide is a measure of their acute sensitivity.

Equally frightening to certain of these characters are the raging of a powerful father and the threat of being overwhelmed by him. The coincidence of Aya's birth with a storm in her first attempt at autobiography is not the simple recording of a real event: the most celebrated and quoted passage of Rohan's prose is a description of a storm in *The Five-Storied Pagoda*. Aya thus focuses on a scene that marks not only her birth as a daughter but her birth as a writer as well. But more important than her troubled sense of her past and her inheritance is her return to a moment in which her anxiety toward her father is most vividly present. She is attempting to clear an imaginative space for herself, to check the force of her father's influence. In Harold Bloom's words, "What can the imagination defend us against except the preemptive force of another imagination?"[13] This problem of inheritance, of resemblance and indebtedness to the previous generation, appears and reappears in her writing.

In her memoir "Miso Dregs," Aya creates the character of a self-deprecating girl attempting to define herself. Her father, she tells us, had been hoping for a boy—his first child, a male, was stillborn, and his second was a girl—and when Aya arrived, uglier than most babies, he registered his disappointment with a cluck of regret for this new, unwanted child. Aya's nursemaid later told her that he regretted her birth and that her mother, Kimiko, apparently sad for her own misfortune in failing to produce a boy, had tears in her eyes. The anxiety and loneliness Aya assigns to this moment lasted decades. Her feeling that Rohan was disappointed remained with her until her father died, when she finally seemed to realize that he loved her after all. For now, though, she thinks that her orange-brown hair, gaping eye sockets, and funny nose must have dissatisfied a lover of beauty like her father. She sees her birth as an impudent though comically impotent slap in his face.

The Kōda family continued to grow, and the disappointment caused by Aya's birth was alleviated by the birth of her brother two years later, an event that Aya claims brought the Kōda family to its peak of happiness. The day of Ichiro's birth, unlike her own, was suffused with the soft sunlight of spring; there were sounds of distant festival drums and a faint smell of cherry blossoms, and Rohan seemed to be praying. The dreamy days lasted until Aya was seven. The day of her own birth could only be imagined, but the day of her mother's death awakened her consciousness to the world and impressed her with vivid memories that she would carry with her and recall years later. She records the minutiae of her mother's deathbed scene with an exactitude that we would expect from a novelist consciously seeking details to use in her work. After describing faces, clothes, and tears, she tries to sketch her mother—her gently smiling face, beautiful but determined looking; her skill as a housekeeper; her talent as a cook; her playful banter with husband. Aya's mother is virtually the only person to appear in her writings whom Aya remembers with unambiguous love and respect. It is a measure of Rohan's power over his daughter's imagination that Aya writes so stintingly of her mother, but it is the brevity of her warm memories that lends them poignancy. Her early departure from Aya's life left Aya with a longing for a lost time of familial happiness and uncomplicated love.

After Kimiko's death in 1910, the Kōda household was cared for by a maid and by Aya's maternal aunt Ohisa and her father's mother, Yū. In time the grandmother appeared less and the aunt more in Aya's life and memory. She was a sad woman, divorced and the mother of a child who had died in infancy. She was also an independent and passionate woman. Before Aya's mother married Rohan, her family had hoped that Kimiko would marry a businessman and had strongly opposed a man of letters as a suitable match. Ohisa had demanded that her sister turn Rohan down and threatened to sever all ties with her if she did not. Kimiko persisted, and on her wedding day Ohisa struck her on the back of the head, and the two saw very little of each other for a long time. The hot blood that ran through this woman, says Aya, ran through her mother and herself as well (*KAZ* 2: 18).

The autumn her mother died, the nearby Sumida River flooded, and Aya and her brother were taken to their aunt Nobuko's home in nearby Ishikawa. Busy with concerts, students, and socializing, Nobuko had no time to keep house. Care of the children was left to the stern and severe grandmother. This first interval away from home seems to have intensified the sense of loss that began to grow in Aya with the death of her mother. She describes herself as withdrawn and resentful of her fate. She buckled under the weight of her grandmother's strictures and would often sit staring out a window at the sky, painting imaginary pictures of her lost home. Aya describes this scene, and like the young girl in it, she falls into a reverie, but she thinks of the motherless children wandering the streets of postwar Tokyo at the time of her writing.

Fortunately, her stay with her grandmother was brief. Aya remembers her father coming to visit her and fighting with her grandmother about how she treated Aya. When Aya finally returned home, it was to a house ravaged by floodwater and mud, stinking from the moldy books spread out everywhere to dry, like dead animals. With compassion she remembers her father silently poring over his treasured books, unable to give them up despite their soggy condition.

But Aya's contact with her grandmother did not end here; Aya often stayed overnight at her house after returning late from school, and their time together seems to have softened Aya's feelings toward her. The grandmother was one of the larger-than-life members of the Kōda family. She had big, powerful hands, wrote a beautiful script, and inspired envy in her son and awe in her granddaughter; she was a talented musician who conditioned her daughter Nobuko's fingers to play the samisen by having her do needlework; she had an unending store of energy for her household duties, which she respected much as artisans respect their trade. Finally, she was exacting in training her child in the proprieties of form and conduct. Once, when Rohan was a child, Aya relates, his hands were freezing, and to warm them, he slipped them into his kimono through the openings at the armpits. But this behavior was unfitting for a young child. His mother dragged him to a pillar and said, "Pull your hands out and try slapping that. That will take care of those hands." That was the last time Rohan put his cold hands inside his kimono.[14]

Aya's memory of her grandfather seems dim in contrast. Kōda Shigenobu lived apart from his wife and had been converted to Christianity by Uemura Masahisa, the man who later performed Rohan's second wedding ceremony and Aya's baptism. He was poor and owned little else but a tea-ceremony set and some lacquer and porcelain. But because of either poverty or religious fervor he sold almost all these possessions when he entered the church. When Rohan left home as a young man, his father gave him what remained—a kettle, a kettle hanger, and a small lump of clay. When Rohan was sick, his father had made him drink shavings from this lump, in whose curative powers he believed. According to Aya, the clay had a shine to it. Once, Rohan's brother Gunji threw it against another rock with all his might to see what magic lay at its center; it bounced back without breaking and let out a dull noise. Rohan wanted to try cutting it open with a saw but didn't dare. It remained in his possession until it finally disappeared during the air raids on Tokyo. After the war a friend of the family found the kettle and returned it to Rohan. This object—on which Aya places such importance—was all that was left to remind her of her grandfather.

What remained to Rohan after his wife died was the responsibility of raising the children. He made his older daughter, Uta, practice the tea ceremony and made Aya memorize poetry. Aya remembers the frustration of not being able to meet her father's standards and the tears she shed as she ran away from him and her aunt as they tried to grab her and make her recite her verses. At times like these, Aya longed for her dead mother, for some refuge from paternal demands. Yet she also remembers a gentle, nurturing quality to her father's strictness. With gratitude and love she recalls how he comforted her after her first painful days at the Terajima elementary school, where she was taunted by the other children for her unusual first name (*KAZ* 2: 43). The name Aya means, among other things, literature, letters, rhetoric, or trope.

A special bond formed between father and daughter during these years. He seems to have demanded more of Aya than of her sister, treating her at times almost as if she were the son he had hoped for. He taught her poetry and told her about the uniqueness of her name, as if to remind her that it held a kernel of her inheritance from him. In spite of Rohan's insistence to the contrary, we can assume that in naming his child he intended to transmit his life of letters to his daughter in some way—even if symbolically. "Names," Aya writes, "are thought to be the first sign of a parent's blessing on a child. What could he have been thinking when he named me Aya?" (*KAZ* 2: 48). The painful feelings that Aya attaches to the mispronunciation of her name at school and the warm bond with her father created by that name together represent the emotional poles of her mixed inheritance from her father.

Aya experienced grammar school as another in a series of separations that exacerbated her sense of being different from everyone else. Two important events followed upon her mother's death and her entry into school. The following year her older sister, Uta, died at age eleven, and later the same year a new mother entered the Kōda household. In remembering Uta's death Aya found another opportunity to create an image against which she paled in comparison. Uta was beautiful and smart and, unlike herself, was loved by her father.

But with Uta gone, Aya was the elder child and only daughter. Rohan nevertheless remained somewhat aloof from her, strangely distant and larger than life. She remembers him as her father but also as a public figure, separated from her by a sea of literary people and pursuits. She first heard of his impending marriage from her teachers at school, who had read about it in the newspapers; the next day her aunt Nobuko led her to what looked like a movie theater but was a church. Her father appeared on a stage surrounded by a group of men; and his wife-to-be, when finally introduced to Aya, seemed to have come from a distant and foreign place: "She had a strange face with white eyelashes" (*KAZ* 2: 61).

Aya's life with her stepmother was not happy. Kodama Yayoko was a devout Christian, stricken with arthritis and ineffectual in running the household and caring for Rohan and her stepchildren. Aya resented her arrival as an intrusion and looked down on her inability to work hard and please her husband. Yayako seems to have resented her husband's absorption in books and devotion to liquor, as well as his permissive attitude toward his children. She grew impatient when Aya's brother became ill, and she was too weak physically and emotionally to handle his delinquent behavior at school.

Aya fumed at her stepmother's feebleness and resented being housekeeper and nurse for her father and brother, but she also saw through her anger and felt sorry for the woman. We can admire Aya's ability to describe—and feel—such opposing and difficult emotions. In the following scene she regards her stepmother, who sits silently gazing out a window as she often did in moments of grief.

> As a child of nine or ten, I couldn't truly understand what lay at the heart of a woman past forty, but I think my pity for her derived from some comprehension of her situation. Her silent figure filled me with deep sorrow. I was moved by the sadness of this woman who so visibly bore the wound of disappointment in marriage. Such a lack of pretense is noble. The impression of honest suffering was not fleeting; it was with me when I was older and, in a fit of rebellion against her, threatened to leave home. At that moment her lonely seated figure flickered in my mind and crushed my spirit. Even now, when I think of her, I want to call out to her from the bottom of my soul. My feelings for her are confused—part nostalgia, part pity—but at their core lies the trust of a young child who depends on a parent. In spite of my hate and resentment, her sad image fills me with a sense of security because I know she was a good person after all. Ever since my rebellious moment, love and hate have been twisted together in me; they have tormented me. Like the bond of blood, this bond, too, was very painful. (*KAZ* 2: 79)

Aya here manages to communicate the intensity and complication of familial bonds in language that is both controlled and passionate, removed from the scene yet deeply involved. Becoming a writer meant weakening those bonds, but the fear of being set completely free haunted her with the apprehension of loneliness and hopelessness, with the threat of being cast out from her secure, enclosing space. The parental fights she witnessed intensified—if they didn't create—this feeling. She felt that the rope tying her to her parents could easily snap, even though it was braided with love as well as hate.

The estrangement that Aya saw develop between her father and stepmother hurt her deeply. She remembers looking on as their taunts grew louder and nastier, husband ignoring wife, shouting out lines of poetry despite her pleas for quiet, she absorbed in her Bible, taunting him with her stubborn and arrogant silence. Eventually they would scream and cry and call each other names, she threatening to leave and he threatening to kick her out. Aya once grew so upset that she began shouting at them both and wound up flying into a violent rage, kicking and screaming, knocking over furniture, pleading desperately with him to stop his drinking and with her not to leave. The next morning, peace was restored, but Aya's father shunned her for having yelled at him; and when her mother, with typical self-pity, shrugged off Aya's behavior as natural for a stepdaughter toward a stepmother, Aya was hurt even further. Aya explains the effect this scene would have on her.

> I didn't dream that that night would give rise to a lifelong sadness and sense of inferiority. When, a few years later, I could bear it no longer and decided to leave that cold home, I realized, as if the mist had cleared before my eyes, the moment of my departure had been determined that night. I continued to cling to my hatred for people, which was born in me back then, and I shuddered at its great staying power. Yet I was still unaware of the nature of that hatred. My feelings were directed not toward my parents, who were such an important part of me, but toward myself, wounded by the undeserved hatred of my parents. It is a pity that so much has to be displayed in front of a child, who instinctively loves her parents and craves peace between them. My overanxiousness about them caused me personal misfortune and, in the end, interfered with their love as well. (*KAZ* 2: 93)

Feeling despised and unwanted put Aya in constant fear of being abandoned, and the insecurity turned her into a quivering, timid child. She remembers a conversation in which her parents threatened to send her away as a foster child. To endure her pain, she buried herself deep inside a bed of flowers.

> It was evening. I emerged from the darkness of the bathhouse. On the flower shelf set up especially for us children, yellow lion-head daffodils were in full bloom. They looked pretty in the evening light. The broom along the fence was tinged yellow. I called to the dog sleeping there, but it merely raised its tail. It was female and quite intelligent. Mother wasn't in the kitchen. The whole house was strangely hushed. Beyond the screen I heard someone say, "Aya . . ." I stood stock-still and listened, not realizing that I was doing so. They were discussing sending me away. "She'll never agree," Father was saying. "She definitely won't like the idea." I quietly stepped outside. I lost control, and my heart began to race wildly. I went to the fields, where the sun was already setting. The mustard was

blooming in profusion, and here, too, it was yellow. I squatted beneath the flowers. There were a dim scent and vague warmth about them.

They're sending me away; I'm to be cast from this house. The tales of evil stepmothers I heard at school and from the maid were coming true. I felt impatient, but I couldn't move. If the flowers moved toward my face, I wouldn't be able to see a thing. Suddenly something cold and wet touched my cheek. I was startled, but it was only the nose of the dog, which sat and pressed the weight of its body against me and busily lapped my tears. . . . By the house the maid was yelling, "Aya-san! Aya-san!" and the dog ran away. But I stayed where I was, frozen at the base of the mustard plants, sobbing. When it grew completely dark, Father and Mother came out searching for me, calling my name.

The situation was desperate. I knew they were planning to send me off somewhere, but I was drawn to my father's voice. He drew me into his arms, and I clung to him. (*KAZ* 2: 75)

Aya describes a frightened child hiding inside a warm space shut off from the outside world, looking toward her father as an all-powerful being who could give love but also take it away. Aya relates that at about this age she became aware of her father's status as a famous writer, and when she writes about it, she begins to lament her inability to write of the past, as if the awareness of her father that she had as a child were invading her once again.

"Miso Dregs" closes with Aya's graduation from grammar school at the age of thirteen. Neither her father nor mother attended the ceremony. By an exercise of will the young girl resisted being saddened by the pleasant nostalgia as the schoolchildren said their good-byes to one another. Not until the singing of the school song, with its call for hard work and success in the future, is Aya's emotional guard broken, and she begins to cry.

In the final lines of the memoir Aya emphasizes her childish sense of being no more significant than *misokkasu,* the dregs of miso. But the word also resonates pleasantly. "It would be better without the word *misokkasu* at all. It would be better not to have it in the dictionary. I'd like to put an end to it. I truly wish for that. The word is already disappearing, and yet I wonder—gloomily. Imagining when not even one child will be hurt by such treatment, I hear love in the echo of *misokkasu* that I cannot dispense with" (*KAZ* 2: 155).

In "Flowering Plants," Aya describes a series of seemingly minor events in her life that hold powerful associations for her. Having failed her high school entrance exams, she winds up at a mission school, where she is exposed to the English language. Though generally alienated from her peers, she forms a few friendships and even falls in love with another woman. Meanwhile, her stepmother's rheumatism has worsened along with her ill temper, and Aya is left with the bulk of household chores. Her father seems completely withdrawn, leaving his study only for brief moments and then only to bark out commands.

Aya infuses the small events that made up her life with a tension and a compression of multiple meanings that saves them from becoming trivial and boring. The scenes she chooses to describe are thick with the emotions and themes that obsessed her imagination—her ambiguous feelings toward her father and her home, her inadequacy as a daughter and as a writer, separations, the dynamic of memory and longing, her retrospective vision of herself as a writer developing her voice.

"Flowering Plants" opens with a meditation on a lost home. After graduating from high school, Aya failed the college entrance examination; her worst moment came when she was asked to write an essay on the topic hometown (*furusato*). "I thought that *hometown* was used only by sad and unfortunate drifters when referring to their place of birth. For a person like myself, who was born and raised in the same place, there is no corresponding word" (*KAZ* 2: 162). Aya describes the irony of being so attached to a place that one never views it from a distance: something not yet lost can elicit no nostalgia. But Aya also seems to be saying that someone can feel so suffocated at home that there is no room to feel a warm appreciation of it, no freedom to think of it as a true home.

The Aya of "Flowering Plants" shoulders an ever more onerous burden of duties and family responsibilities, which threatens to crush her. Yet she thrives in the compact space of this tangled world. Out on a hike, she seems at a loss. "It was difficult to distinguish things in all that open space at the outskirts of town. Everything shone brightly in the light. Wherever I turned my eye, the objects that came into view—the thin blades of grass or the broad leaves of the trees—seemed to blend into one another in a brilliance that could have been either darkness or light. The light far in the distance and close by my feet shimmered in harmony" (*KAZ* 2: 197).

In the final passage of the memoir she is on a small ferry carrying her across the river from her school back to her home. It is dark, and a few soft lights flicker inside the boat, bringing her house by the bank into view.

> In the dim light of the lanterns I could see my house on the bank: a selfish father, a dauntless and stubborn mother, a short-tempered, sullen younger brother. Though not a peaceful home, it reflected in the flickering light of the dark river like a warm, beloved place. Had I ever before stood outside its walls alone in the open air, wrapped in the night—stood in the vast darkness of night with the pitch-blackness coiling around the borders of the kimono I was wearing? I felt tense. I defied the darkness and the night. I steeled my nerves and continued my

journey home. . . . It had been decided that I would be boarded somewhere near school for the winter months. Was I finally to be cast out of the family circle? (*KAZ* 2: 261)

We can see the way that Aya imagines the world. She is extraordinarily sensitive to boundaries—to the separations they cause and to their crossing. She divides her world into what is inside and and what is outside and expresses her ambivalence for her home in scenes that involve crossing from one world to another. When she examines her childhood, she finds a young girl obsessed with the threat of separation; and this threat continued to trouble her as an adult until it reached its emotional peak with her father's death. His death opened up a flood of memories in Aya and forced her to try to give those memories form. The trauma was so deep that very little of what she wrote would not evoke boundaries and crossings, or attempted crossings.

The separation that Aya seems to both court and fear in the passage about the ferry ride did not happen until her marriage in 1928 at the age of twenty-four; when she was a high school student, the security of staying home outweighed the excitement of leaving, though on numerous occasions she reached a breaking point and threatened to run away. As we have seen, Aya's attachment to a place—her need to feel connected—can be traced back to her early childhood. But in reading her memoirs, we must remember that the feeling of loss and the need for attachment derive much of their power from the insecurity and loneliness she felt and observed during and immediately after the war, when she was writing. The feelings that she assigns to her younger self cannot be untangled from her feelings years later as she writes of the war.

Yet the older Aya was not merely imposing her feelings on the past; the younger Aya had good reason to feel bruised, for her life was, in fact, a series of separations or threats of separation. What Aya described must have been close to the truth. The threat of separation so suffused the picture of her childhood that even the very few literary allusions in her memoirs relate to it. In 1923, the Great Kantō Earthquake forced her family into a small rented house in nearby Ishikawa. Aya had made many of the arrangements for the move and faced the dislocation with equanimity. Yet she seemed unable to sever her emotional tie to her old home. On the morning of their departure she copied down a poem from *The Tale of Genji* and placed it in a crack in one of the pillars holding up her house. The poem was by a sobbing young princess about to be separated from her childhood home. Her parents' marriage is in shambles, and her mother plans to take her daughter away before her son-in-law returns home. The girl pleads to see her beloved and doting father one last time and writes a poem on cypress-colored paper, which she inserts into a crack in the pillar at whose side she spent many secure hours. Aya quotes the poem.

> And now I leave this house behind forever;
> Do not forget me, friendly cypress pillar.[15]

Aya's first true separation from her childhood home did not come until her marriage in 1928 to Sanbashi Ikunosuke, with whom she spent ten unhappy, financially straitened years. When it came time for her to move on to married life, Aya had garnered the strength and even the excitement necessary to break her old bonds. But as the wedding day approached, her resolve seemed to waver. "For me, who had experienced life only from behind the strong shield of my father, marriage was the first chance to recognize the basic uneasiness and anxiety of life. Although marriage was something simply to feel happy about, it also brought a vague sense of fear" (*KAZ* 1: 215).

Although Rohan was sympathetic to his daughter's fears and even attempted to comfort her, his attachment, too, had greatly strengthened since the death of his son two years earlier. Having spent her early twenties caring for her dying brother, Aya was late, by the standards of the time, in getting married. During those years Rohan depended on Aya for her emotional strength and at times used her to protect him against his own pain. Ichiro's death in 1926 had a powerful effect on Aya, though in her early memoirs she barely touches on him. Not until after she had established herself as a novelist was she able to turn to his illness, which she treated at length in the novel *Little Brother* (*Otōto*, 1956). In her memoirs, however, she was best able to write about her father and seemed to bring in her brother's death to show how her relationship with Rohan developed.

Rohan had taken his son on numerous trips around Japan to expose him to a variety of life experiences. Now only Aya remained. When she returned from the hospital after a bout with diphtheria, he took her off on their first trip together, to Izu. He spent most of his time reading and writing in the inn, and she, on his orders, practiced calligraphy. But the two were linked in their shared grief for brother and son.[16]

For Rohan to arrange for the marriage of his only remaining child must have been difficult. According to Shiotani San, his biographer, Aya came to serve her father at his desk on her last day at home, as she always did, and he told her he had dreamed that she should stay. He said that he would miss her bright eyes. But parental responsibility led him to arrange for her marriage to Sanbashi Ikunosuke, the third son in a family of successful sake merchants. Aya, inappropriately old for a new wife, nonetheless had many qualities that would make her a good match: she was better than most at cleaning, cooking, and sewing; she was a skilled server of food and drink, and she had passable handwriting. Her husband-to-be had spent time in the United States, and Aya, having attended a mission school, knew English better than many women her age.[17]

But Ikunosuke was ill from the very start, and Aya found him ineffectual, even pitiable (*KAZ* 7: 20). Within two years Ikunosuke's sake business had begun to fail, and his desire to build a financial base for his new family had virtually disappeared. Worried and depressed, he grew physically and mentally weaker by the day. Aya ran the sake business and supported the family. But her husband had sunk as low as he could in Aya's eyes, for he had lost his will to work (*KAZ* 7: 25).

Aya desperately needed to escape the deadening life she was leading with her dispirited husband. She describes their relationship as if referring to fictional characters: "The husband was like stagnant water or like a lump of dirt that loses shape when thrown against the ground. The wife was like water in a kettle that blows its lid off when heated by a flame. Each experienced their life together accordingly: as lifeless, like a lump of earth, or potentially explosive, like a bundle of firewood" (*KAZ* 7: 25).

By 1936, Aya and her husband were living in a small rented apartment in a dark, ramshackle house from which they continued to run their small sake business.[18] She was exhausted and bitter, resentful of the condition her husband had brought her to and resentful of her father, who she felt had betrayed her. Her father, for his part, was drunk and in tears over Aya more than once. He spoke of her often and gave her much of what little money he had.[19]

As the daughter of a celebrated writer who lived in squalor, she merited a news article in the *Asahi shinbun*. Complete with a picture of a smiling Aya dressed for work in front of bottles of sake, the article described her effort to learn the trade and included comments that she made about her father. Rohan laughed off her difficulties, she said, and offered not the slightest sympathy. She herself insisted that her trade had nothing to do with her father's infamous love of sake; in other words, she should not be associated with him so glibly. Her remarks simplify her feelings for Rohan and do an injustice to his feelings for her. Like a child who is hurt and wishes to humiliate her parent into showing her more attention, Aya aired her feelings in public, taking him on in the world of letters that had taken him away from her. We can sense resentment in her comments, but need as well.

Aya returned to her father's home with her daughter, Tama, in 1938. That same year Aya's stepmother moved out. The fights with Rohan had become too abusive. In 1944, Tokyo was being turned to ashes by American bombers, and Rohan, Aya, and Tama were spending much of their time anxiously moving from one house to another in search of safety. In Aya's memoirs, the last years of Rohan's life have an eerie calm about them. He is growing an elegant white beard and suffering from severe headaches, bad eyes, and bleeding gums and anus. There is a calm about Aya, too. Exhausted by her recent economic and personal failures and secure again at her father's side, she seems resigned to her fate and willing to devote her energies to his care, rather than to breaking away from him.

She was troubled by the life of wandering and fear into which she and her father were thrown; she recalls feelings of bewilderment and hatred. Yet inside her father's house she was protected from the turbulence outside, soothed by Rohan's steady stream of words about the poet Bashō, philosophy, Chinese poetry, and the myriad subjects that filled his imagination. In Rohan's final days the house was gloomy, and Aya, distressed by his imminent death and constantly afraid that he did not love her, was by his side less and less. She seemed to hide behind the thin walls of the house, where she could only hear his voice. When he died in 1947, the money he left her did not even pay for the funeral.[20]

CHAPTER 3

Lessons of
the Father

In her memoirs Aya implicates Rohan as the source of negative emotions that render the act of writing painfully difficult. Her anxieties and fears about him accompany her feelings about the creative act. But Aya's evocation of her father is not simply associative. He emerges in her writing as a great teacher and guide, as the source of her creativity and the energizing force behind her career. In trying to understand Aya's imagination, we cannot but return to the web of emotions that knotted her to her father. In her writing she recast the two types of emotion she associated with her father into the elements of a self-conscious literary drama. She transformed debilitating aspects of her legacy into a frightened and passive literary persona and culled from that same legacy the nurturing resources of her growth into a literary artist.

In the semiautobiographical piece "The Medal" ("Kunshō," 1949) Aya dramatizes her feelings toward her father at a time of impending marital and financial ruin and speaks, too, about the problem of writing. The story focuses on a striking contrast: her father has been awarded the Medal of Culture while she is eking out a living delivering sake; he has a shiny new award, and she is clad in tattered work clothes; he writes books, and she lugs bottles.

When the piece opens, a young woman—Aya, presumably—has completed a tiring day of work and is riding a bus past the Sumida River. She watches it flow by and becomes lost in nostalgia for her childhood home. Suddenly, from the corner of her eye, she sees her father's name flash across a screen in neon lights. Her first reaction is concern: he's had a stroke. But a more violent emotion takes over when she realizes that he has won the first national culture award. She stands before the screen, clenching her teeth to keep from retching, her mouth full of bile. She puts down her empty bottles, goes behind a building, and begins to weep. The smell of urine assaults her. She looks up at the sign, and his name passes before her again.

"The Medal" is a psychological exploration of Aya's conflicting feelings toward her father, but as is true of all her writings, it projects into the past feelings and conflicts being worked out in the present; it evokes a younger Aya who cannot be dissociated from the woman writing the story. At the time, Aya was establishing an independent literary identity, and she did so in part by depicting herself as a younger woman who adamantly separates herself from her father and his writing. The Aya of "The Medal" feels more kinship with the band of laborers who congratulate her on her father's success than with literati. Her conscience urges her to offer her own congratulations; and when she finally does visit him the next day, she enters through the back door and waits tensely for him to appear.

When he descends from the upper floor of the house—an appropriate entrance, given his looming image—Aya feels a glow of paternal warmth, which she reciprocates with the small, tender gesture of arranging his sitting cushion. Although she needs to feel close to him, she can do so only when thinking of him as a father, not as a famous author. She insists that they are bonded in domestic acts of filial love and service, but never intellectually, never as fledgling writer and mature writer. Her wonder is at the mysterious forces that brought together such a great man and such an average girl. She is "at the bottom of a pitch-black valley, gazing up at the image of a father off in the distance, obscured by mist."[1]

We can imagine the anxiety that Aya must have felt when she began to write. Had she felt less of an emotional bond with her father, less warmth and respect, she might have dealt with his anxiety-producing presence in a more openly critical and dismissive way. She could have depicted him as coldly unavailable. But her feelings, as we have seen, were more complex: in "The Medal" she feels distant from Rohan the writer, the public man, but close to Rohan the father, the private man. She tries to balance both aspects: "Father was a strange man. With the same whip he cracked, he would suddenly point out and describe the beauty of a flower or of the clouds. With the very knife he used to dissect a belly, he would serve up some delicious delicacy."

Aya realizes that her fear of her father was related to her sense that he was constantly testing her and that she was always failing. After recounting a story he used to tell her as a child—about a lion who pushes his cubs off a cliff to see which would survive—Aya likens her father to "a lion of the literary world" and herself to the whimpering cub whose parent tells it to go off to be eaten by the other animals if it can't make it on its own. Aya reacts this way:

> I have nothing of my father's powerful learning and understand nothing about his art. When it comes to questions of fate, free will, the great complexity of human character, again I know nothing. But although I know little of these things, I have never been so foolish as to fear him because he is "a lion of the literary world." The only thing linking us was the flow of feelings between parent and child. But if I were to try to express these childhood feelings—warped in that peculiar way children's feelings are—I would have to say that there was truly something of the beast about father, something in him that wanted to test me, to kick me down and tell me to go off to be eaten.

Aya's fear of Rohan was diminished by her awareness that she was his daughter and no more. The pain of rejection was likewise deepened because she could not hope that he would think of her as a developing writer, worthy of his approval or even his training. We can assume that Aya did not suffer the struggles of a fledgling writer in her childhood; but as an adult memoirist, she could not help but project her desire to be a writer onto her past.

In "The Medal," Aya's only protection from the frightening lion of a father is her self-sufficiency and strength. She is a hard worker. Her sailcloth work-apron, bearing the insignia of her trade, gives her pride and energy and acts as "a shield against every type of arrow" and as a barrier that "hid my anguish." Yet the protection is incomplete; and her need to close off her inner struggle brings bruises and wounds to her inner spirit, for it separates her from her father and his happiness with the award.

Aya does not resolve conflicting feelings, then, but holds them without diminishing their force. She retrieves moments from the past with which she can examine her present emotional state. The end of "The Medal" returns her to the moment of writing. She has become a writer and has therefore come out from behind her canvas shield, but she still needs to withdraw behind it on occasion. "The medal itself somehow managed to survive the wartime fires, and the words that I put down now provide the solace of tears. The feel of that sailcloth apron on my body sometimes comes back with a living freshness that seems to wrap me in a tight embrace."

The Aya of "The Medal" is an angry, proud woman striving for independence from her father. But this same woman also seems thwarted by her notions of womanhood. Given the fortitude with which she worked with her husband at the sake business, she could have struck out on her own, but the extreme difficulty of doing so aside, the idea probably did not occur to her. Many years of living at her father's side and then at her husband's had taught Aya her proper place.

Living with her father had also taught Aya a language of negativity with which to describe herself as a writer. In most of her prose pieces and in the afterwords that appear with most of her works, self-disparaging remarks are endemic. We could easily dismiss them as the product of insecurity and false modesty, but her repeated and almost strident insistence on her ineptitude points to a more complex process at work. Aya's recurrent apologies and statements of contrived humility suggest that she is creating a passive guise through which the creative personality underneath can speak. "I am no magician. After forty years of cooking rice I cannot all of a sudden become accustomed to writing. Can I possibly write a novel? Or even a haiku? Can I write anything at all? . . . My father never praised me. In his final days he would often say, 'You're unable to do anything at all, but at least you're not the type to do harm.' This made me happy" (*KAZ* 1: 54).

At times Aya's avowed abhorrence of the world of letters is replete with all the anger and deference she felt toward her father: "My father used to say to me, 'The reason you're so stupid is that you don't read books,' or 'For once, why don't you try reading something of mine?' I was born in a literary household. But when I try to read through an entire volume, I recall my exhausted father poring over a book, and I become distracted. If I don't force that image from childhood down into my gut—as if forcing myself to gulp down spit—I cannot read in peace. How timid I am. I can't read, but not because I wasn't surrounded by books" (*KAZ* 1: 25).

Nor did she aim to write: "Like all the other normal girls of the time, I planned on becoming a housewife and was raised in a narrow sphere of domestic tasks. Father's lifelong passion for writing, together with his violent nature, made me resentful and didn't dispose me to scholarship or the arts. But with his death my destiny changed" (*KAZ* 1: 256). In 1963, looking back on her career as a famous and respected writer, Aya remembers writing for publication "without thinking about it, as if in a daze," unsure that she was up to the task at all.[2] Her first pieces do lack assuredness and evince anxiety about the act of writing. In "Miscellaneous Notes" she offered short and almost random descriptions of her father in his final days, interspersed with her own comments about her feelings toward him. The most lucid and effective passage comes when she explains her relationship to her father. She understands the uniqueness of being the daughter of so famous a man but regards herself as an "unworthy child" (*fusho no ko*). The sense of inadequacy that she expresses in her first piece occupies Aya throughout her career.

However strongly she might have felt it in the years growing up with her father, she was now even more deeply its victim, for the moment she began to write, she also began to see herself in a contest with him. At the close of "Miscellaneous Notes" she apologizes for wrestling in his arena.

> What might Father think of these shabby words I've put together? What might people say? Someone who has lived her life with silence as her sole consolation cannot but quake at the thought of picking up this worn-out brush to write for publication. Something in me was moved when the editors asked me to write, saying that everyone seemed to miss my father since his departure from this world. I grew accustomed to rejecting the requests to write that I received in the last two years of my father's life. It was easy to do so—my writing is so terribly unskilled, and I find writing even letters troublesome. But I am no longer able to reject these requests. What can my inherited task [*fukubun*] be but to record for posterity the image of my father as a healthy man? I beg your forgiveness from the outset for the inadequacies of my prose. I remember as a child being stumped by my homework and asking Father to help me write something. Instead, he taught me the song called "The Daughter of the Thread Merchant on Third Street in the Capital." I realize that writing doesn't come to me as easily as that song did. Because I could never get anywhere trying to apply formal rules for composing balanced prose, I have decided to turn from "The Daughter of the Thread Merchant" to something akin to *Essays in Idleness* [*Tsurezuregusa*]. I have scribbled down these inept words hoping that my extremely shallow understanding of my father and my clumsy way of describing him will not offend people too much. (*KAZ* 1: 18)

Aya seems to quake before the image of her father (which she fears to have violated in her writing) and before the task of describing him (which has been forced upon her and which she cannot master). But hidden behind these meek and self-effacing remarks is a literary sensibility that belies her claim to ignorance and naïveté; in denying the literary quality of her prose, she shows herself to be working through a literary idea by figuratively describing the literary position she wishes to take against her father: she will no longer be the daughter of the thread maker, of the man who weaves intricate and formal patterns, but will instead write idle essays, a more formless style (*zuihitsu*) associated with Yoshida Kenko's *Essays in Idleness* since the fifteenth century. She dissociates herself from her father and from the demands of formal structure and associates herself with another literary tradition, thus gaining an authority that validates her own procedures.

In her memoirs Aya tries to domesticate the image of a father, whose presence in her imagination threatens to crush her own creative impulses. She does this in part by disavowing any literary influence that may have come from him, by insisting that she had little to do with other than the most mundane aspects of his life. "What connected my father to me most deeply had nothing whatsoever to do with writing or learning; what bound us together was nothing more than the kitchen and food" (*KAZ* 1: 73). She chooses to recall moments of domestic intimacy, when she served him sake, arranged his cushions, or listened to his tales of childhood. She remembers how he placed his son on his lap to comfort the boy for having wet his sheets. With his face beet-red from drink and with tears in his eyes, Rohan tells how he, too, had often wet his pants. Once he was kicked out of his home with his soiled bedding and forced to make the rounds of all the neighbors to offer his apologies. Desperate to cure his problem, he had gone to see a druggist, who told him to consume a nightly potion of bird dung. It was "black, hard, and smelly," he remembers. Aya writes, "I can't continue putting together my memories without including this tale" (*KAZ* 2: 72).

So persistent is Aya in emphasizing her father's private appearance that she almost lures us into believing that his importance as a literary figure barely interested her at all. Yet in these passages describing filial moments she uses imagery associated with his professional life in order to engage Rohan as a writer as well. "Books" ("Hon," 1954), for example, opens with a childhood memory of Rohan's intimidating appearance as he concentrated on reading a book. Aya remembers feeling bored as she watched him and jealous of the attention he gave his books. As she grew older, she became used to seeing piles of books around the house, and although she found their indecipherable words majestic and mysterious, they raised no interest in her. During adolescence she was taken by the shapes, sizes, and smells of books but most of all by the dust they created and the challenge it was to keep them clean. Her father often scolded her for having too little respect for his books, and she often complained that they made cleaning too difficult: she dreamed of a home free of their clutter. With the war came air raids, and the books were stored elsewhere. Now that they were gone, she understood what it meant to be without them. "I felt as if the books had ended their lives in some storehouse somewhere. Of course, a book is given life by its owner, but now that I had lost them, I realized that they had absorbed even the feelings of someone like me, who had no real connection to them at all. Any book contains the life of its author. One volume equals one person; in ten books one expects to find the brilliant personalities and knowledge of ten people, and in a hundred books, a hundred people. When those books disappeared, my house lost ten, one hundred people, and I realized that I felt a vague loneliness" (*KAZ* 1: 109). Aya ends this brief memoir by returning to the image of her father scolding her for having so little to do with books.

Whereas Aya associates her father with the texture and materiality of books in "Books," in "Paper" ("Kami"), written two years later, she describes the respect that he and his mother lavished on paper goods. The vignette opens with Aya deciding to give fancy white Japanese paper to a friend as a housewarming gift. She sends a helper to the store, but he returns empty-handed. Realizing that her idea was old-fashioned, she remembers when her grandmother treated sheets of paper like valuable and delicate objects: after using one, she would erase it clean and wrap it in cloth to protect it from bugs. Rohan showed even greater veneration for paper. Over the years she watched him write as carefully as possible to avoid damaging the paper with his brush, even though the concentration might be to the detriment of his prose. It was easier, he often said, to correct one's writing than it was to produce a piece of paper. When he finished using a sheet, he would place it in a wastebasket that held other used sheets. Later he burned them to ashes, as if cremating deceased companions.

The Rohan house was always filled with paper, and Aya remembers her father tearing pages out of magazines and holding them up to the mirror to judge their quality. If the quality was poor, he might grow enraged at the lack of concern the manufacturer showed for customers. Sometimes he even became comically frantic. When Rohan died, Aya continues, the house grew paperless, and for the first time the picture of a childhood surrounded by paper and of a father who seemed to generate paper became etched in her mind. The narrative concludes with Aya lamenting the passing of special paper from her life, but she still thinks of it as the best possible gift to give (*KAZ* 1: 94–98). By discussing her father in terms of his regard for books and paper, Aya indirectly approaches the question of writing and his influence on her. Although she explicitly denies any such influence and repudiates any connection to her father's world of literature and learning, she culls memories that imply different answers.

In "Connecting Things" ("Musubu koto," 1955) she describes her father's approach to reading and in the process reveals—though again in roundabout fashion—the lesson he taught her about literature. In his later healthy years, he worked on manuscripts each morning for pay and read poetry and books on geography in the afternoon for pleasure; as he grew sicker, he read essays on medical science. His voracious reading was curtailed during the war when his eyes began to fail, and Aya admires his fortitude when, after the war, he gave up reading without the least sign of regret or bitterness. Although he continued to work on his prodigious commentary on the poetry of Bashō, others read and did his research for him. Shortly before he died, he asked Aya to investigate the meaning of a particular Chinese compound, but she flubbed this opportunity to take part in his literary pursuits. Unable to read the definition, she approached her sick father at his bedside and wound up asking him to read it for her. "I can't forget the sadly ridiculous figure of that unworthy, miserable little child" (*KAZ* 1: 103).

In the conclusion of the essay, Aya recalls an important lesson she learned from her father about the act of reading and understanding. According to Rohan, the process was akin to the formation of ice. One shard of ice, like one morsel of knowledge, shoots to the surface from the water below, and from that shard another is formed and then another, until the points of each closely aligned shard suddenly pull and stretch against one another until they form one piece. Thin ice then spreads across the water. Rohan said that knowledge took shape constantly, like the shards of ice; understanding, in contrast, involved joining the separate shards into one piece (*KAZ* 1: 104). Earlier in the essay Aya recalled her father's lesson that it was next to impossible to provide a guide to the reading of books: "When reading a book, a stupid person will be impressed with something stupid, and a twisted person will admire writing that is twisted" (*KAZ* 1: 100). But she now manages to salvage from her memory a lesson she could take with her. However obliquely, she describes how he taught her the nature of understanding—and by implication the nature of writing—and the process that shapes it.

No matter how much she insisted to the contrary, then, Aya did not grow up in a literary vacuum. Her claim that she received no direct literary training from her father was a way of distancing herself from the pressure of his presence. Yet she did want to explain how he helped form her sensibilities. She remembers being transfixed by the tales he told night after night about his fishing trips, about superhuman yogis and Christian miracles, about battles and heroic feats in days of yore (*KAZ* 1: 50). She remembers him teaching her about sex by referring to stories from the first collection of literature and history in Japan, the *Kojiki* (Record of Ancient Things, 712), openly and without shame. She was spellbound by the way he mimicked the accents and personalities of each character introduced into his stories. She remembers him telling her to read a novel by Nagai Kafu, and she remembers playing a game with him that involved making puns and coining words. She recalls being castigated for mispronouncing words or for speaking sloppily; she recalls writing haiku and being punished for choosing a wrong word or an inappropriate image.

But perhaps the most important legacy from her father was a set of attitudes toward the world. Rohan dedicated his life to books; he possessed a passion for knowledge that extended to all spheres of life. He talked about tradespeople and shopkeepers with as much interest and respect as he did about scholars and intellectuals—and perhaps with greater enjoyment. He was as interested in good fishing and good food, plants and horse racing, as in metaphysics and ethics. "People who don't pick up knowledge in the streets," he told Aya, "are idiots" (*KAZ* 1: 14).

Although book learning was important—as teenagers, Aya and her brother memorized Confucian classics by rote—the tone of their education altered every Sunday when they set out with their elderly teacher, with Rohan's blessings, for the entertainment district in Asakusa to be educated in the world outside the written word. They heard storytellers, they visited bars and restaurants, they went to dance halls, where Aya and her brother looked on fearfully as their teacher and guide became swept up in the excitement of watching the beautiful girls dance and bare their legs. When they returned home, Rohan might have Aya recite a story she had heard; once, when she grew silent, he began to dance about like a performer. After describing the teacher's behavior in the dance hall, Aya begged to be excused from any more such outings, but Rohan merely dismissed her, and the girl's worldly education continued (*KAZ* 1: 198–202).

If Rohan taught his daughter to be constantly aware of the knowledge to be gleaned from the world around her, he also taught her to concentrate her vision on what lay close at hand. In "Lens" ("Renzu," 1949), Aya describes this visual education and the effect it had in altering her self-image. In the course of the piece, Aya is transformed from an unhappy adolescent who stares at her ugly face in the mirror to a self-accepting girl who has learned to love her own reflection. Sensing the pain his daughter feels about the way she looks, Rohan gives Aya a camera; he tells her to use it to look at the world: "The natural world is too big; look for beauty hidden in more limited dimensions. Your eyes don't seem to be very good, so use this lens as your eye—it's very sophisticated and should help you see" (*KAZ* 1: 64). Through the lens of the camera Aya learns to focus her attention on small slices of life and to arrange what she sees into a frame. By looking at pictures of herself, she learns to view herself more objectively, to confront her image in the mirror with greater calm. In one photograph she sees her resemblance to her mother; in others she sees her father's loneliness written on her own face (*KAZ* 1: 65).

Rohan trained his daughter to sit still to observe the world. This training was rooted in Rohan's Neo-Confucian notions of concentrated and reverent contemplation of things, "perfect knowledge of things through an investigation of their true natures [*kakubutsu chichi*]." The exercise was not done merely to acquire a steadfast artistic vision.[3] Rohan intended instead to instill an attitude of respect, even reverence, for the qualities of everyday objects and domestic tasks. He approached the execution of domestic chores with the same seriousness that he did other forms of work, be it carpentry, philosophy, art, or writing.

He stressed respect for the inherent value of work and found primal energy and spiritual potential all around him. "The Way of everyday life is the exalted way," wrote the eminent eighteenth-century Neo-Confucian thinker Ito Jinsai. "There is nothing in daily life that meets the eye or ear that is not the Way." In his own writing, Rohan often took flights of fancy into the world of dreams or metaphysical speculation, but he balanced these abstractions with concrete images of everyday reality.[4]

Rohan's strict Neo-Confucianism, with its emphasis on maintaining one's proper role in life and executing one's prescribed tasks with devotion, defined Aya's identity as a woman. In the words of Yamazaki Ansai, the great Neo-Confucianist of the seventeenth century and founder of the state Confucian school, which later became the private academy at which Rohan studied as a child, "The highest duty is to fulfil one's allotted function (*taigi meibun*)."[5] But this same philosophical tradition also released Aya's creativity by teaching her to interact with her physical environment. Nineteenth-century thinkers such as Ito Jinsai and Nishikawa Joken—to whom Rohan owed allegiance—developed an epistemology for commoners that valorized everyday objects and tasks and taught the ability to understand and control circumstances through concentrated observation.

According to the Chu Hsi school of Neo-Confucianism, of which Rohan was a devotee, all material things possess a particular principle that is an aspect of a universal principle. The universal, in other words, adheres in the concrete (*rikinigenron*). Confucian learning, according to Chu Hsi, begins with the study of principles. "If we wish to extend our knowledge to the utmost, we must investigate the principles of all things with which we come into contact."[6] Through the particularity of individual things one can understand both metaphysical principles and standards of ethical conduct. A true Confucian must have an attitude of seriousness and reverence at all times and must use the mind to its utmost. "The 'perfect knowledge of things through an investigation of their true natures' (*kakubutsu chichi*) simply means that in regard to a thing that comes to our attention, we make an exhaustive study of all its principles. 'The extension of knowledge,' on the other hand, means that after we have studied exhaustively the principles of a thing, our knowledge of it becomes complete. We obtain this knowledge as if we have extended it [from our minds]."[7]

The principle of a thing is the unchanging quality of what it should be, a standard of propriety. According to Ch'en Ch'un, a disciple of Chu Hsi and a loyal transmitter of his teachings, "What a thing should be is simply its being proper, that is, not being excessive or deficient. That is principal."[8] A proper understanding of principle leads, ideally, to an ethical understanding of the importance of living according to proper function and ensures that one will not stray far. But the emphasis on the power of the mind also has subversive possibilities. It allows for a mastery of the things that make up a person's world; in Ying-shih Yu's words, it "can discover, order, and apply" principles. In Chu Hsi's words: "Principles are universally inherent in all things in the world. But it is the mind that takes charge of them. Being in charge, the mind therefore makes use of them. It may be said that the substance of principles is in things themselves while their functions depend on the mind."[9]

Perception, for Rohan, as for his mentors, involved concentration and understanding of the essence of an object; and when he trained Aya in housework, he instilled this same attitude in her. She was schooled in how to clean, how to perceive, and finally how to write, or so she interpreted her lessons. Within this philosophical framework, Aya discovered in discrete things and small spaces ample opportunity for self-expression and creative growth.

From the summer of her fourteenth year Rohan took control of his daughter's domestic education, teaching her everything she needed to know to take on the full responsibilities of a housekeeper. With her stepmother too weak with arthritis to perform her proper function, Aya was put in charge of the household chores. Rohan taught her the precise movements and the proper attitudes necessary to sweep, to carry buckets of water, to cut tofu, to repaper screens, and even to apply makeup. When a child, Rohan had been guided by a stern and demanding mother who required that all her children share the household chores, so it seemed natural to Rohan that he should impose a similar discipline on his own daughter. His son, Aya often reminds us, was spared the hard work.

Aya often insists that Rohan's interest in training her was more practical than anything else: his wife was ailing, and he needed someone to take care of the housework. His exacting demand for proper form in the performance of domestic tasks resulted in great measure from both practical and aesthetic considerations: better form creates greater efficiency, and women should at all times be graceful and beautiful, even when sweeping, even when chopping wood (*KAZ* 1: 171). Rohan was punctilious, used to being served with deference and accustomed to having everything in its proper place.

In spite of the rigors of this domestic training, Aya often points to it when trying to wrest from her past an explanation for her later development into a writer and for the sensibilities that informed her literature. It is through the metaphor of domesticity, in other words, that she discusses the question of literary influence. Her descriptions of learning to clean evoke the image of an apprentice artist being trained in the workshop of a strict but caring master. Aya grew exhausted under her father's watchful eye and wept when he scolded her for failing to meet his standards, invoking the name of Confucius. She sometimes wished to disappear forever from his sight.

Aya's first training session with her father took place, appropriately, in his study, a room devoted to writing that was normally closed to the children. He showed her how to prepare a broom for sweeping, taught her what order to sweep things in, and explained why it was important to sweep quietly and in a certain way. "Think of the broom as a writing brush," he told her. "You have to learn to use it so that its tip is effective" (*KAZ* 1: 150). He taught her how to handle a bucket of water, describing it as though it were a living being to be mastered. "Water is a truly frightening thing—a person who is weak at heart [*konsei no nurui yatsu*] will be unable to handle it" (*KAZ* 1: 154). He guided her every action and forced her to concentrate on not spilling a drop, as if she was carrying some priceless substance. "Faced with the grandeur of water, can one ever be unaware of one's movements?" (*KAZ* 1: 159). He taught her how to use an ax with grace and power, emphasizing the beauty in the woman who swings an ax with all her might. Rohan tried to teach concentration and thoroughness, along with grace and efficiency. The worst possible insult in the Kōda house was to be called "cheap" (*kechi*), not ungenerous in giving but unwilling to take the extra care and effort needed to properly carry out a task.

At Rohan's deathbed, Aya seems to have understood at last what effect this training had on her developing sensibilities as a writer. "Clasping his cold hands I finally understood. What my father had taught me was 'deep concentration' [*isshin*]. This is my guiding law. In the future I might pursue the path of a struggling writer, or I might, as he predicted, continue to live a domestic life. . . . Whatever I do, I want to preserve my pride in his giving me this one thing that I can rely on. I want to live up to the teachings of his final years" (*KAZ* 1: 54). Aya was intensely curious about her father's aged body and often imagined how he might die: she wanted to open him up and look inside his chest.[10] Indeed, it was to her father's body that Aya first applied her perceptual training. Like a nurse, she recorded his appearance in his final days with stoical objectivity. Aya missed his last breath and regretted the lost opportunity to observe so special a moment. But she recognized that her father had supplied her with some of the tools she would later use to create a literature out of the narrow world in which she lived.

As Aya herself realizes, Rohan was, after all, training her not only to care for his own home but also to fulfill her future responsibilities as a wife and mother. My attempt to impart deeper meanings to his training may seem little more than a rationalization of his constricting ideas about how to raise a young girl. Aya knew that her father held such ideas and often resented his attitude. Perhaps she, too, was generous in finding in his training lessons that extended into other (more unconventional) aspects of her life, specifically her writing. It often seems that Aya became so thoroughly imbued with her father's language of social values that she accepted it as her own. Yet her self-conscious use of that language in discussing matters pertaining to her growth and identity indicates that she accommodated her father's values to her own needs.

Rohan's attitude cannot be so easily reduced to traditional notions of child rearing. Even though he did see his daughter's proper place to be taking care of the home, his attitude toward housework had philosophical depth, and he respected a woman properly carrying out her duties. This attitude, and Aya's general acceptance of it, confounds many generally held notions of domestic work and women's place in the household. We may suspect him of devising a way to keep an intelligent and active daughter in a role that might have held little interest for her, but we must appreciate the genuine respect Rohan had for the role that he felt his daughter had no choice but to take on. He can be faulted, perhaps, for his unwillingness to see his daughter outside that role, but never did he condescend to her because of it.

Nor, apparently, did Aya resent housekeeping. She shared his respect for it and thought his training was an effective tool for understanding and controlling her environment. Indeed, Aya's devotion to "perfect knowledge of things through an investigation of their true natures" stayed with her throughout her career as a writer. It is the backbone of her most celebrated novel, *Flowing*. At age seventy-three, on a trip to northern Japan, she discussed weeds, plants, and trees as if they contained the seeds of human truths, or so says her travel companion. A pine writhing in its combat with the wind was the struggle of life against destiny; the resilience of sprouting weeds was the tenacity to survive. Looking transcended observation, because there was no value in seeing a thing if it did not reveal some inner truth. When she realized that the trees she had trudged so far to see were a disappointment, Aya canceled the remainder of her trip. If she could not discover the hoped-for inner depth in those trees, she would prefer not to look at them at all, for merely looking was not seeing.[11]

In her writing, Aya and her narrators concentrate on the material objects that daily confront them in the home. These objects can elicit tenderness and nostalgia or hostility and bitterness, but they are always worthy of reverence. It is through an imaginative interaction with everyday objects that Aya confronts her feelings toward both her father and her past.

CHAPTER 4

War and

Recovery

The intensity of Aya's vision is undoubtedly related to the narrowness of her gaze. But Aya's concentrated view of material shapes was not circumscribed by her father's house; she also looked at the destruction of material life on the grand scale—the rubble into which Tokyo had been transformed by the war. Her sensitivity to objects, which she learned at her father's knee, was intensified as she viewed the post-1945 world around her.

As ensconced as Aya was within her father's world and as powerful as his language and vision may have been in shaping her own, she also belonged to a complex postwar society that influenced her sensibilities and whose image was refracted in her writing. Seeing Aya as a deferential young woman living an uneventful life in the household of a famous father—an image Aya herself fostered—should not blind us to the ways that her writing was affected by the contemporary situation. In her writing Aya transformed years of domestic service at her father's side into a literature that dealt with small worlds and through them engaged larger social issues: the spiritual state of the Japanese after the war and in the decade to come, the relation of past to present, and the way to live with the mixed and troubling consequences of the war.

Still, Aya is rarely mentioned in studies of postwar Japanese fiction or in discussions of writers who express the spirit of the postwar years. She is conspicuously absent even in those studies that attempt to recall writers

who have fallen through the cracks of literary history. She has been rele-
gated to the position of biographer, "seller of memories," and her writing
has been discussed for what it reveals about her father and her relationship
to him. Critics have seen in her small opus only an extremely narrow literary
vision and have failed to notice the ways in which Aya confronted the issues
of her time.

The oversight should come as no surprise: as one critic has pointed out,
literary histories of postwar writing in Japan have been primarily the work
of writers linked to one or another literary coterie and have thus focused on
the members of that coterie. Critics have spotlighted writers who seem
most obviously representative of their time.[1]

Unlike most other writers of her day, Aya was on the periphery of
literary circles, associated with no literary coterie or journal. Much of her
writing, moreover, reveals a middle-aged woman attempting to piece together a personal identity shaken apart by the death of her father, so her
themes can seem intensely personal, removed from any social context. She
seldom, if ever, looked beyond the confines of her personal life to society
and politics or to the West. Aya was not xenophobic or parochial, nor was
she self-obsessed—she always had her father before her. Yet her limited
subject matter does lend a hermetic quality to her prose. Her language, too,
sprouted and grew in the hothouse conditions of her sequestered life with
her father and thus resembled a peculiarly old-fashioned, private prose
rather than a shared modern public discourse. And unlike most of her
contemporaries, Aya did not overtly take on the issues of most interest to
postwar writers and critics: modernity and the modern self, existential
angst, the elimination of all remnants of fascism, and the creation of a free
and democratic society.[2]

Aya was a special case. But she was also a writer of her time—emphati-
cally so. She had lived through the physical and spiritual destruction of
Japan and was constantly aware of a feeling of loss and of a longing for
spiritual comfort. From her divorce in 1938 until Rohan's death in 1947—
through the years of the war—she cared for her ailing father and stayed at
his side as the bombing of Tokyo intensified. In the last year of the war her
stepmother died, and the family house in Tokyo's Koishikawa district was
destroyed. Aya was exhausted. She remembers these years as a time of
insecurity. "The war taught people a life of aimless wandering. Our family
first set off for Shinano but was unable to settle down there. Then we went
to Izu but couldn't settle there either. The feeling of aimless wandering—
might it be the point at which the desire to be securely settled meets the
urge to move forward continually, abandoning each and every place along

the way? And yet there was something about this uncertain life that was slightly sweet. For the time being, we placed our unsettled feet in Sugano, near Kokufutai, fully aware that we would be there only temporarily, until once again we would have to drift on somewhere else."[3]

When the war ended, Aya was finally able to settle down with her father, if only to watch him die; and by grappling with his death, she grew more sensitive to the sense of loss that gripped the nation. Although her way of confronting the emotional conditions of postwar Japan may have been more personal and more oblique than her contemporaries' way, it rendered the bruised spirit of the nation no less appropriately.

Reactions to the surrender and to the state of the nation thereafter depended on any number of personal factors: what one's political leanings were before the war, how one had imagined the war would end, and how (or if) one imagined death. Other factors—education, geographical location, family history—certainly played an important role as well. The portrait Aya painted of herself during the immediate postwar years was that of an exhausted but tirelessly patient and devoted daughter watching over an ailing parent, though feeling a degree of resentment about serving him and about its effect on her life. In her memoirs there are no politics, no wish for victory or overwhelming sadness at defeat, nor much awareness of the world outside, other than moments of compassion for others suffering as she does—especially the many newly orphaned children huddled in burned-out Tokyo.

Although it is impossible to account for the variety of reactions to the war by Japanese writers, certain patterns of response emerge. Writers of the same generation, for example, shared certain emotional sensibilities. It mattered how old one was: people who turned twenty in 1940, having lived under the shadow of the war effort during their childhood, might have feelings different from those of people born in 1940, who were too young to be saturated with the war ethos before the war ended, and, again, different from those of people old enough not to have been susceptible to the prevailing ideology.

A writer like Kawabata Yasunari—already an established and mature writer when the war ended—possessed something of what Miyoshi Yukio calls "the adamancy [*katakunasa*] of the older generation."[4] According to Kawabata, all that was left after the defeat was a solitary return to "the mountains and rivers of old," and all that was left to write about was an ancient beauty, a "sad, Japanese beauty."[5] Aya was forty-one when the war ended, and she possessed, like Kawabata, a store of memories undamaged by the war; her identity as a person had been formed, like his, many years before. But as a writer, Aya was a mere child, lacking purpose and confidence in her own style. Before anything else she needed to piece together her memories and find—or create—her identity as a writer.

In the period immediately following the war, which one critic described as the most vibrant in Japanese writing since the heyday of Naturalism forty years earlier, Aya was still nursing her father and watching him die in her own personal war.[6] The writers who seemed to capture the spirit of the new age—at least those who were strongly represented in contemporary literary journals—were attempting to arrive at new literary and existential beginnings. They considered that past values had collapsed and that society was in need of rebuilding. They were engaged in a "a profound questioning both of the reality of individual consciousness and of the more ideological and political foundations of Japanese society."[7]

For writers and critics associated with left-wing literary journals such as *Modern Literature* (*Kindai bungaku*) or *New Japanese Literature* (*Shin Nihon bungaku*), which were suppressed before the war, the end to many years of enforced silence meant a new freedom, a "second spring."[8] For fifteen years the language that Japanese had heard and read had been a language that extolled patriotism, military valor, and self-sacrifice. An end to the national war effort consequently meant the possibility of reinventing the Japanese literary language.

The "second spring" came to writers in their thirties when the war ended, who felt that their own youth had been lost during the years of crisis. For Aya the immediate postwar years were a bitter season, a time of bewilderment about the world and her place in it. Although to many writers, revolutionary changes in literature and society now seemed possible, to Aya these hopes were largely irrelevant, far removed from her own life and needs. When Miyamoto Yuriko was concentrating her talents on essays with political and feminist intent, Aya, seven years her junior, was interested only in describing her father's final days and was just beginning to write about her experience with him.

Miyamoto, along with other writers, spoke of larger things. She discussed the need to discard one's old self and learn how to live anew; by using the legacy of the previous generation of proletarian writers, she said, society as a whole and women in particular could be liberated from the shackles of the past. Hirano Ken, an outspoken advocate of a literature of renewal, said that writers should establish a modern, individualized self. According to him, a writer should create a literature that fosters respect for the individual and opposes contempt for humankind. For Honda Shūgo, the end of the war made possible "the awakening of the self" (*shutai no mezame*).[9]

When the hopes expressed in many writings of the immediate postwar period had faded and revolutionary change seemed a dream of the past, Honda, in 1958, summed up the experience of the Postwar writers: "The ultimate goal of the search by the Postwar writers, if we are to give it a name, was human freedom. 'The realization of the self,' or 'the realization of individualism,' has a similar meaning, but most Postwar writers didn't think of human freedom within the framework of individualism. Freedom itself was the ultimate goal."[10]

For novelists associated with the Postwar school, such as Noma Hiroshi, Umezaki Haruo, Shiina Rinzo, and Takeda Taijun—all in their thirties when the war ended—the new era meant an opportunity to debunk the myths that people had lived with for so long and to create a new way of life. These writers explored existential questions: the meaning of the self, the difficulty of living in a world emptied of firm values, the nature of individual freedom.[11]

Much of the fiction produced immediately after the war can be described, then, as the response of Japanese intellectuals to defeat, and in this sense, too, Aya was very much an outsider. To a great extent, criticism dominated the first years after the war. Intellectual issues were debated: the connection between literature and politics, the nature of the modern self, the meaning of humanism and freedom. Change and revolution were in the air. All of the writers, their differences notwithstanding, argued for the realization of a modern, individualized consciousness that would be free from the bonds of tradition.

But the sense of revolutionary possibility, the self-examination, and the striving for change diminished by the early 1950s, and with diminishment came censure of the previous goals. Literary critics declared the end of the postwar period, for the vitality that had characterized the previous years seemed to be fading.[12] If novelists before the war had believed in art and those in the immediate postwar period in revolution, individualism, modernity, and freedom, the writers emerging in the 1950s had little faith in these myths. By then, suggests Isoda Kōichi, all the gods of Japanese literature had died, and writers began to search for meaning beyond the individual—in the past, in tradition, in the idea of a lost homeland. And it was during this time that Aya prevailed over her past sufficiently to cast it into literary form.

By the early 1950s, Aya had gained a temporal distance from her father's death, and the nation, too, had moved beyond the initial postwar years of collapse. The change in the intellectual climate was in part related to the changing material condition of Japan. With the start of the Korean War in

1950 the national economy was boosted by a government arms procurement program. In 1951 a peace treaty between Japan and the United States was finalized, and a year later the Allied occupation ended. The subsequent feelings of relief and release resulted in vigorous debates concerning the need to create a new literature for the "people" (*kokumin*)—a word that until then was taboo because of its associations with prewar fascism—and the need to hold on to native traditions that were fast disappearing in the effort to transform the nation.

In Japanese intellectual life, the search for tradition has often been accompanied by rejection or criticism of the West and the modernity associated with it. Such a yearning for the past is by no means peculiar to the 1950s; it represents a vigorous tradition in its own right. In modern Japanese history the urge to return to bygone ways, to hold on to what is fading away, has gone hand in hand with the urge to modernize, develop, change, and leave the past behind.[13] From the end of the nineteenth century through the first decades of the twentieth, Aya's father was a pivotal figure in this tradition. In the 1930s the writer Yasuda Yojūrō sensed that the internalization of Western values by the Japanese and the rejection of native traditions had led to a deep spiritual crisis. This crisis could only be alleviated, he felt, by reviving a feeling for the true home of the Japanese spirit, that is, a feeling for the gods and the poetic beauty of ancient Japan.[14] The critic Kobayashi Hideo lamented a similar loss in his 1933 essay "Literature of the Forgotten Home" ("Kokyō ushinatta bungaku"): "Where there is no memory, there is no home. Without powerful memories, culled from the layers of firm impressions that a firm environment induces, one will not know the invigorating emotion with which the word *home* overflows. Wherever I look within or about myself, I can find no such place." The loss of a home robbed literature of its foundations: "It is simpler to discover the face of the urbanite, the abstract man, born nowhere at all, than to find a Tokyoite, born in Tokyo. No doubt a type of literature occupies itself with this abstract man, but it must lack the texture of reality. . . . From such an abstraction no true literature can be born."[15] Only a writer who felt so lost and homeless could long so much for a home, and in this, Kobayashi shares much with Aya.

The inverse of this urge—the intellectual rejection of home and tradition—has often been the passkey to literary sophistication and modernity, and although Aya herself did not attempt to establish such an identity, there was in her writing just such a battle with the home and family that were threatening to suffocate her. Since the publication of Shimazaki Tōson's novels *The Broken Commandment* (*Hakai*, 1906) and *The Family* (*Ie*, 1911) and Tayama Katai's novel *The Quilt* (*Futon,* 1907), the home has been associated with traditions and a past that shackle the individual; it is a force against which many Japanese writers have fought in establishing themselves as independent modern artists. To writers like Masamune Hakuchō (1879–1962) and Iwano Homei (1873–1920), home life was essentially prosaic and hostile, a cradle of ambivalence, a prison to escape from. In novels like those by Kasai Zenzo (1887–1928) and Chikamatsu Shuko (1876–1944), the home fared no better: it was a force to be denied, a place to break away from. According to Ito Sei, these novelists "portrayed themselves negatively, denying the conventions of home and society, and in flight."[16] Even a writer like Natsume Sōseki (1867–1916), who was tied more strongly to the past than these others and who was unwilling to make a blanket indictment of the family, depicted the home in *Grass on the Wayside* (*Michikusa,* 1915) as suffocating, its rituals bereft of meaning.

In the years after the war these two attitudes toward the home and tradition—the need to reject and the desire to revive—were expressed by writers and intellectuals with renewed vigor. The desire to rebuild a society whose values had collapsed involved an attempt to sweep away the past. But the feeling of loss remained; only when the Allied occupation ended in 1952, and writers began to stand back from the crowd rushing forward, did the feeling emerge with even greater power, seeming at times even to overshadow the urge to be released from the past. The contest between these impulses was the core of Japanese intellectual life in the 1950s, just when Aya was beginning to find her own way as a writer.[17]

The need to hold on to or regain something lost also derived in part from the accelerated pace of modernization in the early 1950s. The economy was booming, the shape of material life was changing irrevocably, and the new developments were leading into an unknown future. To Aya this transformation was lamentable: it meant the loss of traditions, standards, and historically sanctioned forms. Among intellectuals, it was Takeuchi Yoshimi, in an article entitled "Modernism and the Problem of the People" ("Kindaishugi to minzoku no mondai"), who helped to ignite a debate concerning the impasse in literature and the life of the mind. He criticized Japanese intellectuals for slavishly imitating the West and for turning away from their own traditions; he argued that modernism (*kindaishugi*), in rejecting all vestiges of fascistic thought, had rendered the notion of "the people" taboo and had brought a sense of emptiness (*kūhaku*). Takeuchi was disgusted with the abstract, modern, free individual that such a philosophy had fostered.[18]

Because modernity was associated with the West, a rejection of the one meant a critical attitude toward the other. Takeuchi helped bring this collective disgruntlement with modernity and the West into the open. In a number of articles he referred to the literature written during the occupation as "a literature of colonialism," by which he meant not only physical occupation by an alien power but also spiritual occupation by foreign ideologies.[19]

In 1952, with the physical occupation over, discussion centered on the need to recall the past and the traditions of Japan, which had been lost in the headlong rush toward democracy and individualism. This discussion, which involved critics of all political and literary leanings, focused on the intellectualized literature of the immediate postwar period. There was a new sense that "progress" could not solve all problems, that starting anew might require sacrificing too much, that a clean break with the past was not necessarily the most effective cure for the nation's woes. Writers' attempts to restore meaning to the lives of the people through an ideology of democracy and humanism were seen to have failed, or at least reached a dead end.

The "debate over a literature for the people" (*kokumin bungaku ronsō*) represented the desire to regain an authentic voice. In 1955, for example, Yamamoto Kenkichi, a scholar of modern literature who was responsible for a renewed interest in the Japanese classics in the 1950s, published his *Classics and Literature* (*Koten to bungaku*), calling for a contemporary literature reinvigorated by an understanding of tradition.

Yamamoto argued against a "modernist" literature emphasizing the value of the individual and for a language and aesthetics in which both writer and reader might share a common set of myths and beliefs. By reestablishing the continuity of tradition, he hoped to reestablish the link between those who wrote literature and those who read it.

> When a writer has been set free from the rules that bind communal society and the motivation behind his poetry has become no more than the expression of the feelings, psychology, or thoughts of a completely isolated author writing of his own particular circumstances—in other words, when his writing comes to be nothing more than a confession of a sense of isolation—the poems that he writes show the symptoms of an unavoidable disease. He utterly negates the world and those living in it; his poems cease to serve human society; and within the tragic isolation of his ivory tower, his poetry takes only poetry as its goal and concentrates on the secret art of alchemy. . . . In the end what is attained is the self-justifying consciousness of the poet and the cessation of the communicative function of the poem.[20]

The great success of Fukazawa Shichiro's novel *Tale of Narayama* (*Narayama bushiko*) in 1956, which won an important literary award and set off a flurry of critical and popular debates, exemplified this nostalgia. Set in a poor mountain village, *Narayama* is a retelling of a folk tale in which an old woman is taken by her son deep into the mountains to die, according to ancient custom. That the woman is still a vital and useful person increases the tragedy. But more important is her acceptance of the fate dictated to her by the community, an acceptance described as noble. A contemporary novelist, Takeda Taijun, commented: "What makes this novel beautiful is that the old woman wants to climb the mountain and die quickly. The novel could never have come off if she had been made to cry and scream."[21]

Aya's literary visibility and critical recognition peaked during the years that Yamamoto was rereading tradition and Fukazawa was evoking a vanished past. In 1955 her collected works were issued—a sign of success in Japanese letters—and in 1956 and 1957 she was awarded three prestigious literary awards. She was praised for upholding tradition, for repossessing a style that modern Japanese writing had lost. Yamamoto, one of her greatest champions, put it this way: "In general, Aya's writing is quite different from modern writing. After one has read Aya's work, the very desire to become modern seems nothing more than a hankering after the latest fashion. Aya's own writing, on the contrary, maintains a living vitality lost sight of in the modern Japanese novel."[22]

The ways in which Aya's writing may or may not be considered modern and the implications of describing her in these terms will be discussed in greater detail. For now, it need only be noted that her success in the mid-1950s was linked to the perception of her as a writer who maintained a style and sensibility thought to be missing from more modern writing.

Yearning for the past, for the sanction of tradition, for the comfort and security of a lost home, reveals one important aspect of the Japanese emotional makeup in the 1950s. Some writers, however, because of age or tenacious self-assurance, seemed to live outside the contemporary structure of feelings—even further outside than Aya. Tanizaki Jun'ichirō was one such writer: he seemed to live to the rhythm of his own biological clock. In 1956, at seventy years of age, in his autobiographical work *Childhood Years* (*Yōshō jidai*), he explored his past, not to regain something lost but to locate the roots of his firmly possessed artistic identity.[23]

In her own writing Aya did not cast back to an imagined heroic—though also tragic—past, as did Fukazawa in *Tale of Narayama*, for her memories anchored the past strongly within her. She pieced together an existing and still-vivid past, rather than creating one from her imagination. But neither did Aya have, as Tanizaki did, a fully formed artistic sensibility whose sources she might locate in the past. Instead, she used her memories as a source of artistic vision. What comes through in Aya's writing is a more troubled relation with the past than that expressed by either Fukazawa or Tanizaki: she senses that traditions are fading and laments their impending disappearance, but she also tries to forget those aspects of the past that haunt her, tapping only those that might provide a working artistic identity.

What writers like Aya and Tanizaki did share was their search for historical authenticity. The writers and intellectuals who sought change after the war were by and large younger than Aya and Tanizaki but old enough to have matured politically and emotionally before the war effort became an everyday part of Japanese life. They could imagine rebuilding their world according to solid Marxist, socialist, or modernist beliefs.

But the writers most representative of the youngest postwar generation—writers born in the 1920s, like Ishihara Shintarō, Yasuoka Shōtarō, and Mishima Yukio, who gained prominence in the mid-1950s—had grown up during the war. Lacking the memory of an unsullied past to sustain them, these writers had looked to the future with pessimism. They came to prominence when Aya did, at mid-decade, and thus help us understand how she fit into her time.

The writers of this generation were young enough to be her children and had grown up knowing little other than the ideology of empire. To them the defeat did not bring freedom and liberation, as it did to many of their seniors; it brought enervation, demoralization, disappointment, an inner vacuum. Their writings bear witness to their emptiness as vividly as Aya's do to her very different sensibility. The attraction to the abstract and the desire for a release from quotidian reality is as striking in these writers as the attachment to palpable materiality and the present world is in Aya.

The generation separating Aya from these writers accounts for some arresting contrasts in outlook, but because they lived the same history after the war, each writer evoked essential aspects of the time. The appearance of Aya's novel *Flowing* and the success of *The Tale of Narayama* coincided with the spectacular public success of Ishihara Shintarō's novel *Season of the Sun* (*Taiyō no kisetsu*, 1955). Whereas *Narayama* reached back to a time when devotion to tradition could be heroic, and *Flowing* lamented the passing of tradition, *Season of the Sun* expressed the unfocused energy of a younger generation emerging after years of economic difficulty. For the characters in

Ishihara's novel, the desire to submerge the self grew out of a sense of directionlessness and found its end, not in preordained forms or traditions, but in moments of pure physical activity apart from all social and historical ties.[24]

The desire for a release from established forms and the need to be anchored in tradition describe opposite aspects of the same emotional experience. The sense of weightlessness, which the critic Eto Jun called the most pressing problem facing Japanese literature,[25] was poignantly described by members of the younger generation—in *Season of the Sun,* as well as in the writings of others who sought alternatives to weightlessness, not in the past but in enclosed worlds. Like Aya, these writers were attracted to confined spaces, but their sensibility was different from hers.

One writer who seemed most bewitched by small, secure spaces was Yasuoka Shōtarō, who was born in 1920. Yasuoka's childhood and education were interrupted by the war. "Our formative years coincided with the war years; we faced peace with our insides empty, we had no way of dealing with the new life." Yasuoka spent much of the war stricken with tuberculosis, wrapped tightly in a smelly quilt—a proper image for his spiritual state at the time, for he responded to the events of the outside world by constructing an inner fortress. "From 1940 or 1941 we created a small separate world to protect ourselves from the violence of the so-called mobilization of the national spirit, and we tried to hide inside it. When writing novels, I tried to hide myself as much as possible in empty, meaningless words. Of course, now that the war was over, thought and discussion were free, and there was no reason to hide. But no matter how much outside circumstances changed, the separate world we constructed inside ourselves would not be easily destroyed."[26]

When the war ended, Yasuoka felt liberated, but he sensed spiritual danger in the absence of any powerful force to resist. The intimacy of Yasuoka's other world was gone, and he was left with a feeling of emptiness for which he had no cure.

In describing their sense of spiritual loss after the war, other writers also recall the war as providing relief or satisfaction. Mishima Yukio remembers the war as a festival and the absolute destruction as plenitude. Then, at least, he lived at life's edge and could feel things keenly.

> I had some brave friends who did not worry much about their lives and continued sleeping when the air-raid sirens went off. I, however, hid in the damp, melancholy air shelter with my manuscript in hand. I would crane my neck out the hole and gaze on the beautiful devastation of the metropolis. It was like

looking at the distant bonfire of a great festival of destruction and luxurious death. I was happy then, with no worries about jobs or exams, nothing to someday take responsibility for. Food was scant but sufficient. I was happy in my life and with my literature, with no critics, nobody to battle—just the joy of being a solitary writer. Looking back on this contentment, I can't help romanticizing it, but even when I try to recall the past accurately, I can't remember another time when I didn't feel the burden of my self pressing down on me. I was free of gravity. . . . I was living in a secure fortress.[27]

In his 1956 novel *Temple of the Golden Pavilion* (*Kinkakuji*), this secure fortress is a small golden room inside a flaming temple. The novel describes a young acolyte's disgust with the banality that he sees in postwar life and his desire to find a beauty that transcends it. The temple, to Mizoguchi, is perfection itself, but he can go beyond this world into a place of pure abstraction only by burning it down.

For Mishima, when the war ended, the struggle with absolute power ended as well, and life became mediocre and dull. The real temple was gone, and a new, abstract one replaced it. Mishima and Aya both equated the end of conflict with loss and shared as well a desire to hide inside enclosed spaces. But Mishima, in courting abstraction, could hardly be more different from Aya. Just over ten years after the war, Mishima seemed to long for the destruction of the material world that the war had made possible. Aya came to miss the very opposite—the material struggle to survive that the war had forced on her.

In *The Temple of the Golden Pavilion,* material objects impede access to the spiritual world, and fragments of things are beautiful precisely because, and only when, they seem abstract. As we shall see, Aya uses objects to move the reader from the present to the past and values pieces of things precisely because they embody the past. Aya longs for a grounded realm, "built up," in Kobayashi Hideo's words, from the powerful memories "that a firm environment brings forth."[28] She shows little of the abhorrence of social restrictions or discomfort with tradition seen in some of her younger contemporaries, and none of the flirtation with abstractions seen in Mishima. Rather, she exhibits a faith—though a troubled one—in material reminders of the past.

An inner strength, nurtured under the powerful influence of her father, allowed Aya the luxury—if we may call it that—of choosing to live with a set of standards and mores sanctioned by tradition, no matter how vexed her relation to that tradition might be. Her longing to do so undoubtedly grew out of the uncertainty she felt and perceived in the postwar world. Yet this longing could never be fully satisfied, or so we sense in her writing. Aya wanted to be located securely within a place, in a home, surrounded by solidly arranged emblems of the past. But fulfillment was always post-poned, leaving a troubled ambivalence, a gnawing hunger for something that she knew she could not obtain.

A World

of Objects

In her biographical pieces about life with Rohan, Aya released a flood of memories, presenting the image of a woman emotionally drained and creatively spent. She had poured an entire lifetime of memories onto the page and given them coherence in narrative form. She had become a writer, then, but had used up the material she knew intimately. What was left to write about?

Aya was no longer interested in serving up memories at the request of editors. On April 7, 1950, in the pages of the *Mainichi shinbun*, she announced her decision to stop writing altogether: "It is unforgivable that I have been praised for writing things that require no effort on my part. If I continued writing in this way, I would be shameless. Living without struggling is no way for a member of the Kōda family to live." Brave as this pronouncement may seem, it is a measure of Aya's continuing allegiance to the world defined for her by her father and society that she allowed her urge for independence to lead her to a role not dissimilar from the one she had left: she became a maid in an economically declining geisha establishment. She did not set out on the open road and head for uncharted territory, nor did she ensconce herself in a community of writers and intellectuals or immerse herself in writing. Instead, she entered a world of working women whose lives were as restricted as her own in her father's home. There she could rechannel her skills and energies from service to her father into service to others. At the same time, she could try to shake off her father's heavy mantle. She was changing from a memoirist, depicting the world around her, to a writer of fiction, exploring a world beyond her own and shaping it to her own design.

Although Aya's decision to enter the geisha house certainly involved a desire to find materials for her writing, there was more to it than that. Her father's training had been a moral one, stressing the value of ethical and intellectual rigor, of living and acting according to high personal standards. He had taught her to take charge of her own fate: "A great man with a mission to accomplish must have the determination to make his fate."[1] Aya's life and writing had depended on her father for too long; it was time to determine her own fate. Even though Aya was not able (or did not wish) to free herself completely from her past, she needed to enter a world of her own choosing—and she chose one ruled by a society of women living apart from the society in which she had been reared. For four months she abandoned writing, and all the struggles and anxieties that came with it, and entered a new world. After she emerged from the geisha house, Aya began to exorcise her childhood demons and create a new, confident voice, one that found its fullest expression five years later in *Flowing,* her most popular and critically lauded work, which many critics considered to be her first "true," fully orchestrated novel.[2]

For three years after she left the geisha house, until 1954, she edited her father's writings and wrote short miscellaneous pieces dwelling on her past with him. Not until then did Aya distance herself enough from her past to write her most self-consciously literary works. In the following passage she describes this emergence. The qualities of honest self-appraisal and pos-tured self-denigration are typical.

> The many readers who loved my father's work grieved at his passing and wanted to know how he appeared in his final years. They encouraged me to write, which is how it all began. I wrote as a courtesy to them, and my writing was unexpec-tedly popular because nobody knew anything about what I had to say. . . . I was asked to write one piece after another, but apart from memories of my father, I had nothing at all to write about. People jokingly called me a "seller of memo-ries," and why shouldn't they have? But what was there in my past? I didn't even have a life I could call my own to write about. There wasn't a thing I could write about with confidence. All I had were memories of funerals—the only chance women like myself, bound to the home, have to meet people is at funerals.[3]

Aya's reasons for entering the geisha house and then writing about it were personal, but loss and longing are evident, as is a sense that the world was in crisis—all feelings that partake of a more general Japanese literary sensibility. Modern Japanese writers have often sought ways to describe a shifting civilization. Although they have often embraced tradition, they have also seen it, and the objects representative of it, as the enemy. Because they prefer to look for new forms of life and new ways to describe those forms, they have often lacked the stability—or the desire—to invest their culture with meaning.[4]

Like other Japanese writers, Aya writes about material objects that embody the past in the present. She examines her own emotionally mixed inheritance through these objects. The past to which they draw her is potentially suffocating, but it can also be nuturant and vital. When describing her memories of her grandfather, for example, it is his kettle, which survived into the present, that lures Aya into the past; in the remembrance entitled "Fragment," a piece of a tray induces a rush of memories in the young girl who finds it. Aya's father, we recall, took on the form of an object—an empty shell—at his death; and when Aya attempted to describe his influence on her, she did so through images of books, paper, and other literary paraphernalia. Multiple examples can be adduced; they are scattered through all of Aya's writings. In numerous short pieces, with titles like "Various Tabi," "Sleeves," and "Futons," and in her longer short stories and novels, Aya explored the way "the various objects surrounding one's life speak in various ways" (*KAZ* 6: 314).[5]

Reading Aya's prose is at times like walking through a narrow, dimly lit room jumbled with objects. Only as one's eyes focus does each object appear purposely placed, and only then does each exude an aura, as if about to burst its physical confines and come to life. Aya's obsession with the meaning of objects in her work has as much to do with her complicated relation to the past as with any deliberately literary design.

Before examining the ways in which Aya imaginatively interacts with objects, let us look at how critics have discussed objects in literature. This very broad topic, discussed by Marx, Freud, and Heidegger, by literary critics such as Maeda Ai and Gaston Bachelard, by theoreticians of art such as Tagi Kōzō and Rudolf Arnheim, and by many others, can be treated with some specificity in Aya's case. Simply put, if the world available to human perceptions is composed of spaces and the objects situated within them, the gift of the artist is to instill meaning into those objects and spaces. The literary intelligence of writers like Aya includes a vision of objects and spaces that transforms them from dead, recalcitrant matter into forces alive with human meaning. The specific meaning depends on the idiosyncrasies of the mind perceiving and transforming them. In Mihaly Csikszentmihalyi's phrase, they become "objectified forms of energy."[6]

For Aya, this transformation involved a remaking of her world—a struggle, in words, to mold the contents of her environment into art. "Art," writes Rudolf Arnheim, is "a projection of our own mental images upon the world of things." Once alive with the emotions projected into them, things can form the core of a pathological enslavement to their power, what Marx called the fetishism of commodities, or they can become talismans, material objects that are sources of power. They can serve as reflections of the cosmos—the way that a simple water jug does for Heidegger—or as symbols of human connection and community. The poet gathers the world around an object, says Gaston Bachelard; in it is found "the intimate quality of the intimate dimension."[7]

Objects can also serve as symbols of isolation and alienation, of a world hostile to those inhabiting it. Japanese writers have often explored existential and metaphysical problems by focusing on the meaning that objects and spaces hold for the people living among and in them. Objects can embody the past in both its constricting and nourishing aspects, serving as projections of human desire and frustration. The most interesting presentations have used objects to confront issues such as the possibility that human will can master circumstances, and the interaction of the will with the constraints placed upon it by the present and the past.

Perhaps the most vivid example of Aya's obsession with objects can be found in "Hair" ("Kami," 1951), a brief, poetically compressed meditation on a painful inheritance. "Hair" is a first-person narrative that describes the forceful and unyielding presence of the past in one woman's life. This past is brought forward in the various household items sent to the narrator upon her stepmother's death. The past is tightly (and grotesquely) entwined in a pincushion—a ball of hair and needles that cries and squeaks and finally brings the dead woman back to life. The past returns; it may prick, it may poison, but it must be unraveled. The past cannot be disposed of: it can be consumed in flames, but its sharp core cannot be destroyed.

The narrative moves in typical Aya fashion. We follow the story from the present, where the narrator gazes upon the objects, to the past, the memories elicited by those objects, and back to the present. In the course of the story the seemingly dead reminders of a dead woman come to life and bring her, too, to life again. Reading the story can be a jarring experience; Aya can seem unconcerned about the requirements of rational structure and grossly insensitive to the reader who seeks a firm narrative line to grasp. Aya can be difficult, but with patient consideration the structure of the piece comes to seem brilliantly matched to the problem it confronts—memory and one's accommodation to it.

The narrative traverses a number of ellipses and for this reason is best approached in parts rather than as a whole. It begins with the narrator's musings on her stepmother's death.

> It was a long relationship. But she died, it ended, and I alone remained. A strange feeling—vacant, as if something had slipped out from inside me. . . . She had always been a strong person, able to do things I couldn't—how could she have succumbed so easily? I found it hard to believe; it would not sink in. Perhaps that was because for many years we had lived apart and had had few opportunities to be together, so that when she died, there was nothing of the sadness that normally accompanies death, only a feeling of distance. It was similar to some other feeling, one I knew well but couldn't manage to place for several days until I realized: yes, it was the snow, the snow sliding off the eaves; it was a feeling very much like that.[8]

In this opening passage we notice the layering of people and things, a process that will become more overt in the course of the narrative. The human problem cannot even be approached, it seems, without reference to objects. The word "relationship" is a rendering of *tsunagari,* which also means physical connection, link, or cord; accordingly, the word "ended" (*kireru*) means to cut, sever, snap, again in a physical sense. The vacant feeling that the woman experiences, *supon to shita,* is an onomatopoetic rendering of the feeling associated with, for example, a large drawer emptied out. The stepmother's dying, in the daughter's mind, is a snapping, as of a cord.

The narrator now surveys the objects before her, each of which evokes an image of the past. "Each of my mother's stained and battered household implements—which I had once been accustomed to seeing daily but which I now saw for the first time in a while—spoke of old wounds and revived the past. The bulkiness of the open chest of drawers brought to mind the stubbornness of my mother, sitting sullenly, in a foul mood, refusing to eat; the glint of the uncovered mirror was my mother's habit of casting a sharp glance as she rose to leave a room."

The woman has felt only a mild curiosity in rummaging through these things; now she confronts one object in its alluring but frightening specificity: a pincushion, made by her stepmother and found among her own sewing things by her daughter. Mother and daughter inspect the object, a grotesque combination of hair and needles. They press on it with a marking stylus, and the clump gives off a faint squeak. In turn, says the mother, "a loud creaking seemed about to emanate from inside my head, and to keep my daughter from noticing it, I pressed my hands to my temples. The stiffness traced a path between my temples and settled in."

The pincushion shows signs of life, with the power to draw the woman back into her past, to lure her into unraveling it. The pincushion activates her imagination and brings her even closer to her stepmother, toward whom she feels such disgust that she can barely stand to have the stepmother's pincushion mixed up with her own sewing implements. The ball of hair reminds her of the suffering and the charm of childhood forty years before. Her daughter leaves the room, and the woman continues her examination. "Although I was as careful with the needles as if they were poisonous, my fingers fell victim to the fierce pounding of my heart and I pricked them several times. No matter how often I pricked them, I persisted in pulling the needles out; no matter how often I pulled, the ball only stiffened more at the core. The one needle that was thrust into my own core—the needle of being a stepdaughter—was surely quivering. Hairs poked out demurely, reluctantly, as if they meant to remain in hiding, and they seemed all but devoured by the needles; yet the needles seemed endlessly wrapped in hair."

The more contact the woman has with the needles and hair, the more the object comes to seem as alive as she is herself. The past is hardening itself to the woman, closing itself off from her as surely as she is hardening herself to it. Both the ball's heart and her own heart stiffen.

While removing the needles and then unraveling the ball of hair, the woman loses all sense of time. She wonders at the ageless quality of old hair.

Suddenly I felt a shock. A hair seemed to move. The wind? I gazed at it. It definitely moved. Glistening in the sun, it seemed to float up ever so slightly and curve. I pulled out another hair from inside the ball, and just as I placed it on a piece of white paper, it took in the sun and, like a dream, gently wafted up, as I thought it might. For a second it looked like a young girl stretching herself: tightly curled up beside a hibachi or a chest of drawers, deeply asleep for the briefest moment, then suddenly awake, lifting her head, looking about, rubbing her back as she wriggles across the tatami—her chest and hips raised slightly, the line from her toes to her fingers stretched taut, a fast pulse of pleasure racing through her, her energy subsiding, and her chest quieting to its original, gentle calm. This was the bewitching figure conjured by the curved hair as it straightened itself out.

The dead mother appears, and the narrator cannot convince herself, or us, that she is not real.

The sleeping figure of my young mother, that figure of her behind the rattan blinds in summertime, as she often slept—do I recall that she wore a *yukata* with a pattern of sparrows and bamboo?

She planted her hands on the tatami and rose. Facing away from me, she put her hands in her hair and glanced back at me with a smile.

She looked at me with the face she wore in happy times. "I'm so glad . . . I'm no longer a stepmother." This is what she said. No—this is what I seem to have heard. No—not that either: this is what I had her say. But her voice truly fell from above—truly.

Although her stepmother seems to have gained her own release, the narrator is not yet free. She decides to destroy the object, but is unsuccessful.

I hesitated but decided to burn the ball when the fire under the bath was at its peak, in the way we normally disposed of things. There is a certain dignity and power in the roaring of a flame. I wanted to let the hair wither under this dignity, hidden from all eyes, and return to nothingness. This is what I did. But the needles still remain, just as they were, in my needle box.

Without a doubt, Mother smiled and broke loose of the chains of being a stepmother. I, too, should long ago have been freed of being a stepdaughter. When one thinks of it, ours was a relationship that seemed both long and short. The relationship between parent and child lasts vastly longer after they have been separated by death than during their time together alive.

The hair can be burned, consigned to the flames as the dolls are at the close of another short story, "Dolls" ("Hina," 1955), destroyed as the ceramic chip is in "Fragment," but the connection cannot be broken. Aya often describes this desire to do away with objects that embody the past. She envies those people—the women of the entertainment quarters, for example—who do not allow themselves to be haunted by the past, who can allow their troubles to disappear. In *Flowing*, Rika attempts to release herself from the weight of her past by dispensing with the household objects that are associated with it, and she, too, looks on with envy at the geisha who seem to possess this unsentimental lack of attachment to life's little tragedies. In another short story the narrator expresses a similar sentiment:

A quality within the woman of the entertainment quarters allows her, in various ways, to let things flow gently by: something absolutely different from strength of character or depth of knowledge, something fragrant like the scent of kelp stilled in a moving current. Gently taking things in and gently letting them flow by, she conceals in her depths an acute intelligence and a quick wit, never blocking the flow. To flow is to be clear and lucid, and there is a sense of security in lucidness. One could view the unclogged heart of the downtown [*shitamachi*] woman as coquettish or callous, but nothing shows greater depths of sorrow than the ability to allow things to drift away. The reason entertainment-quarter women, compared to other women, find so little to regret, is that their hearts are shallow and clear, that they bear the burden of that which is stilled in the water's flow. This quality moved me deeply.[9]

But in "Hair" the needles stay in the box, presumably forever. At the start of the narrative the woman claimed that the relationship had been severed, but the material embodiments of the past reminded her that a link remained. Readers are left thinking that she will never be released, that the feeling will continue to prick her.

"Hair," for all its strangeness, is only one of the many instances where Aya's imagination fastens on to objects and the human interaction with them. She was already seeing the world this way in her first writings, when she attempted to make sense of her father's death. Or perhaps it was her experience of his transformation into an empty shell that helped fuel her obsession with objects that come to acquire a life of their own.

Aya's antipathy to abstraction and to a world emptied of objects belongs to her earliest memories as a child. Prior to the following scene her father and stepmother had been arguing, she pleading for the virtues of Christian love, he insisting on the essential emptiness behind all things.

> I asked Father, "What do nothingness and emptiness mean?"
>
> He answered simply, "They mean, to be nothing."
>
> But I wouldn't be silent, and asked over and over again what nothingness meant.
>
> "If you think everything really exists, try and explain what that means," he said.
>
> I replied, "There's a hibachi there, right? And isn't there a teakettle there, too?"
>
> "No, there isn't," he said, laughing.
>
> Wasn't this completely absurd? I took Father's hand and pressed it against the hibachi. "Your hand's touching it, isn't it?" I said.
>
> "There's no hand here," he said.
>
> I truly felt filled with a sense of mystery. "If there's no hand, does that mean there's no father?" I asked.
>
> "That's right."
>
> I thought he must be joking. "That's a lie!" I cried.
>
> Father stared at me and said, "It's true, you know." And then, "When you study about it, you'll understand." Then he stood up and left. Mother, too, quickly rose and left. An eerie sorrow remained with me. (*KAZ* 2: 118)

In her abhorrence of abstraction and her attachment to materiality, Aya is set apart from her contemporaries, belonging more to her father's world than to her own. Many Japanese writers have arrived at a sober, if not pessimistic, vision by way of material objects. In much of the writing of Aya's time, the past is a vague memory, stripped of viable meaning for the present. The images evoked are, appropriately, alien and abstract, serving neither as embodiments of a tradition nor as bearers of a legacy for the future.

This tendency to abstraction was especially true of writers in the 1950s. In Mishima Yukio's *Temple of the Golden Pavilion,* for example, we witness a desire to be free of objects, whose materiality is an impediment to the expansion of the human will. One must destroy them to be free. Similarly, the world that Yoshiyuki Junnosuke creates in stories like "Sudden Rain" ("Shuū," 1954) and "The Whore's Room" ("Shōfu no heya," 1958) contains prostitutes whose bodily surfaces provide security and relaxation, but even those surfaces seem no more than abstractions. Shimao Toshio also evokes a world emptied of substance and meaning. In "Life within a Dream" ("Yume no naka de no nichijō," 1956), the protagonist, a young writer, lives a life of aimless wandering, moving from burned-out slums, where he searches for literary material, to his mother, from whom he feels he must run, to a train, which he finds himself on without knowing how he got there, and then in and out of a number of houses, more imaginary than real. Finally, he senses his body turning inside out and feels himself floating in a stream, himself turned into an abstraction. And in Shiina Rinzo's writings, characters become prisoners of the daily objects surrounding them.[10] Examples of abstract landscapes and alienating environments are also found in the works of Abe Kobo in the 1960s and Furui Yoshikichi in the 1970s.

Although seeming modern to contemporary sensibilities in their evocations of an alienating and traditionless society, the works mentioned do not necessarily paint a complete picture of the time. In fact, the closer that writers were to the war, the more they seemed to value contact with the tangible. In the immediate postwar writings of Tamura Taijiro—in novels such as *Gate of Flesh* (*Nikutai no mon,* 1947)—this contact takes the form of attachment to raw and violent sex; in Noma Hiroshi's *Dark Pictures* (*Kurai e,* 1946) as well, pure physical sensation offers the only hope of awaking from a long nightmare.

Sakaguchi Ango balances visions of emptiness with an affinity for the sheer heft and feel of objects, and in his stories, the destruction of forms does not lead to abstraction. Writing immediately after the war, Ango found beauty in clutter and embraced chaos with a spirit of creativity, though the embrace often seems no more than a desperate attempt to find meaning in the physical and spiritual collapse brought about by the war. "I loved this colossal destruction. The sight of people submitting to fate was strangely beautiful. . . . Japan during the war was an incredible utopia, filled to overflowing with an empty beauty." He shared with other writers a fascination with, in Jay Rubin's words, physical minutiae that were "disgusting, alluring, horrible, passionate, but always physical and ultimately, for people who had come to terms with a fifteen-year war, healthy." Ango turned to the "messy and human" in order to reject the transcendental values that may have led Japan to war, and he was attracted by the lack of meaning in the destruction of forms because he was disgusted by the civilization that created them.[11]

Although Aya shared Ango's fascination with the physicality of things, she possessed a stronger impulse toward order and arrangement—as we shall see in "Dolls"—and a more pressing need to invest things with meaning, to re-form them into something whole. Ango has been photographed as a slouching, haggard man sitting behind a desk engulfed in crumpled papers and garbage; Aya has been photographed sitting erect and proper behind a writing table on which are lined up, in perfect descending order of size, twelve used pencils, each neatly sharpened.

This comparison of Aya with her near contemporaries can help us see her own involvement in postwar problems. And yet Aya seems detached as well, guided by a sensibility that is tied to a past for which many others writing at the same time had little feeling. This detachment is due, no doubt, to Aya's long sequestration in a cultural cocoon spun by her father, a man whose own values and sensibilities were developed before the turn of the century and whose powerful personality so dominated his daughter's mind.

Aya was instilled with a vibrant sense of a salvageable past by a father she feared but also respected; she was initiated into a Neo-Confucian philosophical tradition in which daily life and the many objects that constitute it were not only prized but also seen to contain a deep religiosity: she had a feeling, in Lionel Trilling's words, "for the charm of the mysterious, precarious, little flame that lies at the heart of the commonplace."[12] She was trained to respect all that she touched and tended, to lavish as much care on the handling of things as on the handling of people; and she was sheltered, by and large, from a "modern" way of thinking about literature that emphasized human isolation in a hostile society and the need to be free from restrictions. The energy, the passion, and the desperation, that come through in Aya's most brilliant passages are born of the conflict between this positive inheritance and the more negative feelings—anger, resentment, and hostility—that she held for the past.

No mere listing of reasons can fully account for the complexity of influences and personal responses that went into forming Aya's imagination. But to her ambivalence about the past must be added the following— the problem of gender. Objects, according to Judith Fryer, speak "a language of gender . . . of a world in which women are private property to be contained, more or less, in non-public areas belonging to men."[13] In *Flow-ing*, Aya inverts this notion of objects as imprisoners of women. She demonstrates the evocative power and dynamism of objects, the ways they can be manipulated by women, instead of women by them. She shows how women accept the potential containment and weight of the past and of convention that objects embody and how they mold them to their own needs.

Like the women she writes about, Aya was drawn to traditional roles and at the same time motivated by her own creative desires. These conflicting impulses necessitated an acceptance of ambiguity, an ability to hold various and opposing feelings in place simultaneously, and an understanding of the impossibility of ever fully resolving conflict. If Aya's treatment of tradition (and its embodiment in objects) seems different from that of many Japanese writers, and anachronistic when viewed against the work of her contempo-raries, this is in part because she remained attached, however ambiguously, to traditions that other writers resented and resisted.

No wonder Aya was like writers in her father's generation, writers who lived through the dramatic social, political, and cultural changes brought about by the restoration of imperial rule in 1868 and the restructuring of society along new, "modern" lines, writers who could observe once-viable traditions being extirpated by the movement of historic forces. Two of these writers, Natsume Sōseki and Shimazaki Tōson, in equally valid ways, devoted their creative energies to exploring this historically charged mo-ment. Like Aya, each undertook his exploration within the confined and claustrophobic spaces of the home and through an exploration of the meaning of the various objects found there.

In Tōson's *House* and Sōseki's *Grass on the Wayside*, protagonists are caught in a web of familial relationships, which induce feelings of im-prisonment and resentment toward duty. In *The House* the protagonist, Sankichi, is the youngest son in a family whose generations of living and working together have been erased by the forces of modernity. In Sōseki's *Grass on the Wayside*, the protagonist, Kenzō, is likewise ensnared; emotional bonding in the family has become threatened by more rational, economic arrangements. For each character the past is a suffocating and useless anachronism. In *The House* it exists in abstract or partial form in the many pictures and objects that lie scattered about, mimicking life but possessing no essential vitality. In *Grass on the Wayside*, the past is embodied in household objects, which alienate their users from one another.

At the end of *The House*, Sankichi visits his parents' home village, and there an old neighbor gives him a set of objects that represents the legacy of his ancestors: three stone seals that once belonged to his father. But these seals have no symbolic meaning or emotional vibrancy. They are neither more nor less than what they are—three stones. Another object, a mirror, has also been discovered, but it is not given to Sankichi, indicating perhaps that he cannot view himself in the reflection offered by his family and the past. We cannot but recall here the mirror in Aya's "Hair," whose glint revives its viewer's unhappy past.

The disintegration of objects and the evacuation of meaning from them coincide with an elimination of human connection and warmth. For Tōson, objects do not bind people together, as they can in Aya's imagination. Instead, they represent a lack of connection. In the family meal of the close of the novel, Tōson recapitulates the opening scene with irony: we accompany Sankichi back to his sister's home, and though little seems to have changed physically, the familial feelings that once bound together relatives and employees in the family business are gone. The last sentences of the novel link the images of death with the loss of the past, the end of the family community, and the destruction of an object. Sankichi has left his nephew's hospital room knowing that the young man will soon die. Sankichi told him to "forget about everything in the past . . . about the responsibility you've inherited." Now he thinks of his nephew's cremation: "He thought of Shōta's body transported from the hospital to the crematorium before daybreak. Outside it was still dark."[14]

As in *The House,* objects in Sōseki's novel signal a lack of human connection and an inability to love. Gifts are received as burdens, and kindnesses as symbols of manipulation and betrayal. As a child, Kenzō was promised a silver watch by an unnamed older brother. Upon this brother's death, the silver watch was sold to a pawnshop, only to be redeemed later and given to his other brother, Chōtarō. The unnamed brother's wishes have been betrayed, Kenzō has been betrayed, and the connection between the Kenzō and his father that the gift might have sustained is sundered. The watch becomes the focus of Kenzō's feelings of alienation and hostility, tearing him apart from his family. Kenzō long ago learned to sever objects from their human context: as a child, "he very quickly trained himself to dissociate his favorite toys from the people that had given them to him. The toys had to have an independent existence; otherwise how could he enjoy them?"[15]

In a world of broken human connections, objects stand between people and resonate with their feelings of mutual isolation; a defective lamp can stand for an unbridgeable gap between people.

The lamp was a temperamental one, and if the wick was not trimmed with particular care, it would smoke profusely. Noting that its chimney was indeed getting quite black, Kenzō said, "Let's have the maid bring us another one." But the suggestion was received with a marked lack of enthusiasm by Shimada, who now brought his face close to the glass shade with its busy floral design and peered through the transparent patches. "What can be the matter with it," he muttered anxiously.

"How like him," Kenzō thought, "To be so offended by an inefficient lamp."[16]

The despair with everyday life and human relationships is not unlike that expressed by Tōson. Yet there are differences in the vision of these two writers, at least as expressed in these two novels. Whereas *The House* is imbued with a desire for flight from obligation and daily life, *Grass on the Wayside* shows a philosophical acceptance of the unhappy human estate. In each case, however, objects are tangible forces that impress themselves on those living among them.

The world that Aya depicts can be as physically claustrophobic as Tōson's and Sōseki's. She is similarly obsessed with the meaning that objects and spaces carry, and she is equally interested in the connection between these objects and the possibility of human community. The differences in her vision, however, are even more striking than the similarities. Although troubled by the problem of molding an inherited past to the needs of the present, she arrives at a creative accommodation by breathing life into the spaces and objects allotted to her. In *Flowing*, as we shall see, objects can serve to bind a community of women together, though tentatively.

Aya's treatment of objects expresses a creative play with her environment, but just as important to her is the manipulation of notions of space. She tries to find an authentic imaginative space that is not only true to her social situation but also open to her artistic impulses. In *Literature in the Spaces of the City* (*Toshi kūkan no naka no bungaku*, 1982), Maeda Ai analyzes the use of spaces and objects by a number of Japanese writers. For many of them the compromise reached by Aya is not possible: the spatial settings of their fictions are constricted and suffocating. In Futabatei Shimei's *Floating Clouds* (*Ukigumo*, 1889), a small room serves as a retreat from a world too frightening to deal with; in the works of Kitamura Tōkoku (1868–1894), the home is a small prison.

The preponderance of small and confining spaces in Japanese literature had its beginnings in the works of the tenth- and eleventh-century Heian women writers, who almost willfully avoided writing of the world outside their quarters, over which they had no control, in order to concentrate on their private lives. In the modern tradition this narrow focus is seen in what literary historians have called the mainstream of Japanese writing, the semiautobiographical narratives of the "I-novel." This tendency has evoked a recurring complaint, virtually a lament, in Japanese literary criticism. The I-novel has been vilified; Japanese writers have been condemned for choosing to hide themselves in narrow worlds and to write only about the most immediate circumstances of their lives.[17]

In 1959, when Aya, at the peak of her career, was herself writing of such small spaces, the critical energy devoted to this question of narrowness in literature had not yet subsided. Some of the most fervent and articulate pronouncements were made by the critic Eto Jun, who attacked the inability of mainstream Japanese writers to develop a true "literary style" (*buntai*). By style, Eto meant the use of language to transform the world according to subjective design. What he found lacking among Japanese writers was a belief in the possibility of forming a subjective language that might allow the writer to face real-life circumstances and see through them to their fictional and ultimately changeable natures. Such a style could be created only by writers who believed that they could use language to free themselves from the prison of self and circumstance, which was defined by tradition and contemporary society.

Most Japanese writers, according to Eto, have been unable to overcome the circumstances of their lives by mastering them in fiction; they have instead have been mastered by their circumstances. From its inception, modern Japanese fiction has displayed the self-assertion of an intelligentsia that felt inefficacious and rejected by society at large. Writers have seen life and society—and their place in them—as unalterable, not open to manipulation by human effort; they have chosen not to confront the complex reasons for their social isolation and have avoided creating fictional worlds that might offer alternatives. In their lives and in their writing, Eto argued, they have chosen accommodation and retreat.[18]

It is understandable that social-minded critics like Eto should bemoan the willed self-enclosing tendency of Japanese writers, whose lyrical attachments to private moments can seem, especially in times of social instability, unheroic at best, self-obsessed at worst. Paul Anderer concurs in Eto's analysis. During the fifty years of social and cultural disruption that followed the Meiji restoration, when several major schools of Japanese literature arose and expired, when the great masterpieces of the modern language were written, a writer rarely transcended the fictional boundaries of home, family, and self. According to Anderer, when a writer like Arishima Takeo attempted to do so, he was filled with apprehension about leaving the safe boundaries set by the literary tradition, and feared that a fiction that did not embrace the world as a sufficient reality pointed to a life "that has been emptied out . . . denied its concreteness and density." Japanese fiction, Anderer writes, "takes place within delimited borders" and sticks close to the familiar, known, and small. He concludes with regret that "there can be no quest within such a literary system; no reach for an alternative reality, a higher or simply some other world, discovered and revealed by a utopian imagination."[19]

His argument is forceful but seems correct in only the most literal sense, for it implies that such an other world is found away from the familiar, known, and small. Though perhaps true for searches and adventures in the real world, searches in the imaginary world of literature can be undertaken within defined borders and limits and may involve a reworking of a given world rather than an escape from it.

What analyses like Eto's and Anderer's have not taken into account is the possibility of writing within the cloister sanctioned by tradition and instilling it with subjective meaning, thereby moving beyond the borders of individual restriction and isolation. For a number of Japanese writers, according to Maeda, small spaces removed from society were more than places of escape and exile; they also proffered the hope of finding an alternative creative voice. In the eighteenth century, writers like Shikitei Sanba and Ryūtei Tanehiko explored the back alleys of society, evoking them as liminal areas where creative energies could grow unimpeded by the political and social restrictions imposed in the outside, official world. For Nagai Kafu, the dark, hidden corners and byways of Tokyo offered a similar alternative to officialdom while also providing a place where a writer could still speak with some authority about a world he knew.[20]

Aya never left her own inside world in search of a utopian other, and it was precisely to engage themes extending beyond her isolated self that she intentionally and protectively hid herself inside confined spaces; from within the borders of her socially defined role she challenged that role and sought artistic freedom. In her narrowness Aya is hardly distinguishable from her literary forebears or contemporaries, and she is anything but transgressive in her choice and depiction of fictional space. Yet Aya does not bow down to circumstance, though the inhabitant of a world crowded with domestic objects and circumscribed by the daily round; rather, she makes her life accommodate her sense of self. In Aya's imagination the spaces of the house become, in Gaston Bachelard's words, "an instrument with which to confront the cosmos." For Aya, a house is, in Taki Kōji's phrase, a "living space," energized and brought to life by human effort.[21]

In less cosmic terms, Aya finds the house and other confined spaces to be places within which she can speak with confidence and authority. When she thinks of the kitchen, she thinks of the years of work done and life lived there. "Through the kitchen," she writes, "the wisdom of the past is preserved and passed on." The kitchen "settles the unsettled spirit" (*KAZ* 6: 311–319).

But the kitchen and similar spaces do not possess predefined value and meaning for their users. Rather, the users themselves transform the spaces and instill them with life. This process is most vividly at work in *Flowing*, where rooms become energized spaces in which geisha perform their art; but it is also evident in a novel like *Younger Brother*, where a hospital room becomes the setting for a drama of deep sympathies. In these and other cases, we see Aya using a personal language to make her environment conform to the force of her imagination. Critics have often found her writings to lack a literary style. On the contrary, she forms a language to mold the world to her inner needs.

"Favorite Corners" ("Ki ni iri no sumikko," 1957), is a mature example of Aya's self-conscious manipulation of inherited spatial constrictions. Like much of her writing, this short piece condenses into its own limited space a number of issues important to Aya. The opening reveals the movement of mental images and associations while describing her ambiguous feelings about the idea of a home.

> What associations come to mind when you think of a home? A red roof and fresh tatami, perhaps. Or a sitting room in disarray. Or even the fear of not being able to pay the rent. What I think of first are the boundaries, borders, and smallness of a home. Someone once said to me, "What unpleasant associations come to your mind. It's very disagreeable not to have good associations with the word *home*. Even if your present home is joyless and full of problems, the word nevertheless should have good associations. It is natural to think of pleasant, fun, bright things shining out from a home. Images like border, boundary, smallness—they make no clear sense to people." Images that make no clear sense to people are no doubt unsatisfying. I understand what my friend means. It's enjoyable to think of a home as a circle from which a bright light radiates, from which every kind of happiness streams as though it were a small child's drawing of a sun. This image is what people most desire. When they hear words like *boundary, garden, smallness,* or *narrowness* associated with a home, they think all the sun-filled joy is being left out. But that's not what I mean to imply. To me, a home is where you rest your spirit in peace; it is the breeding ground of good things and a place to put your faith in. Associations take on such different shapes in the minds of different people. (*KAZ* 6: 292)

Aya rejects the standard image of a home as a place projecting brightness and goodness to the outside world but endorses the idea of a home as the breeding ground for spirit and imagination. After allowing her narrative to move through a number of images that she associates with the nurturing intimacy of a home, Aya returns to her main rhetorical point.

Boundaries limit things, throw shadows on things, form corners. There is a wide-open pleasure and freedom in the limitless, but something, finally, is lacking. Limits negate freedom but offer arrangement. There is a sense of order and a power in the arrangements created by limits. Shadows infuse the environment with beauty; corners, tight and constricting, have a serenity about them. Once we have chosen the appropriate land and location for a home, we have already made a narrow delimitation, but our feeling toward our home further moves us to arrange and delimit even the positions of our floor cushions with the most subtle care.

There is apparently a phenomenon called "the anguished monkey of six windows." When you place a monkey in a large room with six windows, it runs wildly from one to the other, desperately crying out. Undoubtedly this phenomenon points to some deeper problem, but when I think of just the scene itself, I can't help but sense that monkey's unease. I feel such pity I can barely stand it.

A home where one cannot be still—a life of floating from window to window in spite of one's self: how very pitiful. I wonder what might happen if a log were placed in that room. The monkey might avoid being chased about by that feeling of restlessness; if there were borders and shadows and corners, it could get by without becoming so ill at ease.

A person well known for his talent and hard work told me the following story. He went on an errand to the home of a famous person. The garden and house were large indeed—apparently the garden was wider than a park, and the house bigger than a public hall. He was led into a large room and left there to wait for the master of the house. A number of personal things were lying about, but there was so much space he didn't know where to sit. He finally got his bearings at the entranceway and settled down there. "And it was while I was sitting there that I became edgy. I realized how similar I was to that monkey. Being a person, and not a monkey, I persevered and continued to sit there as calmly as possible, but I was calm only on the outside: my inner spirit was restless—my ears, my eyes, my arms and legs itched. I felt exactly like that monkey, its eyes bugging out nervously. What a poor creature I am to have let all that open space bother me so." I can understand this feeling, and it doesn't take such an incredibly large place to evoke it. Even when people are gathered together in a small room, they hesitatingly desire to inch their way toward the corners. A home, I feel, is created according to how things are arranged, how small corners of serenity are created.

Having summarized her ideas, Aya proceeds to dramatize them in a scene from her past.

I don't know about foreign things, but in an English text of mine there was a description of children choosing a favorite corner and going there to read a book or carrying over a chair to talk with their friends. The foreign teacher who told us about this always used to explain how wonderful and nostalgic her "chosen corner" was to her. Sitting among foreign things, living with foreign people, teaching foreign students, she must have felt a surge of feeling when she thought of this chosen corner in her own country and home. As a child I sensed this in her, and my youthful feelings responded to hers.

But that corner would not have been something grand. It would have been a corner by the frame of a bay window, with people's backs leaning against it; it would have been a wall tacked with faded photographs; or a place where a bright bunch of jonquils sprouted leaves every year—it would have been a small and humble corner. Such a humble place could be a pleasant corner, a serene corner, a corner that offered peace through an entire lifetime.

Aya now comes to a moment that reappears toward the end of many of her pieces, the disruption of the war. Wartime destruction does not end in malaise or passivity, however, but in a remaking of the world according to personal design. Aya, faithful to her role and self-image, is an onlooker to the actual construction.

I lost my house in the war. But having lost it, I couldn't just remain homeless, so I had a small hut built. Unable to do the work myself, I enlisted the wisdom and energy of others. How was it to be built? I didn't want to interfere with the construction of the rooms—materials and labor were all regulated at that time, and it would have been inappropriate for me to complain. So I didn't venture my opinions. But I wanted for myself at least some small corner of the kitchen, some "chosen corner." Just to imagine a small triangular shelf hung in that corner made me happy. I wondered how I'd enjoy arranging things on it. But in such a small and narrow kitchen there wasn't even a corner that could hold my little shelf. Every space was filled with absolutely necessary things. Things were bulging out of their places.

There was nowhere even to put a broom or a duster. I managed to forget that I'd been robbed of the joy of having a little shelf, and instead I searched and searched until I found a nice corner for the broom. I struggled to arrange a small space six inches wide and two feet deep alongside a three-mat-sized bay window, and it was there that I stored the broom. Knowing that the broom could now settle down quietly, without becoming like that wild monkey, without having to chase nervously about the room with its eyes, I felt relieved. The partitions, shadows, and corners of a room are needed not just by people but by things as well.

Finally, I will let my thoughts fall where they will. I always remember with gratitude the smallest room of that house. For some reason it seemed to be made up almost exclusively of corners. It seemed strong and dependable. I'm not saying I liked it more than anywhere else—I just feel grateful. How wonderfully well it was set up! How I relied on those corners! (*KAZ* 6: 300–301)

The strangest moment in the passage comes when Aya searches for a resting place for the broom, treating it as if it were a bruised friend needing attention. The care she shows for objects, the spirit she projects into them, the need to be surrounded by their clutter, represent both an acceptance of the environment and a reworking of it. Much the same can be said of her spaces: they imbibe the spirit of their users and become places of expressive freedom.

At a time of national destruction and chaos, Aya constructed a small world of order and security. Mishima Yukio and Yasuoka Shōtarō, among others, did this as well, but we need only recall the suffocating and escapist quality of their worlds to realize the extent to which Aya embraced her own with feelings of relief and comfort because she was where she felt she naturally belonged. Unlike her male contemporaries, she had always been in this small world and chose to find freedom within it.

In this context, the word *freedom* should be used with care. Aya was no rebel. Freedom for her does not imply liberation from restrictive social standards or expectations, nor does it involve an escape from smothering relationships. A proper place is found for the broom inside the proper place for the woman. When the character assumes her proper role as caretaker, she attempts to put things in order—the way Aya does with her memories of her father. In "Hair" the woman unravels the pincushion along with her feelings for her stepmother and burns her stepmother's hair as if consigning those memories to destruction as well. But the needles and pins remain, and all she can do is put them in a box, in their appropriate place. She is not freed from her past in any way.

For Aya, then, freedom means carving out a secure niche from which to speak with authority. The space and persona that Aya finds are dangerously close to those spaces and personas that could potentially silence her. They belong to an inheritance from the past that she cannot shed but that cannot overwhelm her, either. Carrying the burdens of her past, she finds a place that has the conditions necessary for personal expression.

In "The Black Hems" ("Kuroi suso," 1955), Aya finds that place of expressive freedom at funerals, where women could meet and interact. In the story, she describes a woman who cloaks herself in ritual and ritual clothing, which allow for subjective expression but also threaten to squelch individual impulse. Aya's own voice likewise presents the opposition between expression and repression: it mixes the confidence of the storyteller with the self-deprecation of a shy girl. In the afterword to the story, Aya writes: "'The Black Hems' is nothing more than a product of my desire to randomly arrange my experiences at funerals and the things I heard from people there. The work itself is an essay in the form of fiction, so I am still, after all, nothing but a seller of memories" (*KAZ* 7: 273). But Aya transforms the narrow world of funerals with a sophistication that belies her disclaimer. Though still unsure of her abilities as a writer, Aya is also posing as someone naive and unable to bring literary form to her ideas, unable to create art from memory. She can now have it both ways: she can be a literary artist without forsaking her former identity as the ignorant daughter of Kōda Rohan.

Aya never fully resolves the tension created by these two opposing forces in her life. Instead, she shapes it to literary ends. In "The Black Hems," Aya self-consciously manipulates her world in order to master it, in order to write about problems of female identity, community, time, and aging. As in *Flowing,* she finds a community of women, which frees her to manipulate the meanings of things bequeathed to her by society. She finds those meanings repressive but necessary for self-empowerment. She uses the sphere of funeral ceremonies and the functions and objects related to them to exhibit the imaginative freedom possible in a repressive society. Because Aya thinks that freedom can be realized only within the parameters set by society, she examines the likelihood that it will be realized by focusing on two potentially repressive aspects of female social identity—clothing and service.

Clothing can be either an encasement, wrapping its wearer in a socially defined role, or a costume, self-consciously shaped by its wearer. It can limit identity, or it can allow the expansion of identity. To Virginia Woolf, clothing seemed more a controlling than a controlled force: "There is much to support the view that it is clothes that wear us and not we them; we may make them take the mould of arm or breast, but they mould our hearts, our brains, our tongues to their liking."[22] Clothing can either foster or deny growth. In Aya's "The Medal," for example, clothing provides psychological strength in confrontations with a powerful father.

In "The Black Hems," Aya elaborates on this tension. Her protagonist moves toward self-assertion and freedom, but her attempts are held in check by forces of confinement. She feels both an urge for independence and the sacrifice of human connection that this involves. "The Black Hems" traces the life of Chiyo, a girl whose sole chance for extrafamily contact comes at the funerals she attends. Her emotional life, from her lonely adolescence to romance, a failed marriage, and physical decline, is paralleled by her gradual mastery of the job of arranging funeral ceremonies and is expressed in meaning that she gives the clothing she wears.

Chiyo is defined, in the opening lines of the story, by her drab kimono, unsuited for a girl so young. Like a fresh kimono, "the sixteen-year-old was stiff with strain." When she arrives at the ceremony, she is self-conscious about her appearance and surprises the hosts and other guests by apologizing for her lack of proper attire. This is the first of many ceremonies that Chiyo will help with, and it is here that she meets Ko, the distant relative for whom she will develop a vague romantic longing as she sees him again and again at these events. When she meets Ko, he, too, is defined by his clothing: "He wore a stiff, pleated skirt, through which one could see layers of white on cool black Akashi silk."[23]

In the coming months and years, with the deaths of various relatives, Chiyo achieves expertise in handling funeral arrangements and comes to understand that her allotted role is to be a specialist in funerals. She has her mother buy her a new black mourning kimono for her high school graduation; it rustles with life and makes Chiyo feel alive, too. The fresh blackness of the kimono coincides with Chiyo's hopes of union with Ko.

But the moment she acquires the kimono signals the end of Chiyo's dream. Her formal acceptance of her role, symbolized by her new outfit, demands a sacrifice: before attending her next funeral, Chiyo hears that Ko has married another woman. When she still wore her old kimono, Ko was infatuated with her, and a long union seemed possible.

Unsettled by the loss of Ko and seeking to fill her emptiness with ritual, Chiyo throws herself into her funeral work. Gradually she begins to show her age, but the funeral atmosphere that clings to her now makes her seem more beautiful. Her attainment of this beauty coincides, however, with a lost opportunity for human connection:

Spring passed and autumn came, and after a year, another year went by. Chiyo's marriage was put off later and later, leaving a sadly fresh girl behind. When a woman passes age twenty-five, her internal beauty and individual glow increase, but youth vanishes from the lines of her shoulders and back. Age sneaks in from places the mirror doesn't show, and decay begins to spread from unnoticed corners.

A black kimono now seems most becoming. Every time Chiyo wore her mourning garb, she shone with beauty. The artless, natural appearance of sadness had its effects: in her words of condolence and in her burning of incense she had acquired experience, and she came to be known as the woman of the double-layered black kimono, distinct from all the other women. . . . At work she was called the Black Princess.

Chiyo has become one with her social identity, one with the blackness of her kimono, but at the same time she has become most surely herself.

When Chiyo meets Ko again, for the last time, after a separation of many years, she has gone through an unhappy marriage and divorce and has lived through the death of her former husband. Although she donned the black kimono for his funeral—as she had donned the dark years of married life with him—it had deteriorated considerably. "You're wearing the same funeral kimono as always, but you have none of your former glow," says her mother. Ko, too, has had his share of misfortune. When the two meet, the atmosphere is suffused with decay, death, and sadness about lost possibilities. She has been passively living out the final years of the war.

After a devastating air raid, Ko leads Chiyo to a seaside town where his father is at the point of death. They watch him die on the bare floor of a dilapidated lumber warehouse. In the most unsettling scene of the story, Ko and Chiyo accompany the family and the dead body to a lonely crematorium on a pine-covered hill, where they watch the custodian manage the cremation. "The pines whistled, the sun began to set, and after a long wait the old woman said, 'The ashes are ready.' She pulled the iron tray out of the oven with a clatter and rested it on a handcart, then roughly took it through the darkness out into the open. Flames too large to be called embers drew the fresh breeze and came together in a blaze: the scene resembled the screens depicting hell, with the old witch-hag pulling the carriages of fire. Ko said something to her. The hag turned her red face to him and barked, 'Don't be a fool. I'm doing this out of kindness to you. Without a fire, do you think the women could see their way? I could, but then I'm used to it.'"

Ko and Chiyo remain to gather the bones from the ashes. The old woman observes the two and, laughing, says, "This gentleman and this lady are no couple, are they? I can smell it."

Chiyo returns home sick, unable to sleep for the lingering smell of the cremation. Aya's narrative now moves to the larger world; and in a few brief sentences, events of great magnitude are condensed, as if their importance could not compare to the relatively minor events of Chiyo's life. Hiroshima is bombed, the war ends, her mother dies, and Chiyo attends her mother's funeral as the chief mourner. She then hears that Ko, fearing arrest for certain crimes, has committed suicide.

But Chiyo has one more funeral to attend. She starts to get dressed in her black kimono, but "the hems had worn completely through, and in some places their lining was soiled gray and hung down like a sagging bridge." Chiyo panics when she realizes that she is not presentable. She grows furious and takes her anger out on her old serving woman. Then her kimono takes on a life of its own.

> She tossed both sleeves of the kimono in the air, so it looked like a bat flying up, and threw it down on the tatami. She opened the scissors wide as she cut into the hems.
>
> . . . As she got to the side seam, the scissors hesitated, the cloth resisted, and as she continued, the sound of the cutting, too, seemed like a protest. Unmoved, Chiyo put more force into her thumb.
>
> . . . White silk now protruded below the hems, whose lopped-off edges coiled on the mat like a long dead snake. Irritated, Chiyo grabbed the thread from the old woman, who was scurrying about nervously, but Chiyo couldn't thread the needle without her glasses. Although she didn't look angry, she snatched them up. With quick basting stitches, Chiyo made rough seams sufficient to bring the front and back together. The old double-layered kimono gave off a final murmur of protest.

While she works on the kimono, time stops, but when she arrives at the ceremony after donning her outfit, she senses the passing of time all the more keenly. She has to admit to her wan appearance; like the kimono, she is worn through, and she feels even shabbier when she sees a handsome, spiffed-up young cousin, whose white cuffs gleam under dark blue sleeves. Seeing the young boy forces Chiyo to face her own mortality. Here the story draws to a close. "Through the layers of green leaves deep inside the garden, a balmy summer breeze drifted in with a glimmer. The air passed through Chiyo's hastily mended black hems. She felt that a calm—a funereal calm, the calm of a person's having died—had begun to settle under the roof of the house."

In the course of the story the black kimono is transformed from a material object into a symbolic extension of its wearer and, finally, into a living metaphor of a woman's life: "Are the life of a mourning kimono and that of a woman the same?"

"The Black Hems" tells a sad story about the lost possibilities of human connection. Chiyo's life is one of failed intimacy; her resilience and her independence of spirit have necessitated a sacrifice of warmth and intimacy. Her cutting of the kimono seems a rash and violent act to the old serving woman sitting at her side, who watches trembling and in tears.

> "I can't tell you how I felt when I saw you cutting it up. To do what you did to a kimono—I couldn't imagine doing it myself." The old woman fumbled with the black snake, its bowels dangling out, and dragged her hands across it. "They say it's bad luck to have a mourning kimono made with no specific occasion in mind, but when I thought that I might be the reason for your making a new kimono, a

feeling welled up in me and the tears began to flow. Madam, please take care of everything when the time comes."

The old woman's feelings were perhaps justified. She was old, and the sight of a woman in her fifties in her white undergarments, brandishing shears and cutting the hems of a black mourning kimono . . . the old woman's brittle nerves probably couldn't stand it. In her hurry to be on time for the funeral, Chiyo had wound up showing a living person the specter of her own funeral. It was at times like this that the intensity of a woman living alone revealed itself.

"You're right. Maybe I should have a new one made. But why don't we promise to put off both your funeral and mine for a while?"

It is through an examination of Chiyo's attitude toward her clothing that Aya attempts to negotiate the competing claims weighing on her own mind—between social convention and individual style, between repression and will, between limits and freedom. To what extent is clothing a covering for the body, and to what extent is it a costume designed by its owner? Does clothing offer opportunities for self-stylization, or is it a kind of armor, rigidly encasing its wearer? The absolute identification of Chiyo with her kimono implies a critique of the force exerted by social roles on individual lives—in this case, by feminine roles on women. Aya reveals the degree to which female identity is wrapped within the outer garments that distinguish social role.

At the same time, however, she discloses the transformative potential of that role. For Chiyo, the transformation comes when she cuts up and remakes the kimono that accompanied her to a lifetime of funerals. At this point, she gets dressed and sets off to the funeral. Only after these acts of will can she attend the funeral as a spectator, freed of her former duties as arranger and server. The functionary role has passed on to a younger generation. The newly bought freedom exacts a price, however: she feels isolated. "Now that she counted, there was nobody left for her to see off. She had seen them all off, and she realized that indeed she was seeing off the last of the line today. That was the truth—she had finally seen them all off."

By manipulating the forms that others have learned to accept, Chiyo has succeeded in her world of decorum and ceremony. Her movement toward freedom has been enacted within the confines of her inherited role and ascribed identity. By accepting tradition and convention, she frees herself to explore received truth and the way that truth can be manipulated. Society, then, is both repressive and necessary. Chiyo must master social forms to avoid being crushed.

The conflict between her sense of herself as an independent being and her sense of herself as a member of a community is the same as for Rika in

Flowing. Rika, who longs to belong to the geisha world, feels removed from it. Aya examines this tension between freedom and community by placing her protagonists in serving roles; as servants, her women are both aloof from and submerged in a community.

In Aya's world, a woman's proper role is to serve; and serving, in turn, guarantees connection to a community. In the short story "Dolls," for example, a mother serves her daughter by caring for a set of dolls; in "The Black Hems," Chiyo serves her family and relations by arranging funerals and serving tea; and Rika, too, serves her mistress and the other geisha, who earn their livelihood by serving others. While no doubt related to inculcated feminine values—housework raised to an ideal—service for Aya implies a measure of control over the world. Chiyo becomes a self-empowered adult when she learns to pour tea properly, Rika finds security as a servant, and the mother in "Dolls" feels as if she has taken charge when she sets up dolls for her daughter.

In Aya's notion of service, objects remain central. Service is linked to the life of objects because it is through them that acts of service are carried out. Rika cleans baths, arranges shoes, folds kimonos; Chiyo makes tea and hands out teacups; the mother in "Dolls" arranges dolls.

Service and objects are also related to the notion of community. According to Lewis Hyde, "The giving of a gift tends to establish a relationship between the parties involved . . . [leaving] a series of interconnected relationships in its wake, and a kind of decentralized cohesiveness."[24] The freely given gift binds and connects: Chiyo is presented with a kimono, and the kimono becomes part of her being, creating a unity between object and owner. The spirit of connectedness is destroyed, according to Hyde, when a gift becomes a commodity and loses its intrinsic value. It becomes an object that separates, differentiates, breaks down unities. Chiyo encounters her childhood love at the cremation of a cousin: their first meeting many years before was marked by a gift given to her—a silver makeup bowl with Chiyo's initials on the cover—but their meeting now is marked by the destruction of an object, the dead man's corpse. After the two of them sift through the ashes and pass the bones to one another, as the ceremony requires, Ko offers the old woman in charge a cash payment. The lack of connection between Ko and Chiyo—the lack of erotic connection—coincides with an exchange of money for services. Here, it is significant that the person who receives the payment, the old woman, senses that the couple are not married, and comments on it with a snicker. As in the works of Sōseki and Tōson, financial arrangements disrupt personal ones. When Chiyo prepares for her last funeral, she is alone and no longer responsible for arranging or serving. The kimono she has worn until now, the gift given to her, is cut up and resewn: disintegration of the object, destruction of its wholeness, coincides with the end of service, the absence of community, and the beginning of isolation.

But the fracturing of community seems necessary for the fostering of individual growth. At the end of *Flowing*, for example, Rika is alone after the geisha community breaks apart: "New beginnings are not merely happy occasions: there is also a sense of withering away, of leaving old friends behind. . . . The many paths to be taken, the self that was to take them, seemed to stagnate in exhaustion and loneliness. The days flow into the future. From the dark road ahead comes the rumble of a train passing before her eyes. . . . The heads of the few passengers aboard appear in isolation. 'One in the morning,' she thinks. 'The last train.' And then she thought of something else entirely."[25]

Still, Rika emerges from her community enriched with expressive power. She has become an idiosyncratic presence and an artist—here the figures of Rika and Aya meld—who perceives the world at a distance and gives her perceptions creative form. The artist can conflate a woman with the clothes that adorn her and cast that perception into aesthetic form. In the following description from *Flowing*, women and clothing become a fluid mass of shape and color.

> Rika, of course, looked on coldly. The mistress crumpled to the ground, her knees buckling, the child coiled around her. The child's body showed not the slightest hint of feminine sexuality. The woman that the child referred to as her aunt wore a faded yukata, but from between her collapsing legs there appeared the soft pink of her flesh. Her body settled gradually into a beautifully broken form. The image of her dropping to the floor entwined with her niece was not remarkable in and of itself—everybody has witnessed such a scene. But in this insignificant tableau the woman's true character was revealed. Rika watched this gorgeous form with fascination. The child clutched the body of the woman, who was gently resisting her. As the woman fell over on her side, a tender smile played on her lips. The child was obstructing the woman's chest from Rika's view, but beneath the heavy crepe edge of the sleeve a bare arm was revealed. The woman's leg was folded on top of the other, discreetly, forming a sideways V, and the tips of her white tabi protruded slightly from beneath her hems. . . . Her fall was steady and quiet, her collapse beautiful, her increasing state of disarray a wonder to behold. (45)

The woman and the girl look like objects to Rika, whereas the clothes they wear seem almost animate. In the dynamic interaction with their clothes both control their environment and are controlled by it. Like

Chiyo, they are not turned into lifeless dolls. But if "The Black Hems" describes how the environment can be managed, it also shows how impossible it is to gain release from the pull of circumstances. Only through inherited form can Chiyo dominate form; only through clothing and service can she effect a compromise with the world and nurture an independent identity of her own making. She is never released from the weight of her inheritance as a woman. At the close of the story she no longer serves at funerals, and she has remade her clothing with her own hands; but her release will not be complete, for she will presumably continue to abide by familial obligations and the ceremonies that they require of her.

If Chiyo has to control the circumstances of her life to avoid being turned into a doll, the protagonist of "Dolls" shows her own control in the purchase and display of a set of dolls. Lacking a strong narrative—as do many of Aya's stories, which seem as much like essays as they do like fiction—"Dolls" moves with the thoughts of the main character, a mother who tries to create for her daughter a perfect arrangement of dolls in perfect doll clothing with perfect doll accoutrements. The dolls are described in fine detail—their expressions, their smiles, their clothes, their idiosyncrasies, their resemblances to real people (one looks like Audrey Hepburn)—and as in "The Black Hems," their life and decline as objects parallel the life and decline of the woman associated with them—the mother who arranges them. By the close of the story, seven or eight years have passed, the mother has divorced her husband and returned to her father's home, and the dolls have lost their former luster. "They had all aged a great deal. One doesn't expect dolls to grow old, but their faces were shrunken and pale. The white of their foreheads and cheeks had become transparent, like a cocoon about to open. The once cool and serene black eyes had a look of middle-aged complacency, and they no longer shone." Worm-eaten and scarred, the set of dolls no longer glittered with life. "How sad that the dolls had grown old and that I, too, had grown old, while my daughter still retained the bloom of youth."[26]

In "The Black Hems" and "Dolls" there is no stopping the gradual decay of objects: the kimono becomes threadbare, and the dolls fade. The mother in "Dolls" tries desperately to deny the force of change—or at least quell her fears about it—by setting the dolls up: "The years flowed on. Air raids came one after the other, and Tokyo was turned completely inside out. It was not a time to display dolls. Sensing that this was the end, everyone felt compelled to behave in unexpected and unconventional ways. . . . And for that very reason, against all common sense, I set up the doll stand as in the past." In the end, the dolls are left to disintegrate in the bombed city. The daughter, young and unaware of the process of decay, decides to leave them behind. Aya's narratives inevitably return to such moments of pathos, moments when the attempt to halt decay—through the arrangement of objects, for example—fails.

Rika's endeavor to freeze time with her perception is one manifestation of this urge to create stability from chaos. In *Flowing,* Rika realizes that she cannot stop the passage of time and that she herself stands outside the stream of life. Aware of the force of change yet intrigued by standing beyond it and perceiving it, she attempts to maintain an objective view of the decay that she witnesses, thus remaining outside its ravages. Rika observes moments of great fluidity and complex movement as slices of time. Her aesthetic distance and aestheticized reaction—seeing events as art and casting them into art—come from attempting to stand outside the course of events. But the real world cannot be ignored: the geisha house will close, Rika will leave, and objects will keep on decaying.

In Aya's works, gestures of control are always accompanied by a movement from order back into chaos. The moment that Rika captures—the woman and the girl falling to the floor—is only, she realizes, a "momentary silhouette." The order that she wants to maintain seems destined to be disrupted. "The condition of the room after mother and child had gone bespoke Rika's character. The ashes in the brazier were swept into a neat pile, the tea towels were twisted tightly in their rack, the tables and pillows were all set straight. Even the cat had its head between its legs and was curled up in a perfect ball. But as soon as Someka and Nanako, who were anything but orderly, saw that the mistress had gone, they made havoc of the place" (36).

Although decay and disorder seem inevitable, Aya also feels the urge toward order: in "Dolls" every detail of the doll's display must be perfected and every space must be filled. "In the doll display, which was charming down to the last detail, only the space for the curtain yawned mockingly, as though it were a large mouth, and inside that mouth the red and blue beaded-glass headpieces of the female dolls flickered, irritating me beyond endurance." That which she cannot control threatens her, and she is scolded by her father for arrogantly believing that she can achieve total control. Her mother-in-law is hurt by this arrogance: with every detail attended to, "her spirit could find no place to enter."

To the mother in "Dolls," only beauty is reliable, though her compulsion to create order and perfection must end in futility and emotional coldness. As in "The Black Hems," the past returns in the guise of an old woman— here the mother-in-law—to reproach the younger woman for hubris. In this sense, the past is debilitating; it holds desire in check and obstructs creative vision. But the restriction placed on the woman's will by the past does not squelch her personality completely; rather, it forms her notion of beauty.

Just as Aya's literary persona arises from passivity, inadequacy, and ineptitude, the mother's notions of beauty in "Dolls" arise from poverty and lack. Of the fifteen dolls, twelve are ideally beautiful, and three are downright funny-looking. The imperfect dolls evoke sympathy, and only by combining them with the perfect dolls is an aesthetic developed, one that the narrator calls *hachō no chōwa*—harmony created by the fracturing of harmony. Things that are too beautiful need to be countered by things that are humanly comprehensible. In Rika's attempt to control her environment, her imagination, too, takes in everything before it—the "smell of a sick dog's vomit," as well as "the sparsely falling snow, descending slowly, black and white, as if pushing its way through the air." The serenity of the snow and the stink of the dying dog—both are available to Aya's senses and both, because of their beauty or their disruption of beauty, excite those senses into converting them into art (31).[27]

Aya's attraction to an aesthetic of lack and imperfection is most explicitly rendered in "Dolls." But other moments in Aya's writing express the same sensibility. As portrayed in her memoirs, Aya's father, though famous, did not manage to earn more than a meager living; and although Aya grew up in a culturally and intellectually stimulating atmosphere, materially she had little more than a plenitude of books. When she was a child, she resented making do with a minimum of clothing and food, but she learned to appreciate the little she had. Her father taught her—with a strictness that Aya describes as "weird"—"to open [her] eyes to the beauty in a simple clod of earth" (*KAZ* 1: 186).

Aya learned not just to make do but to find in deprivation a richness and intimacy unavailable in the life of luxury denied her. She came to appreciate a life of economic hardship in poor and constricted spaces—kitchen entrance-ways, back alleyways smelling of garbage and cats, river banks where boatmen barely eke out a living—and sensed a loss when Japan emerged from postwar poverty: "These days the world has settled down, and nothing is impossible to someone with money. No longer do others rely on me to help shoulder their burdens, nor do I offer to do so" (*KAZ* 6: 336). The nostalgia for a time when struggle gave meaning to life is reminiscent of Mishima's and Yasuoka's nostalgia. It associates deprivation with intimacy, and luxury with emotional coldness. The potentially constricting spaces of her childhood that are described in her memoirs become, then, creative spaces.

Aya transformed the wartime destruction into an aesthetic notion that valorized half-formed, imperfect, fragmented things. In this transformation she aligned herself with an important tradition in the history of Japanese aesthetics, exemplified by the writings of Yoshida Kenko in the fifteenth century. She was also responding, however, to contemporary circumstances. She turned a past that had brought loss and ruin into a present that found fragments from the past to be capable of fostering new growth. In a short essay that is essentially a disquisition on garbage, Aya describes this transformation.

> What in the world is garbage? There's nothing that in essence is garbage. All garbage was once something else, something that existed before, something that, having exhausted its purpose, collapsed and was destroyed and turned into dust and came to be called garbage. Garbage is a name for a form that changes. A tree's leaf falls, a crimson flower scatters. When still on the branch they were leaf and flower, but at the moment they separated from the branch, they changed into garbage. Garbage, I think, is something sorrowful. Even kitchen garbage is. A potato wears a skin, but the skin that has been peeled off and thrown away is no longer a potato; it has become garbage. Until the point when kitchen garbage is understood to be garbage, it is things like apples and carrots. Truly, the time it takes to turn into what is called garbage is only the briefest instant. (*KAZ* 5: 252)

The passage evinces Aya's concentrated interest in small and disregarded things—things like herself. It also reveals once again her fascination with moments of transformation, like the moment that her father passed on. What follows the destruction of an object is not, she suggests, devoid of value. "Asked what the word *garbage* brings to mind, most people would respond, 'Something dirty.' By saying 'something dirty,' they clearly establish their distance from garbage. And so, if one asks, 'Doesn't the word *garbage* suggest something familiar and intimate?' the expression on their faces wavers between yes and no, and people say, 'I suppose so. Now that you mention it, garbage is certainly all around me.' This is a fine way of thinking. It's perfectly reasonable. It is natural to think of 'dirty' things that are close to us as disagreeable and far away, and of distant, 'beautiful' things as enjoyable and close to our hearts. And yet—" (*KAZ* 5: 255).

For Aya, memories, too, are broken things, fragments that can be collected and salvaged. Her world, having been blasted by war, is heaped with memories. Her journey into the past was mandated by the war and by the death of her father. Memories, like fragments, lead to intimacy; an unruptured life, free of a splintered profusion of memories, induces coldness, the coldness of luxury, the luxury of living without memories.

Aya's attempt to retrieve objects from the past is an attempt to preserve memories as well. Objects and memories force themselves on her and draw her back, away from the present. They account for the disjointedness of many of her narratives, the moments that interrupt or divert the narrative flow.

A scene in "Dolls," for example, seems wholly out of place in the story: an explanation of why the fabric that the woman ordered for the doll display arrives late. The daughter of the fabric dyer had sobbed all day. After the father lost patience and spanked her, she grew feverish, and the parents called a doctor. "When the doctor came around noon, they were shocked to find that the husband's open palm had left clear red marks on the baby's little behind. The doctor gave the chilling diagnosis: 'A needle.' The father had unluckily hit the child where a needle was stuck in her body and had driven it farther in." After a great commotion the child was taken to a hospital to have the needle removed (*KAZ* 7: 130).

The passage takes on vibrancy in part because it seems to emerge from nowhere. Moments such as this often appear in Aya's writing. They stick out like a needle and interfere with the narrative flow. They belong to what Frank Kermode calls, in another context, "a quasi-magical, non-sequential plot that is at odds with the prevailing idiom of the story."[28]

The needle story pierces Aya's memory and forces itself into her narrative. The image of a father slapping a daughter and inflicting an internal wound is true to her own experience. The pain of memory is represented by a sharp object stabbing the flesh. The image immediately recalls the needle from "Hair," which stuck in the pincushion and in the woman as well, representing the anguish she felt about her stepmother and about her ties to the past.

A similar movement of memory can be seen in the contemporaneous works of Yasuoka Shōtarō, where memory, or the objects that embody it, disrupts the linear movement of time. In Yasuoka's narratives the present is never fully regained, and memories impede the continuation of a viable existence.[29] In Aya's narratives, however, memories are not a barrier. Her narratives often begin in the present, only to be drawn back to the past by a specific object and the memories it stirs; then her narratives emerge once again into the present. Aya herself describes the process of memory as it affects the experience of time:

> It is probably true of everyone that the little things we see and hear when we are young have great emotional impact. They strike us, and then they seem to sink in firmly somewhere deep in our hearts, occasionally floating to the surface with

unusual clarity. At those times we cannot help but marvel at the oldness of a memory. When we stop to count, twenty—no, thirty—years have passed. Thinking of that span of thirty years, which we have certainly not forgotten, we are deeply moved again. And there are various ways of being struck by a memory. There is the positive, expansive way: we can't restrain ourselves from telling it to everyone around us and wind up talking our heads off. And there is the negative, retentive way: here, for no apparent reason, we hold the memory tightly to ourselves, unwilling to reveal it to another person, as though it was better to keep it private. People who experience memory this way often freeze up when someone describes a story similar to their own, and they move their tongues only enough to say, "I also . . ." These people end up not speaking; their tongues become lead, their teeth stones, and the lips clay—though they possess no great secret or anything of the kind. It's not that they can't talk but that they won't talk. But this, too, is a matter of the particular moment. These days, somehow, my lips seem to have loosened. Is there a time when memory suddenly strikes, suddenly sinks, suddenly expands? (*KAZ* 7: 195)

Memories and objects determine the way that Aya's protagonists experience time. In "The Black Hems," time moves according to the woman's relation with her clothes. In "Dolls" the war is mentioned in just a few brief lines; the time of the story moves according to the woman's obsession with the dolls. In *Flowing,* the war and its aftermath lead the main character into an enclosed world where time moves according to the rhythms of geisha life. In these and Aya's other works, the war intrudes in the narrative, as it did in Aya's life, and accentuates the fracturing moment that inspired her own career as a writer.

CHAPTER 6

Flowing

In length, complexity, and beauty of style, *Flowing* marks the climax of Aya's career. Everything she wrote prior to it seems preparatory, and everything after it reads like a coda. *Flowing* represents a literary height that she had not reached before and would never scale again, and our judgment of her entire career as a writer must depend largely on our evaluation of this one work. *Flowing* is also the work in which the literary and personal themes that possessed Aya's imagination are presented with the greatest depth and clarity.

Flowing describes a failing geisha establishment through the eyes of a middle-aged maid who begins to work there at the start of the novel. Little actually happens in the novel: we witness the dissolution of a once-viable way of life in a time of economic and emotional hardship. Through Rika's eyes we observe the various goings-on as if observing a series of tableaux. It is Rika's personality and the quality of her perceptions that hold our attention. The novel may be read, in fact, as a record of Rika's emotional and perceptual reactions to the events around her. She immerses herself in them and removes herself from them when she feels overwhelmed by their force. At these times she takes a solitary walk, slips out of a room to do a chore, or allows herself to drift into a daydream.

Rika sees a world in which standards that once defined modes of behavior, and borders that once separated categories of people, have begun to collapse. Characters who do not fit into clear categories and who do not uphold the standards appropriate to their roles weaken and suffer, sacrificed to the forces of time. The novel can thus be read as a criticism of the diminished obedience to strictly defined prewar modes of behavior. Whether this criticism derives from simple nostalgia, from a crotchety conservatism that locates value only in the past and that laments any change threatening to destroy it, or, rather, from an unsentimental awareness of loss is a question that can be answered only after a thorough examination of the novel.

The character of Rika nevertheless offers an immediate clue to the predominant tone. Rika stands apart from this world whose traditions are dying. She mourns their demise and disparages the weakness of those who have let them die but maintains an identity powerful enough to ensure her own survival. Her cold and often cruel observations of a world tearing apart at the seams make *Flowing* more than a nostalgic lament for a lost past. Rika understands that the traditions of the geisha are no longer viable. She loathes the geisha's inability to cut their ties with the past when it has become destructive to them and admires men for being able to forget about former sorrows. After witnessing an old geisha and her former lover meet and then part, she observes: "Perhaps she felt the pathos because he was a good man, devoid of nostalgia, who had completely severed his ties; but the lingering, clinging heart of a woman seemed offensive to Rika, though she, too, was a woman."[1]

Though a woman living among women, Rika is never wholly part of the community.[2] She moves about demurely on the periphery, but she becomes, in the end, the strong, still center of a crumbling world. Hers are the eyes and the ears through which the reader experiences the world of the novel. She is the first and most fully developed protagonist in Aya's writings who is completely disengaged from the life of a family, utterly free to observe what she chooses to observe, and highly confident of the quality of her perceptions—as is Aya, with whom she seems to share an identity.

Rika is a refugee from an obliquely alluded-to nuclear family with a vague history of postwar impoverishment. She enters the entertainment quarters in hopes of shedding her identity and releasing herself from the burdens of her past. When the novel opens, she is looking for the entrance-way of this haven. Having found it, she enters, is examined by her prospective employer—who immediately recognizes her as a woman of proper breeding—and is hired as a maid, even though she is too old for the job. In keeping with her new identity she is given a new, auspicious name, Oharu (Spring), thought to be more appropriate to her changed life. She will, however, continue to be called Rika by her employers, indicating to the reader that she never fully enters her new role.

In this new environment Rika feels "helpless and alone, engulfed by strange waters" (5). She feels inferior to her new companions and her employer. They are professionals (*kurōto*), insiders, owners of special skills and talents, and she is an amateur (*shirōto*), an outsider unschooled in their secrets. The novel begins in the contemporary postwar world but quickly passes into one that moves to the pace of traditional modes of behavior.

After one day's service Rika's past has been wiped away: "Familiarity grows in the span of even one day. Surrounding her now was one day's depth of familiarity to attest to who she was" (18). Rika's conditions of employment release her from her past: she needs no references and is asked no questions.

Rika can lose herself in any of the various dramas taking place within the house. She is immediately struck, assaulted almost, by voices emanating from behind the door she is about to enter. They belong to the madam of the house, a great beauty, talented musician, and skilled businesswoman, who has only recently begun to fade; to her daughter Katsuyo, whose looks and lack of talent disqualify her to follow in her mother's footsteps; to the madam's niece Yoneko, a petulant, slow-witted, and long-suffering girl; and to Yoneko's daughter Fujiko, the helpless victim of a troubled adult world. Other characters drift in and out of the story, including three commuting geishas (there used to be seven); the madam's older sister Kishibōjin, cold, powerful, and rich; another older geisha who owns a lucrative restaurant; the young geisha Namie, whose situation helps bring down the house; her uncle, who squeezes money from the madam for hiring his under-age niece; a lawyer; a policeman; a dashing young man who saves the day; a dying dog; and a mischievous cat.

Rika chooses to live among geisha because it allows her a temporary escape from the sorrows of her life, both present and past, and from her memory of them. The entertainment quarters are a refuge for fallen people, a place where no social opprobrium attaches to a woman's status or past, no matter how sordid. Rika often seems like an anthropologist witnessing the final days of a dying culture, and when *Flowing* was published—a year before prostitution was legally abolished and the pleasure quarters decimated—it was certainly read as such. By way of Rika's steadfast gaze we learn details of economic life within the geisha world: there are various classes of working women, from cheap whore to skilled entertainer to wealthy proprietor, and there is movement up and down the class ladder; each geisha buys her clothing on loans made by the madam of the house, who can charge her exorbitant interest; New Year gifts are usually exchanged for money or for other gifts to give to other geisha, thus lessening the geisha's burden of debt and obligation; the payment system is complicated indeed, the cash moving from the customer, to the geisha union office, to the madam of the house, and finally to the geisha herself.

During the 1950s, with the national restructuring of the economy, cultural life seemed to be gradually centralizing. Skills associated with distinct neighborhoods were giving way to large-scale industries associated with no locale in particular. Differences in class, language, skill, and profession were disappearing. In the geisha world a vanishing landscape and economy still existed. Here, in the old downtown area of Tokyo, the *shitamachi,* the past seemed to live, and cultural authority had a locus. The writers and craftsmen who had always frequented the geisha quarters respected the activities and language of certain shitamachi neighborhoods. Aya learned from her father to associate cultural authority with the downtown; he was a connoisseur of its crafts and literature, and the heroes of his fiction were more likely to be dedicated artisans than self-absorbed intellectuals.[3]

Like Aya, Rika is drawn to the geisha world, but not exclusively because of its cultural authority; it also provides her with an environment similar to the one from which she comes. She feels most at home in a nurturing role, defined by chores and by responsibilities to others. She wants a life where a set of rules organizes behavior—where various codes determine how to dress, eat, and talk, where distinctions of class are still immediately and clearly recognized by nuances of speech and etiquette. It is a world very much like the one created for Aya by her father. And like Aya, Rika assumes a role that allows her to feel anchored.

Rika takes on the responsibilities of cleaning and serving. At first, she shops, cooks, washes toilets, searches for stray cats, and cleans up mouse droppings. But in time her other, more elegant and superior self, hidden behind her pose as a maid, emerges.

The full revelation of her identity must wait, however, for the final moments of the novel, when the geisha establishment is on the verge of collapse. Only when the geisha relinquish their identities as geisha can Rika step out of her role as maid. When the novel opens, the boundary between geisha and non-geisha is still firm, and Rika can find her place only by assuming her strictly defined role. But her entry into the geisha house—the Tutanoya—also coincides with the geisha Yukimaru's departure, the first in a series of crossings from the inside to the outside world. The wall between the two worlds has begun to weaken, so Rika can slip in between the cracks and find her own place of strength.

The following passage describes Rika's first act of service, her first attempt to bring order to her environment.

Try as she might to arrange the jumble of Yukimaru's shoes, Rika was unable to figure out which went with which. She was crouched down attempting to match them when a puppy, its paws wet with urine, jumped up on her shoulder and affectionately pressed itself against her. Yukimaru pulled a pair of fancy sandals from the back of the shelf, bowed slightly to Rika from behind the lattice door, and departed. In Yukimaru's uncertainty, Rika sensed a desire to express something, a suggestion of some hidden tragedy. It was Yukimaru's tragic look that lent her the air of a geisha. The wind, picking up the stench of dog, blew in through a small crack in the door; dusk had descended. An inexperienced maid, Rika was momentarily overwhelmed by the pathos that Yukimaru had left in her wake. She looked at the swarm of white intestinal worms in the dog's feces, and at the white dog itself—its hair thinning, its frame sagging, its body trembling. For some reason, Rika felt she could settle down in this place. (8)

Not only does Rika arrange the footwear; she also arranges the scene in her mind with the power of her perception. Although she is not completely successful, the chance to sort out the confusion and wipe up the mess invigorates her. She can exert a measure of control over her cluttered environment through acts of service; even more important, these acts of service bring her imaginative control as well. Service seems to lend Rika the authority of a writer, to authenticate her in her role as an artist. The arranging of Yukimaru's footwear is the first in a series of attempts at control that leads, finally, to control of the entire establishment.[4]

Rika's control is dependent upon the spatial constriction of her environment:

The bathroom was filthy; the tub looked as though it hadn't been heated in ages. Carefully stepping onto the drain board, she wasn't surprised to find a collection of mouse droppings in front of her. If she didn't hurry and do a proper job the bath would never be ready on time. . . . When she opened the small wainscoted window, which appeared never to have been opened before, she saw that she was barely six inches from the clapboarding of the house next door. The light bulb inside the house was unbearably bright, and the planks that ran across the ceiling had no doubt been stripped from another building. The holes left by nails were lined up like black stains. A rack for drying clothes hung from the ceiling like an umbrella with only its skeleton showing. On one side, dried socks drooped listlessly, and on the other, a scarlet collar meant to be worn with an under-kimono. There was a beauty in this confined space. Very often, narrowness implies poverty, but when it is used cleverly like this, it gives a sense of abundance, of things packed in to the very limit, so that they burst out the sides. Left without even a pillow for her head, Rika had experienced many poor and narrow places since her financial collapse after the war, but now she finally understood what narrowness meant. In the end, narrowness exists where people and things exist. Because there are things, there is narrowness; the absence of people and things is the absence of narrowness. (9)

In the course of the novel the narrow parameters of her world allow Rika ever-expanding possibilities for action. She begins as a complete stranger and neophyte: "After sleeping there only one night, Rika sensed that outside, beyond the peddler's voices in the street, there was a world of ordinary people, the world she had lived in until the previous day" (45). She acquires a sense of camaraderie with those inside: "Rika remained seated in the kitchen but felt, in the end, unable to stay without doing anything to help. She worried [about the crisis], not as if looking down on a mass of people, but as if the problem were her very own" (46). Eventually, she becomes an emotional and practical support, taking care of the house when the madam is detained at the police station for tax evasion and taking charge of a petulant young geisha, managing her when nobody else can. By the end of the novel Rika displays greater strength than the madam herself. At the point of imminent ruin a wealthy young man steps in and, with the aid of a wealthy geisha, buys the house, moves the madam to a new, lower-quality establishment, and installs Rika as the head of the old place, which will be made into an inn. Her intelligence and skills have been recognized, her role transformed from server to overseer.

Rika can show admiration and concern for the women she serves, and often feels secure in their presence, but she is never fully one of them. Even though she shares the poverty, the bitter cold and inadequate diet, the struggle to meet the demands of everyday life, and even though she is bound to them and is, like them, free of marital ties, she maintains her distance from the small community of which she is a member by remaining an observer. She has a double identity, reminiscent of Aya's: on the one hand a domestic servant, on the other a trained and lucid observer; on the one hand a maid, on the other an artist.

Rika is not unconscious of this dissimulation, but is, rather, constantly aware of her superiority. She regards weakness with icy detachment, at times with royal condescension, confident of her own correctness. Although she admires the geisha's skills, she despises their self-pity and loathes the way they ingratiate themselves with men and depend on them in times of need: "Both the geisha and the madam had a wisdom about their faces, and each had the strength to make her way on her chosen path, but somehow it seemed that they stinted with their powers. They did not use all their energy and strength, half relying instead on their lovers. Even the madam, uncertain of her strength, lacking confidence, and unable to lean on her husband, who was himself failing, naturally began to weaken and to give in to her coquettish and cunning heart" (69).

When the madam allows the young man Saeki to take control during the financial crisis in the house, Rika's disapproval is more explicit: "For her to throw away the strength and pride culled over the long years so easily, to be stripped of authority so swiftly, made Rika feel both chagrined and disappointed" (119).

Rika revels in her more refined speech and writing, her greater emotional strength, her more thorough domestic training. But she also tries to appear naive and obsequiously feigns surprise and admiration at appropriate moments. Her true self, however, cannot help but reveal itself, often with an elegant slip of the tongue or a graceful slip of the pen. She despises everything that does not meet her standards of propriety, cleanliness, and strength, but she tries to keep her judgments in check. Any criticism is shared only with the reader, never, except at the end, with the other characters. The narrative voice at these moments is Aya's; she speaks as the proud daughter of Kōda Rohan, gazing upon the scene in the guise of a maid.

Rika's condescension is balanced by her admiration for the geisha. She values the economic independence and freedom from "normal" responsibilities that the women share, their verbal and social skills, their stress on ritual and custom, their dedication to work and to the tools of their trade—their kimonos, their musical instruments, their bodies—and to the fruit of their labor, their money. These women instill meaning into the material objects of which their world is composed: "The money of amateurs is meaningless, insipid, dying, valueless, thought Rika; but the money of professionals is alive and intelligent: cut it and blood pours out, strike it and it gives off a sharp ring. Even among professionals' coins there are differences in charm and attractiveness" (38).[5]

The geisha can transform empty spaces into vibrant places. A simple room becomes a *zashiki*, a place where they ply their trade. Rika is fascinated to observe the madam at work and realizes that the creation of a zashiki does not depend upon beautiful and elegant furnishings but upon talent and taste. "The madam had been working in the zashiki. Rika had never seen a geisha's zashiki, but she knew this was one the moment she saw it. It was entirely different from the room [*cha no ma*] that the madam usually occupied and was two or three times as wide. A rainbow seemed to span the madam's body. . . . Her beautiful face, endowed by nature, and her skill as a geisha, acquired through many years of training, generously filled the room" (55).

The geisha's work requires transformations of this sort. Their clothing, their makeup, their bodies, are tools to manipulate. Although Rika remains skeptical of the geisha's obsessive rituals of self-transformation (makeup, she feels at one point, is nothing more than a mask) and is disturbed when their changeovers seem to be simpering coquettishness, she often feels shabby herself. Once she watches a geisha rise from her bed.

Still on her side, she first reaches out her thin hand and flips each layer of the *yuzen* blanket off her. Then, gently raising her upper body with her other hand, her lap crumpling, she shifts into a sideways seated position. She rises smoothly, as if extracting her body from inside the futon, leaving behind not even the wrinkles of her sleep. A silver-gray collar is attached to her long underkimono, on which there is a weeping cherry tree of white and purple and a green willow; the area around her breast is folded in a bit, and she has loosely wrapped around her an undersash with a green bamboo design and one golden bar. There is no crimson anywhere, but she looks radiant and bright. Although she manages to look youthful, one cannot help but realize her night was that of a woman already on in years. It was not a night spent with a lover nor a night in which a lover was desired—but that is the conjecture of an amateur.

Within this woman dressed in deep purple, deeper than crimson, Rika sees all that could burn, even with an almost spent passion. Perhaps there is nothing left but the memory of a burning past, yet even now she arises from sleep with such elegance. If it is indeed the remains of an art deeply imbued over the long years and no longer capable of being extracted—rather than an eroticism merely gushing up from inside her—this technique of a lifetime is a beautiful thing. Nandori gently places her hands between the blankets, opens an old-fashioned folding pocket mirror, and smooths her loose hair. As though in slow motion, she rises gracefully and, without the slightest hint of being rushed, arranges her hair in the mirror. In distant and faded memories, Rika, too, can recall mornings such as this, but how long it has been since she has known such beautiful awakenings! To what end does she wake up halfheartedly, brush her teeth hastily, and rush through her meal? In contrast, this old woman had probably awoken like this each and every morning, awoken as if another person were there, awoken with motions suggesting that she was even in love with that person— supply extracted her body from a bed shared by two and, without a sound, arranged her hair. That was the difference. Although outside the sun is high, the shutters remain shut; her undergarments are shining brightly, wrapped in the light of the electric lamp. (113–114)

Such alchemy is, however, increasingly rare in the geisha world.[6] Boundaries have begun to disintegrate. The distinctions in style and skill that once separated amateur from professional are disappearing. At one time the geisha had complete and exclusive control over their social identities; now their mode of being is standardized and widely available. Strict categories of social life have become forms of commodity. The geisha have been illusionists, specialists in skills specific to their social status and identity, owners of a repertoire passed down the generations. Now these skills are on the market. Geisha recruits are drawn from a class of women unschooled in artistic accomplishment and less conscious of their role as artists, less able to exercise their strength as manipulators of form. Even their makeup—which once created an opaque boundary between geisha and customer but which also allowed a woman to transform herself—has grown thin and no longer fulfills its proper function. The illusion is attenuated; creativeness has been replaced by shamming. The geisha, women who exploit their own bodies, are exploited by the pressure of financial crisis.

The geisha's ability to transform their bodies and their environments diminishes in the course of the novel until they become objects susceptible to the forces of change. Rika senses this, and senses her own superiority as an amateur; she spends much of the novel battling the madam. Rika unmasks the geisha, removing them from the category of geisha and reducing them to mere women. That they can be exposed so easily is as much a sign of their already-reduced powers of illusion, of their slip into commodification, as it is of Rika's acumen. After a scene in which the madam seems to have been defeated by the usurer, Rika is critical, but cautiously so.

> In the relationship between an accomplished woman—the owner of an establishment—and a woman on her way to becoming accomplished, there are many troublesome feelings. And so that night, Rika couldn't fight her initial feeling of condescension. And yet she wondered if her judgment wasn't hasty. It simply couldn't be that the madam would allow herself to be defeated like this, that she had no more tricks, and that she could be walked out on so summarily. The wisdom of the geisha would undoubtedly be revealed in her mastery of the aftermath. Neither her ability nor her victory or defeat could be determined at this midway point. Even allowing herself to be forced to kneel might be just another technique. The more complicated the strategy and the more violent the thrust and parry, the more opportunities there were for reversing the situation. (60)

Rika realizes that she can be victorious over the force of crippling change by combining her own lack of coquettishness with the erotic transformative potential inherent in the geisha's skills: "Rika felt that she wanted to grasp the nature of a great geisha [*meigi*]. The madam possessed some quality that filled Rika with admiration, but in this evening's appearance there had been nothing to praise. One couldn't call it anything but a clumsy, ugly failure. What, then, was a geisha? In the glimpses of a great geisha's talent that the madam unconsciously revealed day to day, Rika saw the power of attraction, and at those times she admired her unreservedly, but at other times she was scornful" (60).

In the course of the novel the differences between Rika and the geisha become less distinct, because the geisha lose their special qualities as geisha. The outside world, no longer so strictly separate, impinges with ever-greater force, and the inside world cannot withstand the economic pressures and cultural changes from outside. The outside world enters the geisha world in the ring of a telephone, signaling a call from a patron, or in a visit from the police, investigating a legal infraction, or in the arrival of a handsome young man, come to save the fortunes of the house. It bangs on the door of the inner sanctum, relentlessly battering down its self-sufficiency.

Rika's entry into the geisha house is, I have suggested, the first of a number of crossings in the novel. The outside world invades the inside more imperatively in the guise of the old usurer who extorts money from the madam for illegally employing his underage niece. His actions cripple the geisha's ability to control their environment. That the house maintains its tottering solidity at all is a testament to Rika's strength, but that strength derives from her amateurism and as such signals the inability of the professionals to fend for themselves. Like the geisha house, hanging in a precarious balance between self-sufficiency and collapse, Rika and the madam of the house are situated at their own personal boundaries, between middle and old age, between self-sufficiency and possible collapse. The trajectories that their lives will take are different, however. As the establishment and its madam head toward ruin, Rika gains authority.

Though gradually integrated into the community, Rika remains aloof. She is accepted by those she serves because she is respected as a worker, but she is also recognized to be brighter and more sophisticated than her station in life implies. Her handwriting and her speech, for example, belong to a cultured world different from that of a maid.

Her status as an outsider allows Rika to look upon her world the way a painter looks upon a busy scene; it is there to perceive and capture. The world can even seem to exist merely to satisfy her desire to cast things into aesthetic form, much as the novel often seems an elaborate exercise in Aya's own aesthetic transformations. This accounts, perhaps, for the jarring disjuncture between Rika's rigorous antisentimentalism and the stagy scenes of geisha tragedy that dot the novel. Rika often looks coldly on emotional disarray, observing rather than becoming involved. Her reactions to difficulties can be impersonal and aesthetic. Katsuyo, the daughter of the madam, has been lamenting her inadequate inheritance and worrying about how to earn a living in a trade she is unsuited for. Later in the novel Rika is able to sympathize with her situation. "Rika felt keenly how unfortunate this parent and child were. What could there be between a beautiful mother, extravagantly talented at seduction—one who had skills and an income—and a clumsy daughter whom nobody could like, a woman with no interests or income? Somehow a special relationship, difficult to imagine, had developed between them" (136).

But she lacks the power to fully sympathize. After briefly analyzing Katsuyo's emotional state, she continues to observe and comment:

> Katsuyo had exposed her inner feelings and was speaking with passionate honesty, yet her cheeks seemed too full, like swollen rivers, and her narrow eyes, shining with tears, looked like pieces of straw. The sight was not beautiful. Even her mouth, whose protruding lower lip was considered quite attractive, displayed a certain commonness in its rows of uneven teeth. That, too, was not beautiful. Although, in the present situation, the appearance of her eyes and teeth was of little importance, things that are not beautiful are not pleasant. Rika continued to observe with precision, and despite herself, her eyes filled. What moved her and brought her to tears was not that Katsuyo was pitiful. What moved her was the thought that everyone, regardless of the situation, wants to look beautiful. (128)

Rika has listened to Katsuyo's long, angry speech about the way she is treated for being ugly and clumsy, about the jealousy she feels for her mother, about the anguish she feels for having failed to live up to the standards of the previous generation. Although reminiscent of Rika's, and Aya's, own anguish, Katsuyo's does not elicit sympathy; Rika responds with a removed, aesthetic judgment: "Not only beautiful women look beautiful when angry. Someone can also look awkward when angry without feeling awkward at all. Rika listened to Katsuyo's selfish complaint and could not reject outright what she was saying. When hurt and anger are not resolved overnight, they develop a certain pungency. Katsuyo's words were stiff, but they contained a hint of sorrow" (72). What Rika observes here is that a combination of frustrated anger and passionately but awkwardly expressed sorrow can create an effect of beauty. And although there is a hint of emotion in Rika's response, it is that of an observer toward a stimulus: "The reason Rika didn't leave Katsuyo and go to the kitchen was the tenderness of Katsuyo's youth. The image of youth was shining sorrowfully in her tonight, and it kept Rika in the room, oblivious to questions of right and wrong" (72).

Rika's sympathy succumbs to her stronger instinct to observe. This perhaps accounts for the harsh statements "The sight was not beautiful" and "That, too, was not beautiful." The writing leaves the past tense of description and enters the present tense of Rika's thoughts, disturbing the forward movement of the passage and accentuating her role as an onlooker. Aya's own voice enters the narrative at moments like these. Rika observes Katsuyo, and we see Katsuyo through her eyes; but when the prose enters the present tense, we are jarred out of the scene and seem to be listening to Aya's voice, which has merged with Rika's. Shifting from the past tense of description to the present tense of Rika's thoughts, easily accomplished in the Japanese language, also freeze-frames narrative moments. Aya uses the technique throughout the novel; it represents her (and Rika's) imaginative control over the decaying movement of time.

Katsuyo's words stimulate Rika into examining her own life and bring her to the realization that it is her outsider status that allows her to empathize without losing her precious distance. "It seemed to her that a great deal of time had passed since she had first come to the house. Having learned so many new things, she had the illusion that it had been a long while, though in reality it had not been at all. And especially now, as she listened to the problems of this young woman and to the sound of her voice—creaking like bamboo—she suddenly felt the tide of years catching up with her. . . . Perhaps it was due to her position as a maid: an outsider, she was able to sit by and coolly observe, and precisely because she was detached, she was able to empathize completely" (73).

Katsuyo's lament, which appears late in the novel, signals the collapse of the world that Rika entered at the start. The movement of time that rules the outside world, the tide of years, has overtaken the circular movement of time—impelled by the seasons and seasonal rituals—that has governed the geisha world. The demise of the house is imminent, as is the end of Rika's role in it. The collapsing of the boundaries between the worlds naturally hinges upon a character like Katsuyo, for she, like Rika, is not firmly within either the amateur or the professional category. The daughter of a geisha, she has inherited none of the qualities necessary for a geisha; yet because of her birth, she is unsuited for life in the outside world. But even though both transcend their boundaries, Katsuyo is a victim, and Rika a victor. Rika will leave, but she will begin life again in a position of authority.

Objective, aloof, self-sufficient, self-confident, Rika is also keenly aware that she is cut off from others. Independence leads to isolation, as Aya points out in an afterword to the novel. "From the time I was small, I watched the river. The water, eager to flow, would rush down, yet, wanting to pause, would hesitate, falter, pool, only to flow on again. There was a bridge over the river, and people would cross it calmly, indifferent to the fact that it was a bridge built over flowing water. I would do the same. A bridge is not significant in and of itself, but when I approached it, I would pause a moment and gaze upstream and down, from one side to the other. The river flows; the bridge runs across it. Though I call this novel *Flowing,* I am captured by that moment on this side of the bridge when I feel my heart suddenly pause" (151).

Aya hesitates, aware, in one moment, of a flow that she cannot stop and of herself standing outside the stream of time. In that moment she can observe the world without participating in it. As an observer, Rika, too, can stem decay. One aspect of the geisha world that attracts her is its merging of the categories of old and new: "What was new in the morning had already become old by night. Nobody seemed to distinguish old from new. Having arrived that day, Rika was new, but she felt that she was already being treated . . . as if she had been around for many years" (11).

Because Rika observes movement in clips of time, as in the description of the geisha waking up, and maintains an aesthetic distance and aestheticized reactions, she can mold events and people in her imagination. But Rika has no control outside the household, where there are dangerous streets, newspapers, politics, marriages, deaths, and poverty—where everything seems uncertain and unmanageable and changes too quickly. Inside, in contrast, poverty has potential—the women living with it understand how to transform what little they have, and Rika's imagination is invigorated by their constant struggle with privation. Inside there is also protection from the Tokyo of the early 1950s, now emerging from poverty and confusion into a new age of growth and change. Rika, a woman of breeding and refinement, enters a geisha house where "the filth at the entrance was disgusting; the smell of a sick dog's vomit and shit left to putrefy through the night mixed with the sharp odor of ink from the newspapers" (20). Indoors she finds something compelling—linked somehow to the smell of suffocation and decay—that makes her choose the closed-off world instead of the wide-open world. Deterioration offers the possibility of creative action. "I cannot say exactly what draws me to this place, but the richness of these past two days, the many bewildering sights I have seen, the intricacies, . . . the sense of richness is due in the end to the narrowness, a narrowness that is fascinating and easy to comprehend. Because it is narrow I feel I can capture it in its entirety. Understanding it so completely, I am filled with assurance and hope. The world outside is too wide. It makes me feel the kind of anxiety one feels when the sun goes down over a broad, empty plain. I hate that wide and empty world; I like it in here" (33).

Time moves inexorably forward in the wide and empty world, regardless of the humans occupying it. Space there is emptied of human meaning. Inside the entertainment quarters, time moves according to human design. It is replete with meaning for those who experience it. When Rika stands at the threshold to the geisha house, between the two worlds, the foul-smelling newspaper she notices there, representing recorded, linear time, is mixed with dog vomit and excrement, representing time as it moves through natural cycles of decline and rebirth. The amalgamation of the images implies the amalgamation of the worlds; and in the course of the novel the invasion of time from the outside world becomes irreversible.

Still, through most of the novel, borders remain, no matter how shaky, and Rika thinks her world is crisscrossed with them. She is obsessed with borders, with the differences between her own status and skills as an outsider and those of the geisha as insiders, between the world from which she comes and the one that she has entered; she senses borders everywhere, in the voices of the women, for example, and even in the cat: "Is everyone whose role is to entertain trained to have two voices, an interior and an outer one? Both Nanako and the madam had such voices; and the cat, too, had a battle scream and the lovely purr of a prized pet. Between the scream and the purr an entire musical scale was missing" (11).[7]

To understand Rika's peculiar obsession, we must look through her to Aya herself. About the same time Aya wrote *Flowing,* she revealed her interest in borders and their impending collapse in a number of essays. During this period of postwar reconstruction, the mid-1950s, her attention turned to housing, the changing nature of which had disturbed her during and immediately after the war, when she saw the many homeless people and when she, too, with her father and daughter, experienced a life of aimless wandering. Even though culture critics and government white papers alike announced the end of crisis and recovery, the housing shortage was still severe; half of those without homes in 1945 were still without homes in 1956, and hundreds of thousands still lived in temporary barracks.[8]

Aya's concern at the time, however, was less with the lack of housing than with its quality—with the concrete and glass buildings constructed by the government. To her the modern, efficient, bright, white living units were poor replacements for the darker houses where she grew up: the wood-pillared, clay-walled, paper-doored spaces of the old Japanese home. Because modern kitchens (like modern makeup and modern language) lacked the years of human use that provided historical depth, Aya felt they could neither preserve nor perpetuate the wisdom of the past.

But it was not only the cold surfaces of stainless steel kitchens, impervious to the gradual layering of human experience, that repelled Aya. She was also troubled by the way that domestic space had been rearranged by new urban design. Traditional Japanese architecture delineated the public and private spheres, a separation that also fostered an interaction between the two. The entranceway served as a meeting point and social space where two spheres of human activity could mingle, as they do in *Flowing*. Inside the house, beyond the entranceway, a parallel distinction existed between the private sitting room and the semipublic parlor. The removal of the entranceway and the installation of cylinder locks—undertaken on a mass scale for the first time in the 1950s—disturbed this long-abiding arrangement. The fiction of writers such as Shimao Toshio exemplified the new sense of space and bespoke the isolation and enclosure now felt by the young writers of the so-called withdrawn (*naikō*) generation.[9]

Aya's response to the changing domestic spatial order was to lament the loss of strictly defined borders—not because she craved restrictions or feared freedom of movement nor because she found enclosing spaces suffocating. In a reversal we have come to expect of her thinking, Aya eulogized gates for creating the possibility of freedom within restriction. As the point separating and conjoining the outside and inside worlds, a gate imposed order and lured people into a place of comfort and freedom.[10] The word *freedom* here, however, should be qualified, as before. It is a freedom that includes an acceptance of restrictions and conventions, as the geisha Katsuyo implies when she bemoans her lack of suitors: "Yes, free. But freedom isn't desirable, nor is anything else, when one doesn't feel the need for it. I may be free, with no partner and nobody to belong to, but freedom doesn't seem to have any value" (127).

Borders guarantee this freedom, and their elimination threatens it. Aya accepts the sanction of convention and the rigidity of roles, but she also recognizes the practical necessity of surviving in a world where such standards are doomed. While Rika thus regrets the loss of tradition, she is also able to exit from and return to the geisha world in order to survive. As a character possessing two identities, one inside and one outside, one submerged and one apparent, Rika displays Aya's sensitivity to the interplay of surface and depth. This sensitivity is behind Aya's attempt to create an authentic literary voice that could accommodate her continuing allegiance to her father and the ethical standards he set for her, as well as her desires as an independent artist. Such sensitivity is at the very core of her development of a literary persona that adopts a conventionally feminine guise but works in creative ways behind it.

The dynamic of depths and surfaces is also at work in Rika's desire to live within the entertainment quarters. She chooses a way of life that seems to suit her demure and obedient persona: during her brief stay with the geisha she is ensconced in a space that seems to offer a reprieve from the force of change and struggle. But hiding in this outwardly protective environment, she gives her more independent self free reign. When she enters, she seems frightened and intimidated, but it soon becomes apparent that she is neither, and she leaves the geisha house self-assured and decisive.

In choosing to set her novel in the geisha quarters, Aya behaves in much the same way as her protagonist. She chooses a world that seems matched to one aspect of her identity, but within that world she continues to express another aspect. She chooses as a setting a place that is primarily the province of a male tradition of writing about a particularly and essentially feminine world, and she writes about a class of women who have been the focus of the mainstream literary imagination in Japan. Having chosen this established literary setting, however, she reveals from the inside a world quite different from its usual depictions. Aya takes a conventionally male literary topos and re-forms it according to her own sensibility. Where male writers have discovered femininity in its idealized, abstract form, Aya discovers femininity in its de-idealized specificity—femininity writ small.

Flowing offers a potentially stable environment as an antidote to a life of aimlessness. It depicts an anchorage in a world in flux, a place tendering a reprieve from national politics and broad social change. In these ways *Flowing* shares much with other novels that have treated the demimonde. In her *Cultural History of Courtesans* (*Yūjo no bunkashi*), Saeki Junko has traced the depiction of the courtesan from the historical chronicles and the poetry anthology the *Man'yōshū* of the eighth century, through Heian court poetry, the Nō plays of the fifteenth century, the Genroku-era (1675–1725) dramas of Chikamatsu and novels of Saikaku, and on to the novels of the modern period. In these various periods and genres women have been associated with sexuality and sacred power, with the ability to make a bridge between the profane world and the sacred one. They were goddesses and shamans— metaphors for the pathos of humankind's fleeting existence. They guided men to ecstatic moments where death and life, love and death, could meet. They offered the possibility of freedom from earthly attachments.[11]

Late in the seventeenth century, according to Saeki, the spiritual power that men understood to reside in women was held in check when government decree established legal entertainment districts to which courtesans were confined. Their power was secularized, but they continued to be a focus of the male literary imagination. In the first literary work to treat these confined women—*The Tale of Rōten* (*Rōten monogatari*, 1589)—the geisha (*daiya*) was evoked as an unearthly beauty, representing a world of fantasy and dreams, able to lead men to a more sublime realm. The demimonde itself came to represent an alternative to grinding reality. It became the object of longing, the lost home, a place of security.[12]

This longing for a home also characterizes Izumi Kyōka's *The Saint of Mount Koya* (*Koya hijiri,* 1900), one of the first modern novels to treat the demimonde. In it, a young man leaves his own life and travels to another world, where he meets a woman who can transform men into animals through sex.

A projection of male fantasy and desire, the image of an alternative world ruled by women maintained a strong hold on Japanese writers in part because of the ambivalence they felt about the quickened pace of economic, social, and political change that accompanied the massive influx of Western technology and thought at the end of the nineteenth century.[13] Kyōka's characters travel to timeless worlds where modernization has made no dent in myth and mystery. In Nagai Kafu's *Strange Tales from East of the River* (*Bokuto kidan,* 1937), a young woman guides a disgruntled man away from his present life into alleyways that recall a Tokyo unsullied by change; in Kawabata Yasunari's *Snow Country* (*Yukiguni,* 1937), a man is led away from his life by the bewitching image of a woman; and in Yoshiyuki Jūnnosuke's novels of the 1950s, whores offer an escape from the "real" world into one in which time has stopped.

In their presentation of a world apart from national politics and bourgeois life, the novelists of the demimonde have much in common. Their differences, though, are equally notable: if there is a tendency in Kawabata and Kafu to idealize their subjects, there is as strong a tendency in Tokuda Shūsei and Higuchi Ichiyō (one of the few women who wrote about the demimonde) to maintain a sensitivity to harsh economic reality.

Yet an aimless wandering and a possible end to that wandering set much of this writing apart from Aya's. Kafu's *Woman of the Dream* (*Yume no onna,* 1903), for example, tells the story of a prostitute set adrift from a stable family, searching for a man to moor her life. At the conclusion of the story she is reunited with her lost mother, and her life of wandering ends. In Kyōka's *Pilgrimage to Yushima* (*Yushima mōde,* 1899), a pair of lovers journey to a temple, hoping to put an end to their wandering and become united in bonds of love. In Chikamatsu Shūkō's *Black Hair* (*Kurokami,* 1922), a young man hopes to find a resting place for his suffering heart by settling down with a woman. And in Tokuda Shūsei's *Festering* (*Tadare,* 1913), a man wanders from house to house with his lover, all the while desiring to put down roots.

The desire to escape a life of insecurity and be settled in a home—in a place removed from the world at large—may be Rika's initial impulse to enter the geisha house, but what she discovers there, and what Aya reveals, is the transformation of a once-static world. The demimonde seen from without by male novelists seems to move in a continuous and comforting flow of time and seems, too, to represent unchanging values and to be a haven for the wandering spirit; but when viewed from the inside, it is anything but stable. There is no place to rest here, just a never-ending traversal of borders, which themselves will not last long. Only Rika, the messenger from the outside world, seems to represent solid values and strength.

Flowing is a cold novel. The energy and warmth that Rika finds upon her entry into the geisha house soon dissipates; the early protective warmth later seems like a childish illusion. Gusts of bitter wind blow through the run-down house, and Rika, in a parallel decline, internalizes the cold and falls ill. The forces ripping the house apart reach their most critical point at the moment Rika herself is on the point of collapse.

The crisis originates in the household's annual struggle to make ready for the observance of the New Year, cleaning, preparing clothing and food, and exchanging gifts. To complete these religious and traditional rituals, each geisha must fight to secure adequate work and funds. The struggle to execute the rituals is a struggle to affirm the movement of time within the geisha world, as well as the ritual function of the geisha.

But before the New Year there is little work and less food, and Rika, as if symbolically taking on the pathos of her world, becomes exhausted by the frenetic fight against poverty. The feverish activity of the geisha preparing for their final engagements of the year seems to push Rika past her personal threshold. She has been watching their preparations when suddenly the narrative shifts from inside her mind and follows her as she attempts to calm herself by going outside to gaze at the falling snow. Rika temporarily removes herself from the geisha world and moves back into her own. She reacts in typically dual fashion, as both artist and housekeeper. "Rika began to go indoors but turned around once again. The lamps along the side dimly lit the black fence across the way. Chased by the wind, the snow seemed like white stripes passing from one side to the other—tonight, she thought, there would be boiled tofu and no fish. Although boiled tofu couldn't be called tasty, it made one feel one had eaten good tofu without spending much money on it. Cooking in a kettle allowed one to disguise things this way. As she stood in the poor and lonely kitchen, she thought the snow made a desolate and forbidding scene" (83).

Rika becomes lost now in a daydream, far from thoughts of boiled bean curd. There are many such moments in the novel, when Rika evades the rush of stimuli by turning inward. Modern Japanese literature is replete with protagonists who seem to walk about more than anything else. The rambles of Sōseki's characters, of Shiga's and Kafū's, are haphazard, however. They are the movements of errant spirits. Rika's walks are always purposeful. Even a simple errand is an opportunity for perceptually capturing a scene.

> As far as the eye could reach, the snow pressed down and fell darkly. But from the eaves, from the fence, and over by the garbage cans, it suddenly flipped and turned white as it fell. It made one think of feathers, or cotton, or something warm, and it fell as if driven from farther and farther beyond, as if coming in and spreading out above her head. Perhaps because it attached itself to the wind, the fine snow fell as if it were galloping madly in. And yet there was something relaxed and deliberate about this white stuff. As it fell through places like the ring of light around the lamp across the way, it seemed to be chased by the wind, and when it formed into a horizontal flock, it seemed to escape, to run off, laughing as it went. Wind and snow are entirely different things: the snow arrives warm, soft, gently wrapped; only the wind is cold and cuts through one with its chill. Snow falling on her shoulders, Rika looked up and down, down and up. The snow seemed to pile up without even one flake melting. (82)

Rika manages to stave off her illness through the New Year, as if only her energy could guarantee a safe passage through the holiday. The next morning she collapses. The outbreak of her fever represents the first emotional climax in the novel. The geisha world has successfully, though barely, taken its proper place within the ritualistic world of circular time, and equilibrium has, if only temporarily, been achieved. The scenes that encompass Rika's exit from the geisha world are perhaps the tensest in the novel. They test her commitment to her new status, as well as the ability of the geisha house to function without her. Realizing that proper care of the sick is not a talent of the geisha, she goes to a cousin to be taken care of, but the experience holds more emotional pain than succor. The moment she leaves the entertainment quarters, everything is transformed in a flash to brightness and bustle, and Rika feels "as if she had been dragged out of the burrow in which she had buried herself" (89).

Her cousins are as cold as the winds blowing through the geisha house. Her aunt is a proud woman who has come through the war better than most—better, Rika realizes, than the geisha—and she begrudgingly and patronizingly gives Rika permission to stay. But Rika soon comes to see that she can no longer be at home in this world; her family lacks sincerity, and the food they serve her is prepared without loving care. In the geisha world the merest morsels could be transformed into delicacies. In this world, on the contrary, everything is still, dead, like "the stale air at the base of a mountain" (90). Where she came from, everything was in constant motion, and now, temporarily away from it, she longs for swirling change.

Rika finally feels ready to commit herself to the geisha world, but before doing so, she needs to free herself more completely from her past, to cut the cords that still tie her down. Because Rika's connection to her past is embodied in the objects that remain from that past, she needs to clean out her old room and dispose of everything related to her former life: her hibachi, her tea kettle, her heater, and her old kitchen implements. She is stoical about this, even ruthless, and without the slightest hint of sentimentality she wraps the clothing kept as a memento of her dead son and has it sent off to her husband's relatives. She does not regret that "the time to cut all bonds has come." She longs "to escape from everything that has entwined her and to lightly let go of her feelings" (91).

Even at this moment, however, Rika finds no peace. Alone now, and cleansed, she is impelled by a desire to move on, but she fears that she has nowhere to go.

> She wanted to go somewhere and say something to someone, but at her age and in her circumstances, what could she say and to whom? She did not especially wish to speak to her husband or son. She knew she had nobody to speak to, and it was vexing to have nowhere to go. Where should one go at a time like this? She wasn't particularly interested in mountains or rivers, and she wasn't devout enough to make a pilgrimage to her temple. Surely she could not go to the zoo. There was no other place to go but the graveyard. A graveyard was not merely a place of graves. She wanted to go somewhere removed from the shabbiness of things like living and dying; she wanted to go to a good, different place, a pure place, a place, indeed, without kitchens or toilets. Is there any such place other than a graveyard? A gravestone is tranquil, and as Rika faces one, there is no agitation in her. (91)

Rummaging through objects and returning to the dead, to the end and origin of generations—these actions evoke similar scenes in the novels of Sōseki and Tōson and others, where male characters often journey from Tokyo to their country homes only to find objects there that no longer possess inner significance and a past that they cannot control. Rika, unlike many of these other characters, acts assertively and disposes of the objects precisely because they resonate so painfully for her. Rika's gesture is twofold, comprising both a desire to draw sustenance from the past and a wish to be released from it. She needs to visit the graveyard but also to destroy the objects that link her to it. Rika desires release from all sense of community but returns to the community of the dead for spiritual replenishment. When she leaves her cousins, she feels a human connection to them at last, and they exchange words appropriate to blood relatives. Rika has now become a fully individuated human being.

The stark loneliness of the scenes away from the entertainment quarters make the depiction of Rika's return all the more striking. Away from the geisha house the narrative eye focuses on Rika's inner turmoil, on her judgments about her family and her realization of her aloneness. The difficulties of others have no room to enter her life as they did while she was surrounded by geisha. Conscious and contemplative of her sufferings, Rika is alone outside the geisha house; inside she is in a network of people.

When she returns to the geisha world, she takes the peripheral role she has grown accustomed to—as a maid, but as an observer too absorbed by the world around her and by other people's problems to focus on herself. There are moments, of course, when this method of forgetting fails Rika, and she is drawn back to her past and into herself, as when she smells an apple that reminds her of the fruit she once brought her child or when she converses with a handsome driver whose elegant language makes her flush with feelings of vague sexuality and nostalgia for a world to which she once belonged. She remains aware of her status as both insider and outsider but allows the dramas occurring around her to engulf her.

When Rika returns, the house is in filthy disarray, and the geisha welcome her back with the anticipation of harried children awaiting parental guidance. She immediately loses herself in their lives and in her judgments of them and in this way manages to stay her loneliness. In the rest of the novel she watches as the forces that tear at the geisha house gain momentum and force it apart.

The forces that bring the house to ruin were set in motion early on. The rough and randy uncle of a young geisha—a poor miner from the countryside—has been demanding payments because his underage niece has been employed as a prostitute illegally; later, the case is settled out of court, but the incident affects the madam's real and perceived self-sufficiency. While she is held at the police station, Rika takes charge of the house, and the power balance shifts significantly and permanently in her direction.

In the declining days of the house another geisha, the skilled, elegant Tutaji, also leaves, though, unlike the madam, for greater solvency. She marries a company president and settles into a secure life on the outside. Other geisha are less fortunate: the intelligent and educated Nanako meets her former lover and returns bitterly disappointed; Someka, still clinging to a once-glorious past, finds herself increasingly in need of the solace of liquor. Used by a young man for the money she can bring him, squeezed by the painful debts she owes the madam's sister, and hated by Katsuyo, who attempts to turn the madam against her, Someka becomes hysterical and unleashes a barrage of lamentations. Yoneko, daughter of the wealthy but unspoiled Kishibōjin, is forced to leave her own young daughter and serve as a maid at a less reputable establishment. Finally, the madam, the owner of a flourishing establishment with a reputation to uphold, is forced by debt and taxes to relinquish her business and watch it be converted into a new establishment with Rika at its head. Aya originally planned on calling the novel "This Side of the Bridge" but changed the title to *Flowing*, not because the geisha will be swept away but because Rika will flow on.[14]

If *Flowing* is a cold novel, it is also a noisy one. Rika experiences a world filled with voices and music, with special languages belonging to a system of communication different from her own. Voices seep out to her through the cracks in the door as she awaits entry at the start of the novel; voices float down to her from upstairs and remain a constant murmur throughout the novel, like a tape recorder nobody can stop. At various moments Rika approaches her breaking point and attempts to escape these voices.

The language spoken among the geisha is often so elliptical, so replete with code words and intimate references, and so dizzyingly quick in communicating its message, that Rika often feels like a foreigner. She admires this language, however, for it often seems to cut through the dross of her own and allows for an immediacy of communication. The geisha language involves more than words. Its most subtle and complex messages are passed in other forms, in the donning of a kimono, the preparation of food, the playing of an instrument, or the application of makeup. In the geisha's attitude toward makeup she sees the essential difference between the professional and the amateur: to a professional it speaks of self-transformation; to an amateur it is only a mask (80).

But the language most characteristic of the geisha, Rika feels, is the language of music, the plucking of the samisen—which fills the final scenes of *Flowing* with an ever-increasing din. In the face of imminent economic collapse, and with the sad awareness that her own special status and skills as a geisha will soon be things of the past, the madam practices for an important musical performance. Stuck on one particularly difficult passage, she is desperate in her struggle to perfect it, as if only a proper execution of the music could stop the forces of decay. Rika, as usual, observes her as she herself scurries about chopping food and cleaning; she judges the madam and confirms her own superior knowledge and sensitivity. Suddenly she can no longer contain herself. When the madam hits a bad note, Rika accidentally cuts herself with the chopping knife. We recall here the scene from "Kitchen Sounds," in which a young wife cuts herself with a chopping knife because of her husband's surveillance. The situation is now reversed; the female protagonist is the observer, the hearer of sounds who becomes offended by their unpleasant tone. At last Rika's discipline buckles, and she lets a criticism slip out. The madam forces her to explain herself, and for the first time in the novel Rika seems to speak in her true voice—perceptive and confident.

> "That's the feeling. This morning the tone is truly clear and good." The madam seemed like a woman who possessed only clear and good feelings. She seemed removed from her profession as a geisha and from of the bonds of being a wife. Neither noble nor beautiful, the expression in her eyes was merely friendly and calm.
>
> "Really," Rika continued. "In fact, for the past few minutes, I've been sharing in the gift of your good feeling. This morning you were very fine—completely different from what you had been until yesterday."
>
> "What's that you said?"
>
> "I'm sorry? You were talking about your practicing, weren't you?"
>
> "That's correct. But . . . "
>
> Rika was about to retreat into the hallway with the empty kettle.
>
> "Just a minute! You, you . . . "

Rika realizes that she has overstepped her bounds, that it is inappropriate for her to judge the madam so openly. The madam is shocked that an amateur could make such judgments and grows suspicious of Rika's hidden past. She presses Rika to continue, and Rika realizes that the madam is attempting to fight and defeat her. But Rika avoids the battle. Her thoughts run like this: "Even a maid who buys a ticket and attends the theater can be a discerning audience. She has a pair of eyes and two ears, and even if there are thousands of maids, each may judge freely. A person who sings in front of others doesn't distinguish between the professionals and the amateurs listening" (137–139).

This is a crucial scene in *Flowing*. Not only is Rika's mask torn off, but two languages, two semiotic systems, are mutually recognized. If the geisha have *gei,* the skills appropriate to their profession, Rika has *kan,* the sensibility developed in her own life in the outside world, which allows her to judge the madam's music without ever being able to play it. Rika has also mastered the geisha language in another way. She flatters the madam with humble apologies and generous praise and then reflects that what she has said is half a lie—that she has learned the geisha's way of manipulating language to smooth out difficult situations. The hierarchy that separated her from the madam has collapsed: the two are equals.

Even before this climactic scene the geisha had always recognized Rika's gift for language and her elegant handwriting; the madam relied upon her verbal skills to deal with problems she herself could not manage—problems with the police, for example, or with the usurer. Rika's sensitivity to language even makes her suffer at times. It awakens in her the sexuality still carefully buried within, and it saddens her and draws her, against her will, to the past. Rika is startled when she hears a ricksha man speak beautifully: "The youth of his sharply parted hair and the nape of his neck. That a man so very young, a ricksha puller, could use polite language like this, as if it flowed. That a ricksha puller could speak to a maid in such smooth, good language. In good language there is an echo of fleeting sorrow" (31). The two exchange words, and Rika's mind begins to wander: "She peered at the snow falling sparsely, slowly, black and white, cleaving the atmosphere. How can something that comes from the heavens be so refreshing? Rain and hail are both refreshing, but what of this magnanimous quality of snow? And again, why would the good language of the young ricksha puller be so evocative? Guided by the snow, Rika slowly took the route home, feeling as if she had met a person for the first time in a long while. For no particular reason she felt as if she had met a delightful person" (31).

Never before had Rika's deep sensitivity been recognized, and never before had the madam realized that Rika possessed a gift for speaking the geisha language, for hearing the musical quality inherent in things. Rika's mastery of this language represents her final victory over the world of the professional. At the end of *Flowing,* when she emerges from the fractured community, she is enriched with expressive power; she has acquired a strong personality and become an artist (here the figures of Aya and Rika merge)—someone who can observe things at a distance and give her perceptions creative form.

Aya has also attained the status of autodidact. She entered the geisha house in part to discover a world and find a voice apart from her father, and she exhibits her discovery in *Flowing* by creating an observer who presses personal judgments on the reader. Defined almost solely by the quality of those judgments, her literary persona—a combination of Aya and Rika—presents perceptions that are the expressions of an active intelligence.

Rika's mastery of the madam's musical language raises the important question of Aya's own language. Language was the first, and remained the primary, link between Aya and her father and hence perhaps elicits from her feelings of pathos and loss. Language still evokes her father's world. To describe Aya's prose as old-fashioned has become commonplace; critics say it belongs more to her father's time than to her own, having evolved in his handspun literary and philological cocoon. But there is much to support this view. Aya employs antiquated words with such naturalness that one wonders whether she knows that they belong to the eighteenth century or earlier. Her syntax often more closely resembles her father's than her contemporaries', for she relies on ellipses of grammatical particles, sentences ending in nouns, out-of-use Chinese characters, and the combination of dialogue and narrative within single sentences—a technique that her father perfected, moving against the stylistic currents of his time. Certain passages are even close to the neoclassical prose of Ōzaki Kōyō, who wrote in the 1880s.[15]

Aya exploits the traditional genius of the language: she employs ellipses to truncate great movements of action into single paragraphs or sentences, as did the seventeenth-century novelist Saikaku, whom her father helped revive in the early years of the twentieth century; she drops transitions in an idiosyncratic way that can make her prose virtually impossible to follow; she avoids personal pronouns to a degree unusual even in Japanese, a language that readily excludes them; and she crafts sinuous and fluid agglutinative word endings and sentences that betray her greater interest in euphony than in clarity of meaning. It is often difficult to determine who is speaking, or about whom something is being said. The narrative can be inside Rika's mind—as in the opening lines of the novel—or Rika can be referred to in the third person, or the narrator and Rika can merge. Like the early modern stylist Izumi Kyōka, Aya chose her readers and seemed willing to sacrifice those who lack the desire—or the patience—to keep up; and like the philological misanthrope Saitō Ryokū, she clung to a style that made her, in many eyes, a literary anachronism.[16]

The quirks that made Aya's prose difficult for and even opaque to readers in the 1950s make her even more so for readers now. Yet Aya's obscurity is not an attempt to warp and break traditional diction and syntax, as in the postwar writing of Noma Hiroshi or the young Ōe Kenzaburo. Her idiosyncratic use of language derives in part from her un-self-conscious use of past styles, which others writing in the 1950s did not have the knowledge to imitate.

Aya's reliance on traditional language no doubt derives from the influence of her father, a writer known for his dislike of the clear, bland style created by the language reformers in the first years of the twentieth century.

It was this style that came to characterize Japanese writing in the years to come, and by the 1950s only the rare writer eschewed the by-then-authoritative notion of literary language as a transparent conveyor of ideas. At the end of his life, when he was too ill to write, Rohan dictated a study entitled "Ongenron" (1945) in which he investigated onomatopoetic words and argued against the Saussurian notion—represented in Japan by the linguistics of Hashimoto Shinkichi—that the meaning of a word exists apart from its sound, that form and content are arbitrarily connected. Rohan argued that a word's meaning inhered in its sound and questioned the creation of a "modern" literary language that would strip language of its surface quality and attempt to separate the inner voice from its outer vehicle (*genbun-itchi*). In his short story "Picture Viewing" ("Kangadan," 1926), the entire world is enveloped in sound.

> For a long time he thought that the world was boundless, but now he wondered if the world was nothing more than this *zaaaa* and, thinking it through again, if this thing *zaaaa* was, precisely, the world. He felt as if the voice *ogyaa-ogyaa* that he first gave off at birth and the voice *gyaa-tto* made by others and then the entire array of voices created in the various commotions that one makes—the *kyaa-kyaa, gan-gan, bun-bun, guji-guji, shiku-shiku* made when reading books, singing songs, laughing in joy, or screaming in anger—and the sounds of a horse neighing, a cow bellowing, a car jolting, a train booming, a steamship churning the waves, and the faint sound of one needle falling on a wooden floor—he felt as if all these, without exception, came together and entered into that sound *zaaaa;* and then if he concentrated and listened quietly, he distinctly recognized that all these various sounds most certainly did exist in the one sound, and while he was thinking that yes, this was the way it was, before he knew it he could no longer hear the *zaaaa*.[17]

Rohan favored a language that displayed its surface qualities and reveled in its beauty as language, and Aya was one of the few writers in the 1950s who shared his belief. She seems to have bypassed the influence of all the major schools of modern Japanese writing—Naturalism, the White Birch Society, the Postwar school—and taken her father's insular linguistic approach. Like Rohan's expansive world of sound, Aya's smaller world inside the geisha quarter is also filled with sounds—of voices, of the samisen, of Aya's own plentiful use of onomatopoeia. It is in part from Rohan, then, that she gained her sensitivity to the musicality of things.

In the short piece "Deafness" ("Tsunbo," 1957), Aya reveals the importance of musical sound to her language and displays a personal philosophy of language that is akin to her father's. To Aya, the sound of a word is intimately connected to the emotional resonance behind it.

Each defect of the body has its own special name—*tsunbo* [deafness], for example, or *domori* [stuttering]. Although it may seem that to speak of this is to dwell perversely on something unfortunate, that is not what motivates me. When I use these words I am inevitably taken with their resonance, and I wind up lost in thought. This group of words compels me because it contains so many different expressions. No doubt they sometimes reverberate with a condescending or mocking quality, but the reverberations are those of the people using the terms. The original formation of the words reflected a desire to create an accurate verbal expression of a particular characteristic. Of course, within that desire there was a sense of surprise, as well as feelings that grew out of the surprise, like wonder. But in any case, these words developed from a naive honesty, and it goes without saying, the words' reverberations originated in the sympathy that is an essential part of the natural goodness of humankind. These are words created from a steady gaze. So, for example, when one refers to a person's very flat nose as *hanapechya* or to a nose that has been smashed as *hanagake*, one defines the person's entire being. And the word *hanakuta* refers to a nose whose shape and sense of smell have totally disappeared.

Aya continues in this way, describing the fine distinctions that go into creating appropriate words. She is most interested in the way that the sound of the word "deaf" expresses its meaning:

People went out of their way to make distinctions like these, but not out of mean-spiritedness. They did so out of a simple respect, which couldn't help but make such minute distinctions.

But more than the defects of noses or eyes, it is *tsunbo* that most compels me. Whether the word *tsunbo* derives its meaning from a combination of *tsu* and *nbo,* or of *tsun* and *bo,* or from the entire *tsunbo,* a person lacking education like myself cannot tell. *Tsun* is usually used to denote a sharp, pointed object thrust into something. The sound *bo* evokes something that is shrunk down and then pops open, with the sound *bo*. It is used when something inside expands, and the outer surface bursts and spreads out. Draw out the sound and make a long *bō*, and it refers to something whose borders are indistinct. In *bo* one feels an expansion that meets resistance; in *bō* one senses expansion that meets no resistance. As opposed to *tsun,* which connotes an intense thrust into the ear's cavity, *bo* connotes an expansion that encompasses both resistance and nonresistance. I should like to think that with the word *tsunbo,* people were attempting to express something like this: a sound meets resistance and sticks; the sound is inside the ear, but at the bottom of the ear it explodes and expands and cannot be transmitted.

She now discusses a musical instrument, and in so doing touches upon the question of her father's influence: "I don't know whether my father talked to my aunt after seeing the koto or whether he just introduced the salesman to her and saw the koto after she bought it." Her father was, Aya tells us, unsure of the quality of the koto and told Aya to have her aunt show it to her, but death interfered. Later, Aya recalls her father's remarks on the koto and then turns to evaluating it herself, describing it as if it were a living being.

There was no reason I should be able to judge the quality of the koto. I squeezed my eyes shut and pressed my hands to it, and with my eyes closed, I found it somewhat easier to feel: it was smooth indeed. I felt a smoothness that captivated my heart. As I looked at it I wanted fiercely—the word *fiercely* may sound odd, but it is exactly what I mean—to draw a sound from this koto. The wish pressed on me, and I felt an unendurable urge—damned koto! Play!

A koto dealer came and removed the tattered strings, which twanged as he did so. With a soft cloth he wiped the instrument reverently. The new strings wanted to rustle, even as they sat there on the tatami floor. When the first string was attached, my face was already burning. When the first bridge was set in place, the dealer touched the strings and made them emit a sound, as if doing nothing special at all. There was a heavy feeling in my chest. I listened to the sound. I listened as the koto was tuned, anguished that something had been exposed, that he had done something very cruel. He plucked the strings a bit and then stopped.

The koto has remained quietly in my alcove, untouched even during my daily cleaning. Since I am unable to play, the koto has made no sound since that time. The other person sometimes calls on an errand but never offers to play. In a word, the koto has been dutifully enshrined. Because I have been entrusted with it, I have been even more captivated by the word *tsunbo*. At times it seems to me that an unplayed instrument makes a person deaf somewhere. And at times it seems that a person who possesses an instrument that could sing if played but who cannot play should be called *katatsunbo* [half deaf]. But wait—wasn't there also a word *katte-tsunbo* [purposely deaf]? I wonder if that word has some connection to this koto.

Supposing I could play just a little—that would put an end to the matter. The koto would be disturbed and tampered with terribly and would probably be ruined. And a deep attachment might be born in me as well, in some form or another. But things have turned out happily. The koto sits quietly in the alcove, and it seems splendid to me without its even making a sound. I merely gaze at it. Beneath my eyelids I am thinking of the past, when my father placed a beat-up koto—whose single string looked as if it would snap if touched—in his alcove and laughed, saying, "Sometimes I entertain myself by playing it in my head." And I am thinking of a certain person who, on New Year's Eve, while reciting a poem that contained the words "playing the koto," said, "The sound of the koto, devoid of sympathy and scruples, is indifferent to the many people struggling at year's end," and of how he changed it to "The end of the year; a koto being played at Master So-and-So's house."

The koto entrusted to me doesn't sing even at New Year. (*KAZ* 2: 314–319)

The passage describes the passing of the gift of sound from one generation to the next. The koto is a gift from Aya's father's time. The person who once played it is dead, and the instrument remains silent. But it has the potential to create sound, if only through the power of the imagination. The father makes it play without even touching its strings. The daughter reveres the gift and is disturbed when a stranger handles it. She faces the object with trepidation, for it seems to contain the legacy of the past. It contains a language she is unable to tap—it makes her feel deaf. But the daughter has learned the father's lesson and can finally touch the instrument. It remains silent, but touching it invigorates her imagination. A palpable reminder of the past, the koto is enshrined as the source of Aya's creativity, the source of her own music. Although it never plays to the world, it plays to her imagination.

That Aya was so attached to the language of music does not imply that she fully accepted her father's language as her own. Rather, she forged a personal language out of dead objects. She carried Rohan's legacy, and was most certainly his literary child, but she needed, in addition, to distance herself from his language. This desire, combined with an equally strong attachment to the traditional genius of the language, created a literary style unusual in the postwar years. If her traditionalism is a legacy from her father, her originality is her own manner of distancing herself from that legacy.

Aya searches for the unfamiliar turn of phrase and deliberately obscures her narrative voice—dropping personal pronouns so that who is seeing or speaking often becomes unimportant—in order to emphasize the quality of perception itself. This way of writing exploits the possibilities of the Japanese language and recalls a premodern prose style, but Aya's repudiation of contemporary stylistic clarity in favor of a style connected to tradition represents not merely an affirmation of tradition but also a conscious effort to register her perceptions on the page. Her writing must be intimately close to herself. When she sees something, she does not describe it "as it is" (*aru ga mama*), in the manner of the Naturalist writers, but as it appears to her (*mieta mama*), in the style of the Heian court poets. The reader is constantly reminded of the peculiar subjectivity of her perception.[18]

Aya's preference for inscribing her own sensibilities onto things, rather

than describing what those things objectively appear to be, is best illus-
trated by her abundant and original use of onomatopoetic and mimetic
words, which help her capture everyday speech and allow her to transform
her perceptions into language as directly as possible. In descriptions, she
avoids saying "as if" such-and-such were something else (*no yō ni*) because
an analogy separates her from the object of her perception; likening one
thing to another allows writers to rely on standard notions of similarity
("she wailed like a baby"), rather than on their own "pure" perception. Aya
would not write that a roofload of snow crashes down "like thunder" or
"like the sound of a bomb exploding." She is interested in recording how
her senses register the sound; sensibility takes precedence over reference.
Onomatopoeia—a rich and traditional part of the Japanese language—is a
means of transferring her perceptions to the page. She invents onomatopoetic words and uses mimetic words and often avoids descriptive words
that permit an intellectual understanding of an emotion.[19]

Aya's reliance on onomatopoetic and mimetic words has placed her, in
many critics' minds, within an ancient heritage of Japanese feminine writing. According to Mishima Yukio, the defining characteristic of modern
Japanese literature is femininity. The roots of the literature are in the poetry
and prose of the Heian court women, who wrote of interior emotional
states in enclosed and private environments and who were more concerned
with lyrical evocation than rational thought. All writing that is abstract,
concerned with logic, reason, and argument, has been the province of men
or has been associated with foreign modes of thought—with Chinese
thought and language in the case of the Heian court. Onomatopoeia
represents the clearest case of linguistic gender differentiation, according to
Mishima, for it is a child's and woman's language that depends on an almost
intuitive apprehension of the concreteness of things. Because it does not
allow for abstraction, it is, to Mishima's obsessively masculine imagination,
a fallen language, for the mere transcription of impressions. When reading
Aya's prose, Mishima feels that he is almost touching her skin, and this
makes him uncomfortable. He longs for the intellectual rigor and abstract
distance of a writer like Mori Ōgai. Mishima laments the feminization of
Japanese literature in the 1950s and looks back to a more "masculine" age.
Aya is, to his mind, a main culprit.[20]

Although Mishima's historical analysis backs his distinction between
masculine and feminine writing, such a theory is hardly absolute. Any
convincing argument would have to involve close comparative analysis of a
large body of texts, a task neither Mishima nor I have taken on. The
abundance of counterexamples makes it impossible to extract a pattern: too

many male writers rely upon onomatopoeia—Mishima himself cites the postwar writer Ōda Sakunosuke, and Yasuoka Shōtarō immediately comes to mind—and too many women write the rigorous, controlled, argumentative prose that Mishima dubs unfeminine.

But Mishima's response to Aya is not as idiosyncratic as it seems. Other critics, both men and women, have relied upon physical images to describe Aya's prose, claiming that she communicates more with her body than with her mind, that she lacks the ability to cast her feelings into rigorous form, that she cannot think or write abstractly. Honda Shūgo, spokesman for the Postwar school of writers, went so far as to claim that the reason for women's lack of involvement in his literary movement was that they lacked the ability to establish important founding ideas. But even though other critics agreed with Mishima about the feminine quality of Aya's writing, most valorized her style as essentially Japanese and thus an antidote to male overintellectualization and overreliance on foreign, abstract modes of thought. To these critics "feminine" language was somehow more authentically native and could restore a true, untainted, and life-sustaining quality to Japanese cultural and literary life. Both men and women looked to women's writing as to a savior. According to the feminist critic Miyamoto Yuriko, it could offer a remedy to the hopelessness and despair of male writing.[21]

Perhaps the question is better left to those who have experienced both the despair of masculine writing and the hope of feminine writing. What can be said, however, is that for Aya, onomatopoetic language was tied to feminine experience. When Rika recognized the madam's skill with the samisen, what most irritated Rika, what most prevented the madam's music from flowing out beautifully, was that it sounded like "men's language" (*otoko kotoba*). That "authentic" feminine language was also used by critics in a broader cultural discourse of modernity and tradition has more to do with Aya's audience and the context of her cultural moment than it does with Aya herself.[22]

Aya wrote during a time of cultural stress, when the desire to maintain a hold on tradition seemed essential for the preservation of national self-identity and culture. Her writing became a touchstone for certain values deemed important by the literary and cultural critics of the time. They looked to her for solace because she seemed to reinstate a lost language and set of values and because she seemed to retain an unmodern, peculiarly Japanese sensibility untarnished by Western influence. But when critics refer to the old-fashioned quality of her prose, they also mean that Aya eschews arid intellectualizations and abstractions and engages the realities of "everyday life" (*nichijō seikatsu*).

"Everyday life" has been a catchword among Japanese culture critics. The eighteenth-century thinker Motoori Norinaga attempted to create an epistemology of the common person that valorized daily life and an emotional understanding of it through poetry and thereby to counteract foreign (Chinese) modes of cognition. For him, common things, and the commoners' way of interacting with them, represented a layer of indigenous life. Through the nineteenth century, thinkers like Ito Jinsai and Nishikawa Jōken esteemed the commoners' way of perceiving and controlling their environment, their ability to "understand the authenticity of an emotive truth in a situation, person, or thing and to act empathetically."[23] The phrase "everyday life" has continued to evoke that which is authentically Japanese, referring to the material reality of Japanese life sanctioned by time itself.

In this view, femininity has been seen as most authentically linked to everyday life. And it is everyday life that can, like women's writing, save Japanese intellectuals from their abstracted, modern, masculine fate. While Aya was holding to her quotidian existence, and was thus presumably spared from this fate, Yasuoka Shōtarō's protagonist, in his 1968 novel *After the Curtain Falls* (*Maku ga orite kara*), was experiencing "a decomposed daily life that seemed about to crumble away."[24]

The arguments for describing Aya primarily as unmodern or conservative—as firmly attached to an authentic Japanese everyday life—are compelling. In *Flowing* she leaves us with a lament for the collapse of traditional standards. She bemoans the loss of traditional modes of behavior and the material aspects of life that have been handed down through the generations. The smell of an apple draws her back to the past, the speech of a geisha draws her back, the figure of a woman rising from her bed seems soaked with lived experience, and this, too, draws her back. Younger writers contemporary to Aya—like Yasuoka and Mishima—also wrote narratives in which the past interfered with the present and kept characters from projecting themselves into the future. The quality of the past in *Flowing* is altogether different, however. When Rika seems about to be swept away by the force of her memories, she regains her composure and returns to the present. When sentimentality seems about to overwhelm her, the spell of emotion is broken by an austere reminder of natural time. In one scene the backward movement of memory is interrupted by the natural movement of time in the form of animal feces.

Flowing is certainly a novel of loss. Its characters are tied to a past they cannot regain—Nanako to a man she can no longer have, Someka to a long-vanished personal glory, the madam to a time when her skills still mattered. The heart of the novel, the event that embodies its theme, is the absence of the young geisha Namie. She is the lost center of the world and the impetus for its downfall. But *Flowing* is not a novel of nostalgia. It is too cold, too unsentimental, for that. Rika's emotional toughness, her ethical foundations, make nostalgia incongruous. She feels loss but remains beyond hope or grief.

If the transformation of socially imposed space—so crucial in Aya's literature—seems difficult to locate amid all this loss, it is because the geisha's ability to transform their world is part of the process of decay, and this sense of decay is what dominates the novel. To locate this transformational aspect of Aya's imagination, we must return to the idea of the writer's work as an act of performance. The novel's final pages move quickly to the fall of the house. At the climactic moment, when all hope is gone, we are given an abrupt, shockingly sentimental and stagy happy ending, at odds with the prevailing tone of the novel. Suddenly, the handsome young man Saeki—with the aid of the wealthy Nandori—saves the day: "Nanako continued as she was, unable to conceal her trembling. A woman without a strong inner core, she was certain to get caught in the shallow currents. The madam and her daughter, Rika and the cat—this life of three people and one animal was dishearteningly dreary. . . . At that moment, strangely enough, a phone call came for Rika. Saeki asked her to come quickly to Nandori's establishment" (149).

It is tempting to despair at such an ending, to find in it Aya's capitulation to literary and social convention, to see in it a weakening of her rigorous ethics. She seems to have failed us—unless we understand that she herself is being self-consciously theatrical. In such a reading, the entire work, which she has presented to us as a faithful depiction of a particular society, becomes nothing more than a play, a staged performance. The narrative has been dotted with phrases used exclusively in the theater: a scene is described as being "like a stage set" (*kakiwarimekashii*); Rika recites dialogue and then "withdraws" (*hikitoru*) as in a play; Nanako "[has] a bad role" (*wari o kutta*) as in a play; and Rika sees the madam's discussion with the usurer as a play she must be sure to see (15, 18, 95). After being lambasted by Katsuyo, Someka turns on her and declares her departure from the geisha world with self-conscious theatricality: "I suppose I should be on my way. I'll be going. I've shed some tears, but I haven't cried because of your brilliantly malicious words. These tears were shed when I thought of people . . . dear to me. What would someone like you know about that? And one more thing. Here's a parting gift for you. Listen: when your lower jaw sticks out, your lines have no impact. Good riddance!" (149).

All this acting is natural for people who control illusion, as if in a play.

The last lines of the novel concern the preparations for a grand performance that involves the entire geisha district. We now recall Rika's early perception of the madam's voice as "a voice learning something," and we see that the novel has been a preparation for this final performance. Rika has been performing and watching the women perform, and in these last scenes she listens to their long and tortured speeches, presented to the reader with little or no narrative interruption as if spoken by actors on a stage.

As the novel reaches its conclusion, Aya reminds the reader that it has been her intelligence and imagination that have controlled the world of the novel. The moment of Aya's revelation coincides with Rika's own unmasking: she, too, has been performing, and it is her performance that has controlled the geisha house. As both Rika and Aya reveal themselves as self-conscious performers, they merge again into a single identity. Having stepped out of her role, Rika must leave the geisha world; having stepped out of the play, Aya must end the novel. The final line reminds the reader of this shared but fluid identity and leaves no doubt that the show is over: "When Rika came, the madam found her name annoying and so gave her the name Haru" (151).

Aya's performance, then, has been a playful and transformative one because of its self-conscious irony. She has played a role, and although she seems to have fully merged with it at times (in the figure of Rika), she has maintained her distance. Like the geisha, Rika has learned the art of illusion. By casting her whole life as a play, she has circumvented its potential constrictions, performing in it not as a full participant but as a distanced, ironic actor.

CHAPTER 7

Return to

the Father

When her father died, Aya was left stranded on the side of a border she could not hope to cross. Her career as a writer sprang from this abandonment, and in her writing, she never ceased to return to that moment when a boundary was established—between her and her father, between past and present, between life and death.

Such an irreversible moment of separation occurs toward the end of *Flowing*, when Rika listens to the geisha Tutaji describe the sympathy she feels for her lover's sickly wife, whom she has been tirelessly nursing during the past few months. Rika admires the empathy that could prompt such an act of service and ponders the new role that awaits Tutaji when the wife dies: "She felt relieved now that she knew the rest of her life would be secure, but her security was bought by the death of a person for whom she felt deep affection. The married couple had suffered constant anxiety, and with an effort, they had finally brought their life together to a beautiful end. When a baton is passed, death is at the center of the enactment."[1]

The other women seated in the room are unable to respond to Tutaji when she declares her freedom from the geisha world and her entry into a new life as the wife of a businessman:

It truly was a strange time. Nobody knew what to say to Tutaji, who was attempting to face it, who had no choice but to face it. They couldn't offer congratulations or regrets or express joy or sorrow; they had never imagined that her future had been set for her so securely. Nanako remained leaning against the mirror stand; Someka remained seated, her glasses off, a needle in her hand; the mistress continued to hold the cat: nobody spoke a word. An indescribably sad and heavy feeling seemed to fill the room. Perhaps it seemed to them that the impassable boundary between the amateur and professional worlds might now be passed by Tutaji alone, and they were being vividly reminded of their own quickly declining lives. At Tutaji's destination a light was shining, and in that light appeared a home with a solid foundation, and in that home there was a husband sitting on a sofa, and next to him were a growing son and daughter, and servants serving them. In their own future, by contrast, there was nothing but the sense of a gloomy downward slide. The unambiguous atmosphere of separation had quickly filled their hearts. (123)

In the novel *Little Brother*, written shortly after *Flowing*, Aya again creates a character—Gen—who moves toward the edge of impassable boundaries, who comes close to crossing over and sinking herself in another's identity. (Gen's attempt to merge with her brother certainly reveals a desire in Aya, too, to cross an impassable border.) The novel is filled with the sorrow of Aya's parting from her father and her attempts to achieve again a moment of unity that, like the past, cannot be recaptured or named. "Thoughts," Aya writes, "are like the dew, and a pencil like the sun."[2]

Little Brother is the story of a young woman's sympathy for a troubled and sickly younger brother, of a compassion so strong it becomes self-abnegation and a desire to merge with another. In the novel the urge is always restrained, in part because Aya understands that the goal can never be reached and in part because the desire to merge would involve too great a sacrifice of self-identity. What allows Gen to stand back from Hekiro and maintain her identity as a discrete and self-empowered human being are those very qualities that might also have led her to lose her identity in him—the conventionally feminine attributes of passivity, self-sacrifice, and selflessness. These are the qualities that might have prevented Aya from becoming a creative artist but that served, we have seen, as the very resources of her art.

Tapping these resources was not an untroubled process. Much passion and energy needed to be spent before she could loosen the tie to her father and clear an imaginative space for herself. In *Flowing* she developed a personal voice so insistent on its presence and so sure of its powers of perception that it can be felt in the very rhythm of her language. *Little Brother* marked a new stage in Aya's development, with the narrative more certain of itself, or at least more settled: sentences are shorter and clearer,

diction is simpler and more contemporary, phraseology far less idiosyncratic, and imagery gentler.

Flowing was Aya's first attempt to write a long novel, and perhaps in
writing it she gained the skill to smooth over the bumps: gone from *Little
Brother* are the many personal digressions that interrupt the progress of
Flowing, and gone are the jarring personal judgments that dot the novel,
reminding us of Aya's—or Rika's—presence. Perhaps insisting on her role
as observer allowed Aya to establish a secure literary self. But the calm with
which she sees and writes about the world also makes *Little Brother* a less
passionate and complex novel. We miss the current of subtle perceptions,
the idiosyncrasies of language, the conscious complexities and willful energy that make *Flowing* so compelling.

Aya emerged from the writing of *Flowing*—like Rika from the world of
geisha—as from a greenhouse: replenished and resilient. This strength and
assurance allow her to return, in her writing and in her life, to the world she
had left behind upon entering the geisha house, the world of her family and
of her father. *Little Brother* is a fictional work with strong autobiographical
roots. She focuses on her brother, describing their parents along the way: a
stepmother—a weak, ill, mean-spirited woman who elicits little more than
feelings of distance and anger—and a father, an emotionally removed
literary man who spares nothing in earning the money needed to care for
his sick son but who stints greatly in direct gestures of intimacy. The father
figure, so looming for Aya herself, is only a secondary character here.

Aya's emergence from behind her father's image signals a victory of
sorts; and the immediate creation of a protagonist who submerges herself
in another person's life should not be taken as a sign that the victory is brief,
nor that a burden is being carried once again. In *Little Brother,* Aya is
working in the realm of symbolic inversion, where she is very much the
master of her inheritance. Gen, like Rika and Aya's other creations, de-
velops an active personality through her secondary role as watcher, guard-
ian, and nurturer; from its opening line to its last, *Little Brother* focuses on
this point. The first passage picks up the image of movement that closed
Flowing, but the image here is more tranquil. The woman who became
independent in that novel has been brought back to dependent status, but
unlike her forebear, she need not prove herself worthy of being accepted by
the world of the novel; she already has a secure place:

> The deep river flows. A bank of cherry trees stretches the length of the path.
> Without a sound, fine rain falls on the surface of the river, on the leaves of the
> cherry trees, and on the embankment. At times a gentle breeze blows up this way

from the river, causing the rain and leaves to flap and bend, but they soon straighten again. Far ahead on the bank, the shapes of Japanese and Western parasols can be seen moving forward, all facing ahead. It is still early morning, and students and workers from the village are heading off to town.

Gen, carrying on her shoulder a heavy umbrella with a bull's eye design, is running up the gravel path in her sandals, whose worn straps make it difficult even to walk. On one side is the large river, on the other the low roofs lined up along the embankment—it is the kind of morning when nothing seems to exist other than the row of cherry trees on the bank. Gen rushes by people who are walking vigorously. One block ahead her brother, too, is walking at a brisk pace, displaying his dark-blue uniformed back. He has just this year advanced to the first year of junior high. Across his slightly large new student jacket hangs a white, unsoiled canvas bag; no umbrella in hand, he is soaking wet. Hands stuffed in his hip pockets, his upper body slightly hunched, he is walking like a madman. "She'll never catch up with me!" is written in his appearance, and Gen understands. Her brother can't control his anger and walks along, enduring his wretchedness. He wants her to leave him alone, however pitiful he looks and feels; he doesn't want this half-hearted affection. . . . She chases after him boldly, but her brother notices and lunges desperately ahead with all his strength. Umbrella-less herself, Gen, too, became soaking wet. (*KAZ* 3: 3)

In this passage everything except Gen herself is seen through Gen's eyes or filtered through her mind. She reads in Hekiro's appearance his desire to be left alone; his anger, his temper, his obstinacy, and his pathos are presented as judgments she makes. When he lunges ahead, we see his desperation only because Gen sees it; Gen is the eye into which everything flows: the wind blows off the river "this way," the pedestrians face "ahead," going "to" the city and "away" from the village; the soundlessness of the rain is the soundlessness Gen notices, its apparent movement from river's surface to cherry tree to embankment being not actual movement but the order in which Gen observes it. Gen is defined solely by her perceptions of and care for another person; her eyes are glued to her brother, and her only concern is to protect him from the rain. Her role, then, is a passive one, but as we have learned to expect of Aya, this passivity reveals control. The world presented here seems to flow through Gen as through a sieve, but Gen also actively brings the world within her perceptual net and lets it flow through herself to the reader. She is always present, and the scene unfolds as she sees it, in the present tense. Only with the final line does Gen become the object of inspection. The passage moves into the past tense when the scene is encompassed by a larger eye, that of the narrator or of Aya herself.[3]

The concentration and calm that permeate the passage result in part from Aya's capturing the energies that pulsated in *Flowing*. Like Rika, Gen is the perceptual center of the world of the novel, but her range is reduced. She belongs to a small nuclear family, rather than a busy geisha establishment, and has far less to confront—fewer human problems as well as fewer sensual stimuli—than her predecessor. Rika is constantly battling her environment, but Gen belongs in hers; Rika's mind darts here and there, but Gen's gaze is focused on one primary object of attention.

In other words, Gen has a greater sense of assuredness, a more confident and authoritative vision, than Rika. If we understand Gen to be a transformed Rika, we can attribute this increased authority to the catharsis that *Flowing* provided. But we can also understand it as an outgrowth of the more authoritative sphere within which Gen lives. At first glance, Gen seems to move within a far broader social setting than Rika. She often stays at home, but she often goes out—to school, to the hospital, to the embankment, or onto the river in a boat. In actuality, however, Rika's obsessive awareness of two widely separated worlds, and of the difficulty of moving in and out of them, seems absent in Gen, or at least the boundaries that Gen experiences seem less obviously drawn. Her boundaries have not completely disappeared but have moved closer. The border that Gen faces is that of the skin, which separates two people, and her flowing is not in and out of two worlds but into and out of another's being. In the course of the novel she becomes confined in an ever-narrower world, and as her world narrows, her perceptions sharpen, and her sense of authority—her sense of confidence about the way she perceives the scene before her and her sense of being at home in that scene—increases. The smaller her world, the more authoritative her vision.

Throughout the novel Gen watches her brother, worries about his delinquency at school, protects him from scolding parents, cares for him when ill. She mends his clothes and puts off her own marriage to tend him when he is sick. Again, she almost seems a cipher: the emotions she feels are elicited by him and for him, or they are extensions of his feelings. When he feels despair, she feels despair, and as her understanding of his pain deepens, so, too, does her own inner life.

The emotional identification between the two—present from the start of the novel—increases as the novel progresses, though often blocked or diverted, sometimes even temporarily destroyed. In the opening scene Gen cannot reach Hekiro. She stops just this side of the bridge when she sees her brother about to cross over to the city, into which he will be "swallowed up without a trace" (*KAZ* 3: 6). Bridges are painful reminders of separation in *Little Brother,* especially because they offer the hope of passing to the other side. On one fine morning the brother and sister walk happily to school along the river when suddenly their peace is disturbed by the sight of a bridge: "When they came to where the bridge was visible, she suddenly grew anxious" (*KAZ* 3: 24). Gen is worried about her brother's delinquent behavior, and as she talks to him, they cross over the bridge and arrive at the train station, only to separate there.

The drama of the novel lies in scenes like this, in the movement between moments of profound sharing (usually of loneliness) and moments of painful separation. One such moment comes when Gen, looking from a train window, sees her brother steal something. His actions sink into her— "placed inside her empty heart with a reality of their own" (*KAZ* 3:71)— and trigger a series of meditations. In a troubled home such as theirs, where parental quarrels threaten to destroy all intimacy, siblings are often alienated from one another. But their case was different; she and her brother were close. Now her accidental witnessing of his crime has established a distance between them: "Time passed, and the New Year, too, went by uneventfully. The school semester began. To avoid Gen and leave the house one step ahead of her, Hekiro would rush about the moment he awoke in the morning. The distance of eighteen blocks had once represented the time when brother and sister could talk, but now it held no pleasure at all. While Gen was still packing the lunches, Hekiro would snatch his and rush out in a panic. To stop him from doing this, Gen would put off making his lunch until last, but every time she did, he would look about the kitchen silently and rush out angrily, without his lunch."

Gen feels desperate and abandoned. The appearance of the river has changed accordingly. It no longer flows on, merging and separating and merging again. "Gen wanted to do something. It was terrible to have been discarded by him. She thought she had won some kind of victory when she confronted him, but look how she felt—wretched and pathetic. The days of February passed, one after the other. It was the season when the wind from the river blew coldest. The embankment became a long and unpleasant path. The previous year Hekiro had still been in grammar school, so Gen had often taken this path alone, but being alone now was true loneliness. The path was frozen hard, the cherry trees naked and stiff. Silently the river ran down and yet farther down. The tips of the waves were cut into triangles."

A bleak wind whistles up from the river, so cold it stings, so painful it seems cruel. This is the feeling that Gen is left with when separated from her brother. She now wonders about the source of the river: "Where might the far reaches of this river be found? Might not its source be in the single drops of water seeping from under the weight of rocks pressing down, down,

down into the depths of the earth—large rocks without life, inside a silent mountain, inside a far distant mountain somewhere? And so, no matter how many tens or hundreds of miles the river flows down, when winter comes, the river draws in its power and stubbornly bears the ghastly coldness it possessed when it ran deep, deep, deep down, under the ground" (*KAZ* 3: 73).

In this dark, cold, bleak passage, Gen searches for sources and sets forth images of distance and separation. But Aya's narrative, in characteristic fashion, does not settle at this extreme; it moves on: the brother and sister have their moments of communion, though only when their energies are roped in and their spheres of movement curtailed. These moments occur with greater frequency and depth when Hekiro is stricken with tuberculosis and finally confined to a hospital room: "Hekiro was alone; the tuberculosis had cut him off from everything outside his immediate self. But Gen felt that Hekiro's illness had drawn her into the net of the hospital. Even the home where her parents lived was already outside the net" (*KAZ* 3: 165).

Within this net, faced with her dying brother, Gen grows strong, not unlike Aya when Aya cared for her father. Gen has learned to "sit quietly and observe." Like Aya, Gen receives her true education in these subtle, concentrated moments occurring within a constricted space. "The hospital raised Gen" (*KAZ* 3: 167).

As Gen focuses her attention on her brother, the outside world fades, and the small world before her expands:

> Although it was quiet, the hospital was inside the city, so noise was continuously pouring in. The reason it seemed so still was that in her heart Gen felt still. The ice packs gave off a sound that seeped into her heart. It had been like this: her father had gone to the trouble of coming to see his son and appeared to be praying, his eyes shut, before the boy's sickly figure. Gen sat close to her brother's bedside. There was a dry, cracking sound. As the ice in the pack began to melt, each fragment stirred and let out a crisp sound as it separated from the frozen block. Whether the sound was of each piece separating and falling away or of each hitting the other at the moment of separation, it was a crisp, parched sound. It was a sound that momentarily made one sense the presence of bones. Nobody can know such a sound, of bones bleached in the sun and withered by the wind, hitting against one another. But the sound of the ice in the packs brought it to mind. How often had Gen heard that sound since entering the hospital? It was not unpleasant; rather, it lacked sharpness. But it suggested the sound of dried-up, exhausted bones. (*KAZ* 3: 168)

This is another image of separation, one occurring within a body. Gen's imagination has penetrated her brother that deeply. His being comes to consume her, but gazing upon him from the outside becomes her only reality: "I am here now, watching you. This made her feel secure" (*KAZ* 3: 169).

Hekiro recovers temporarily, but the experience that he and his sister shared inside the hospital has cut them off from the outside world. When they return home, they do not find a haven of security and warmth. "Hekiro continued to improve, and he returned home with Gen for one night, as if practicing for the actual move. Naturally he was overjoyed as he left the entrance of the hospital and entered the car. He was cheerful about returning after so long, but in reality he felt, as did Gen, oddly ill at ease there. He told her secretly: 'I can't relax. Does a place close itself off to you if you stay away? And when you're there, is a new place created?' " (*KAZ* 3: 177).

Their home is not the place to carve out spaces for themselves. When they return to the hospital, they reenter more intimate territory and come closer to joining their selves together. Gen phones her father to report on Hekiro's condition and says: "Father, it isn't I who is crying. It's Hekiro who's crying. I'm crying in his place" (*KAZ* 3: 165). From this point on, the narrative becomes almost completely engaged with the siblings' emotions and sympathies. The world outside the minds and emotions of the two suffering characters is all but absent.

Still, although Gen urgently desires to feel her brother as part of herself, she is unable to do so. Her failure to submerge her identity in his—like Rika's failure to submerge herself in the community of geisha—leads her to a vivid understanding of her existential aloneness.

> The infectious nature of his disease had now made Hekiro an outcast from everyone and everything. He had become isolated by his tuberculosis. When he had first been diagnosed, both he and Gen had felt that the world around them had suddenly become extremely narrow. But they had nevertheless felt that there was nothing to complain of. It had seemed to them that the people around them, abhorring tuberculosis, had been trying to surround them with a fence. Of course they had understood that the disease was contagious: that was why society had built the fence—it feared the disease and wanted to avoid it. Hekiro and Gen had thought of the fence as built for the sake of others, as a fence behind which everybody—including family and friends—could escape from Hekiro and his disease. But things were different now. They were made to feel that the fence was no longer such an expansive and easy thing. It was a fence built tightly around Hekiro's body, with his first layer of skin as the outer border. . . . Hekiro felt completely isolated by it. Gen understood him and could guess how he felt. (*KAZ* 3: 169)

The fence encloses Hekiro from the rest of the world, and Gen, too, is locked out. But her love for her brother impels her to cross the dangerous boundary of the disease, and he also struggles to break down the barriers separating them. The final pages of the novel poignantly describe the brother and sister moving closer to one another. Hekiro tests his sister's love by asking her to feed him noodles, and Gen, understanding her brother's need for human contact, complies with the request. With this last barrier removed, Hekiro is able to open up to his sister completely, and both realize the degree to which they had formerly been unwilling to yield to and give to one another. As so often happens in Aya's stories, the female protagonist's act of will is an act of service—in this case, feeding a brother.

Gen and Hekiro enact a symbolic though temporary union. Gen has forgone marriage to care for him, and she agrees to come to his hospital room dressed in her wedding gown. The sicker he grows, the deeper her feelings for him become, and the more willing she is to sacrifice herself for him; but their separation is inevitable. "This was the brother she had taken care of for so long, since he was a little boy; the brother she had always in one way or another held close to her. Gen had always been the elder sister. Yet now it seemed that Hekiro, since coming to the hospital, had become a person different from the brother of before. . . . Gen wondered why it was that only she felt excluded when she and her brother were together. Although Hekiro was here now, why did she feel separated from him like this? Gen felt she had been left alone, marooned. They had not separated, yet she felt as if they already had. The loneliness pierced her, a loneliness so forlorn that it did not even bring tears" (*KAZ* 3: 77).

When Gen risks infection by feeding noodles to her tubercular brother, small hostilities and problems disappear. The siblings spend his final night together, sleeping in his room, tied together by a ribbon, and wake up to make the tender conversation of parting lovers. When he dies, she, too, loses consciousness.

> Could this be the end? Could this be death? She saw everyone there, standing, except for her mother, who was seated in a chair. Father had placed his hands together, and Mother had assumed a posture of prayer. Nobody moved: there was a stir and also a hush. Was this truly death? Such a simple thing—Hekiro's fingers were cold, but his arm was warm. . . . Through the large glass window behind the drawn blinds the dark dawn sky, jeweled with stars, could be seen. One star suddenly flowed by, leaving a trail of sparks behind. Then suddenly a second, third, fourth, and fifth star streaked across the sky, each tracing a line as it fell. There was a great rattling sound, and everything went black. (*KAZ* 3: 78)

When Gen awakes, she puts on an apron and prepares for her last act of service—cleaning and dressing her brother. She imagines that the stars and the sound in the sky signify the entry of her brother's spirit into heaven. Like *Flowing,* the novel closes with the separation of a woman from the object of her service and hints at a future solitariness—a consequence, it would seem, of the character's identity as outsider and onlooker.

But as always in Aya's work, this sense of isolation is opposed to the potential value to be found in a narrow sphere and in acts of service. Aya's rebellion—if we can call it that—against the confining role of servant did not take the form of a rejection of that role or the house in which she served. Rather, like her characters, she took on the passivity expected of her and turned the world she had been given into the fount of her art.

Kōda Rohan told his daughter when she was young that it was best to communicate with him without words. He also warned her before his death that their separation would be final. Aya did not heed his advice or his warning. She spent her career attempting to communicate with him—and in some way rejoin him. Her dialogue with her dead father guided her evolution as a writer and led her, in the end, back to a world like the one in which she was reared.

In her last sustained piece of writing, *Battle (Tō,* 1965), Aya describes in vivid and relentlessly painful detail the frightening consequences of fatal diseases for the bodies and minds of patients living in a hospital. *Battle* is a novel about death, and it raises the questions that haunted Aya throughout her career: Can a family avoid being destroyed when one of its members departs? Can peace or the semblance of peace ever be restored to those who mourn? Is the experience of a loved one's death wholly singular, or can it be shared?

The novel focuses on a single man, Shōgo, a patient who has battled leukemia for ten years and lives sequestered in a hospital. He, and we through him, witness the gradual but sure decline of various patients, whose families break apart. That Shōgo is himself without family only intensifies the scenes of family breakdown. To his mind, families succumb so easily after death because they were built on weak foundations: sick old men are ignored by children; a frightened father waiting numbly for a son to die is sur-rounded by a family too emotionally cold to provide support; a husband feels released when his wife's brutal suffering comes to an end; a lonely friend commits suicide. Shōgo's vision of family life is not a happy one.

In *Battle,* Aya has returned to her father's world. The world of the hospital is a closed one, where all eyes are concentrated on disease and death, where care for others is the only humanly redeeming value—indeed, nurses and doctors acquire heroic proportions.

Summer. White turns to silver. The doctors and nurses coming through the pine trees emerge from the green shadows and are bathed by the sun. At that instant, their luminous white clothes turn to silver: this is what the eyes peering from inside the rooms saw.

The nurses' caps sparkle brightly. They have sharp edges, so with even the slightest movement of the head they refract the sunlight and become silver. Nature crowns the women with a moment's splendor. But they have never thought twice about their "crowns." They have nothing to do with crowns. No, they know the word and on ceremonial days can see crowns with their own eyes on Her Majesty the Empress Michiko; they can see them in photographs. They see star singers like Hibari-san and Chiemi-san on television. Perhaps the head-pieces of these singers are made for the stage, or perhaps they are of real diamonds, but theirs are the crowns that the nurses talk of and see. That is how far removed from their lives these crowns are. What each nurse wears on her head is a white cap, and not even in her dreams is it a crown.[4]

Aya no doubt saw herself in these women. Rohan had trained her to see, much as these nurses were trained to see, and she had perfected her vision by gazing upon his dying body. It is only natural, then, that in *Battle,* Aya's descriptions sharpen as they concentrate on the specific manifestations of material decline. In each scene and character that Shōgo witnesses, there is a glimpse of Aya, of her experience with death. But not only the funereal atmosphere of the hospital is reminiscent of Rohan's home in his last days. Although the hospital is a closed world, like a prison, the patients confined there are a surrogate family for Shōgo. The hospital can offer a peaceful reprieve from the difficulties of family life in the outside world—much as the geisha world did for Rika, the hospital did for Gen, and Rohan's home did for Aya. The problem of leaving this inner world is serious—again, as it was for Aya and her fictional protagonists. The hospital, like the geisha establishment in *Flowing,* is a place where time moves differently from the way it does in the outside world—according to the natural movement of decay and death. It is a place where meanings are stable and people are anchored within a familiar and manageably small environment. For one recovered girl, Uiko, release from the hospital has not been an altogether happy event:

For the ailing person, the time spent while ill is made up of discrete, important moments. But after recovery, time becomes a blank. One recovers and finally becomes normal, and when one has become normal, the time one spent ill becomes wasted time. But who can warn us of this? Neither she nor her mother had noticed in the slightest. During the period in which nothing existed for Uiko outside her own illness, girls and boys her age were receiving junior high and high school educations; some among them may even have embarked on careers. How much they had learned about the home and society, while she herself, she realized, knew nothing. She had recovered, to be sure, but she still possessed no confidence and could not deny the residue of malaise within her. Her mother would say, "You're better, so be strong," but how was she to be strong? "Now life begins," her mother would say, but how could someone who had not even satisfactorily completed grammar school begin now? "Take it easy for two or three months," her mother would say, without herself expecting to enjoy such a luxury, and it was obvious that Uiko couldn't find a new job and immediately receive an advance. Uiko felt she had to earn quickly at least the money needed to pay for her own food. "A factory would be good," her mother would say, but the mere thought made her shrink. It was even doubtful whether she had the physical strength to be a café waitress carrying coffee cups all day long. In a cheap candy store or sundries shop there were too many items, and she wouldn't be able to manage the calculations; and the job of caretaker for someone's house, which her mother had mentioned, was not readily available. Uiko felt only hesitation, fear, misgivings. She could not imagine happiness. It may have been worth the struggle to battle her illness, but she realized she had had more purpose while sick than she did now. The desire to get better, which she had felt so deeply that it had become instinct, was now completely gone, and no new goals for the future arose. All she could see before her was the stuff of despondency. Her body had regained its health, but her spirit had taken a terrible blow. (264–265)

We hear echoes here of Gen and Hekiro's experience in their hospital. But in *Battle* the anxiety and turmoil of the patient comes into greater relief than the emotions of the person caring for her.

While completely masking her troubled state before her mother, Uiko became more anxious by the day and felt as if she were roaming atop a precipice. She trembled at her mother's words of joy—"You've finally recovered, haven't you?"—and at her mother's phrase of encouragement—"You're healthy now, so . . ." These words gave Uiko an unbearable sense of being driven away. She realized now that it had been fun when the words spoken between them had been, "Let's get well." She and her mother had always been as one: celebrating together, lamenting together, they possessed the same emotions. Uiko never doubted that. And now the two were separate beings. Her mother worked hard on her own and pressured her daughter to be strong, but Uiko felt reproach in her words. Before, it had been nothing for her to watch her mother as she worked, but now she felt even that as a pressure. She felt as if she wanted to ask forgiveness for making her mother struggle so because of her illness; and she felt a gap because she was unable to keep up with her mother's robust health. She felt that the curing of her illness had destroyed her purpose in life and that liberation from the sickbed had thrust her into a deep darkness. (265)

Hermetically sealed from the outside world, the world of *Battle*, like much of Aya's fiction, seems to raise issues of only the most personal or existential consequence. That Aya's imagination is more expansive than this can be glimpsed from the way that she moves from character to character, expressing with equal integrity the inner anguish of each. She displays an overwhelming concern for individual lives and suffering. In *Battle* this empathic quality has become so extreme that Aya herself disappears completely. There are no Rika and no Gen to stand in for her—all that is left is the empathy with which she dips into each life and draws out an integral experience.

Although Aya was not a political allegorist—indeed, she was not political at all—this empathic ability allows her to reach out beyond individuals and create a literature that speaks of the national experience. In addition to being a novel about personal suffering, *Battle* tells the story of Japan's postwar struggle for physical and spiritual recovery. Although the patients in the hospital want to be cured, once they leave the hospital their lives have no meaning. *Battle* concludes where Aya's career began, at a scene of physical decay and death, closely observed in fine and relentless detail. Shōgo has succumbed to death; and the careful placement of objects provides a stoic backdrop to the emotionally tense scene in the autopsy room, at which the character Shinya gazes.

> The room was bright and wide—the ceilings, walls, and floors were white, and large windows had been cut out on either side. Not quite in the center, well inside, there was, of course, the autopsy platform. A white sheet had been spread over it, and underneath was Shōgo's corpse. Toward the base of the table, a largish drain board and a wash basin. Next to the drain, a table and, on top of that, a balance and scale. Another table, a pus bowl, medicine vials, various other items. In the back of the room, next to the window, equipment cabinets with glass doors. In front of that, a smallish concrete drain board. Alongside the door to the morgue, a stretcher. In the corner by the wall, a narrow bed. From somewhere came the sound of purling water. (321)

Shinya is self-conscious about his presence in the room, and attempts to place himself at a comfortable physical and emotional distance. He fears what he is about to see, yet musters the strength to properly assume his role and serve the occasion well. He understands that Shōgo, too, "was now about to give over his entire being in a final act of service and that he himself must not forget the discretion appropriate to an assistant serving a superior. Understanding all this, he realized it was not absolutely necessary to observe the autopsy from afar, as a curiosity. But even more than this, he realized that he must not interfere with the people performing the autopsy. Shinya moved himself to a position near the window" (322).

When the corpse comes into view, the intensity of the observer's gaze freezes the scene, collapsing a lengthy process into a moment of perception.

All of a sudden the sheet was removed, and the stark naked corpse was placed on the platform. Shinya stared in shock. This was unmistakably Beturō Shōgo, but equally unmistakably it was a corpse from which the life had flown. He had grown thin. And his skin was a dirty yellow earthen color. Death had clearly burned itself into his eyes. Dr. Natsukawa stood with the corpse's head to his right and its legs to his left. Dr. Katō, working as assistant, was facing the corpse from his position across the table. Dr. Iwakuni, the notetaker, was at the side of the table. One couldn't tell from where exactly—from the collarbone, perhaps— but the blade quickly glided across the body. Shinya watched the white upper bodies of the two doctors leaning and pushing, their white hats bobbing. Clipped words, German perhaps, spoken intermittently in low voices, their meaning unclear. Soon these words, too, became insignificant to Shinya, as he looked at the open belly before his eyes as if gazing upon a distant view. Even when the intestines were removed, he was unperturbed by their color and shape, thinking, "So that's what they're like"; even when the brain was measured on the scale, he merely thought, "So that's what one does"; when the removed intestines were scrupulously unwound and examined or when cotton was stuffed into the now-empty abdominal cavity and chest, Shinya's eyes gazed with great intensity but vacantly, as if he felt nothing, nothing but the coldness in his fingertips and toes. He lingered in absolute stillness. (322–323)

The next passage immediately invokes the image of hair from another Aya story. "Hatayama drew in his chin as if to say, 'Isn't that so?' Then he took out a comb and nimbly worked it through Shōgo's hair. It was the style Shōgo had always liked. But his thick, stiff hair, perhaps because of the stitching, would not take shape properly. Hatayama massaged the surface of the skin and arranged the hair nicely, then suddenly spoke to Shōgo with a grin on his face. 'I'm going to wake you up now. It's time to get up.' He then moved around to Shōgo's feet" (323).

Like Shinya, like Aya, Hatayama has a special perceptual relationship with a dying man.

"Ready? Up you go."

Bolt upright, the naked Shōgo was straight as a pole. As he stood there his entire body dripped water. Hatayama-san had grabbed his legs and was lifting him with all his strength. It happened in a brief moment. Turning red with exertion, Hatayama-san gently put the body on the table on which it had been resting. He wiped the body with a towel. "Well, you're not a patient anymore.

Wake up and go off to heaven." Even Shinya had heard that very occasionally Hatayama did this kind of thing. It was said that such an act was so rare because it could only be done by someone like Hatayama-san, who constantly looked on such scenes, who carefully observed them and pierced to their essence and then could comment, "This was a good patient." (323)

The motifs of transformation, of service, and of the desire to exhaust one's energies and efforts are linked in this final scene with Aya's obsession with objects. The story concludes:

> The autopsy itself was a legacy Shōgo bestowed to this hospital wholeheartedly. No, not to this hospital, but to this nation. No, not to this hospital, not to this nation, but to the cause of fighting tuberculosis. And yet the intestines and lungs of this legacy were so ragged they were useless: they were shining rags. Shinya hid his emotions as he prayed in silence with the doctors. Although he grieved with Shōgo sincerely, his heart and his senses—how could one explain this?— his heart and senses apprehended something ghastly and frightening. He sensed a shocking, terrible smell in his nostrils as he bent over in prayer. It was an odor rising up from between the seams of the white gown that Shōgo was wearing. Now, for the first time, he noticed: this was the smell of autopsy. The forlornness of spirit and flesh and of life that becomes its opposite. The forlornness of knowing that when you die, you just die, and your spirit and flesh together disappear. Wanting to wipe away the smell stabbing at his nostrils, Shinya walked off into the pine grove. And then, there, he thought, Ah, the massive patient file labeled with the name Beturō Shōgo has finally been closed.
>
> The coffin was carried out at two. People saw it off in lines stretching all the way from the vestibule to the back gate of the morgue. A chill wind chased the back of the hearse. A sound lingered in the tops of the pine trees. (324)

Shōgo's life ends in peace within the walls of the hospital. For those like Uiko, who survive and must leave the hospital, the future is more troubling. Spiritual recovery will not necessarily follow physical recovery; indeed, physical recovery—and the subsequent release from a nurturing environment—creates new and frightening anxieties. If one has become accustomed to the struggle to live, what does one live for when the fight is over? Aya seems to be asking this question of herself regarding her struggle with her father, and in doing so, she asks the question of Japan, a nation newly recovered from postwar devastation. Here her private experience touches that of the culture. Freedom from restriction inevitably brings meaninglessness.

In the novel, Aya's descriptions of death and decay are stoical and cold. What we see is an attempt to emulate the ability that she so admired in the geisha—the ability to be both in the midst of emotional entanglement and outside it, to gently accept what comes and then to gently let it flow away.

This image of flowing sums up Aya's career as a writer. Society offered Aya a script—a limited number of symbols—with which to imagine and then re-create her world, and flowing was the most vivid of these. Flowing is an image wrapped in layers of cultural and social meaning. It evokes the classics of Japanese literature, especially the opening lines of the thirteenth-century prose-poem "Hōjōki," by Kamo no Chōmei: "The flow of the river is ceaseless and its water is never the same. The bubbles that float in the pools, now vanishing, now forming, are not of long duration. So in the world are man and his dwellings."[5] The image is both universal and time-less, evoking the sorrows of change, but it casts on Aya's works the light of Japanese tradition. It is only natural, then, that Aya came to serve as an icon of conservative cultural rejuvenation.

Flowing is a cultural image, but it is also a social one, evoking the conventional feminine attribute of pliant passivity. In the writings of other twentieth-century women writers in Japan, despite a self-declared struggle against social and sexual restrictions, the image of flowing is often used to represent overpowering force: Sata Ineko often writes about flowing in the passive voice—swept away (literally, flowed away; *nagasareru*)—to de-scribe a woman's entrapment in the forces of political change. In Enchi Fumiko's more eroticized prose the force gushes out irresistibly: "A force that flowed unceasingly like a raging stream carried [Tome] on despite everything, allowing her only to gaze back with many a deep sigh to the land left far upstream."[6]

But this cultural and social image was, for Aya, also a personal one. The ostensible passivity of flowing always involved an act of subjective will—an ability to *allow* things to flow through one. Such an ability was no doubt useful in countering the influence her father exerted over her, both before his death and after. But in her writing it became more than that. If Sata Ineko writes about the search for new ways of imagining one's life as a woman in society—in other words, the search for possible happiness—Aya writes about the search for imaginative control over one's environ-ment. Flowing is thus an image of perceptual movement, of the psychic energy that gathers in the objective world and then restructures it. Flow-ing organizes the chaos created by the war, flowing shapes the clutter of memories within Aya, and flowing gives control over the environment to Aya—or Rika or many other characters found in Aya's fictional world. Finally, flowing stands for the literary identity that Aya created in her writing, for the merging and uncoupling of identities—Aya's and Rika's, for example. Flowing allows Aya to remain within conventional roles while moving outside them; it provides a gently ironic distance from which she can assert an idiosyncratic self without rejecting the conventions surrounding it. It allows her to accept her father's influences without having them crush her.

Flowing breaks apart the world, then restructures it.[7] It is apt, then, that after completing *Battle,* Aya devoted herself to rebuilding a five-storied pagoda in the ancient capital of Nara that recalled the pagoda in her father's most famous novel. Indeed, Aya even took up temporary residence near the temple and used the royalties from her father's book to aid in the reconstruction, as well as prepared a series of essays and lectures on the subject. Rebuilding the pagoda would repay her debt to her father for the artistic legacy that he had bequeathed her, the legacy that allowed her to write. It would also symbolize Aya's mastery of her father's literary forms. In writing *Battle,* Aya seems to have written herself out; she had returned almost fully to her father. She could completely return only by devoting herself to an emblem of his world.

Four Stories

by Kōda Aya

The Medal

I wore a jet-black striped kimono for work clothes. The designs on the calico obi were threadbare. A sailcloth apron hung heavily from my hips and lay on my lap like a shield, like a plaster cast, like a barrier.

At thirty-four I had abruptly fallen from being the representative of a sake wholesaler in Shingawa to managing a miserable, wretchedly small sake shop. The shop sounded impressive, and it was an official retail establishment, but in fact it operated without a license or proper premises. It was the end of April 1937, and the world, still not recovered from the February 26 incident of the previous year, was rapidly becoming absorbed in the events that would lead to the China affair three months later. The wheels of danger had begun to spin, we were battered about in a violent whirlpool of events both large and small, one after the other, and even the most insignificant scraps were drawn out of hidden corners and buffeted by hardship. And the very first such scrap was I myself.

Because the business had only one telephone and I depended on a single errand boy, and because I wanted to spend as little time as possible facing my husband's pale, weak face, I drove my nerves and body to their limit. What happened was this: I was making my first delivery to a customer deep in the Horinouchi area, but the map the errand boy had dashed off for me had everything backwards, so I wound up wasting time and effort, and the woman of the house was angry at me for being late. To spite me, she had me take away five empty bottles at once. Taking away empty bottles was part of the arrangement, so I didn't object, but customers understood that I didn't ride a bike and never had me take five at one time. With cord I had brought, I tied the bottles in two bundles.

I had powerful arms. I was known as Rohan's little princess, and it had taken awesome strength to endure the annoyance of being treated as though I were a delicate sprout too weak to bear up against the wind. A twenty-gallon barrel weighs about two hundred pounds, but somehow I learned to lift one, and I shocked people. Once, for an order, I had even taken six five-gallon bottles—weighing seven pounds each—up five flights without an elevator. Taking away five empty bottles was nothing at all, but the woman had me rattled. No matter how I tried, I couldn't rid myself of the haughtiness that came from being raised in the Rohan household and the arrogance of having once been a woman of the upper class. Both feelings often rose up in me, and though I rapidly improved at my work, I couldn't easily control the way I felt in my heart.

The way I looked! The apron had been given to me as a gift by my mother-in-law, who was born with the blood and spirit of a merchant. The obi was thickly layered to keep the calico from wearing out, and the sailcloth apron was so called because it was made from a boat sail. It was as wide as a cape, and in its center the emblem of the sake store was printed boldly. It served as a type of billboard, with slogans such as "Flower of the Sake World," "Heaven beyond Compare," and "Famous the World Over." There were also ads for breweries and customers' stores all over it, bright enough to awaken even the drowsiest eyes.

Wearing such an apron, I, too, served as a good advertisement. I didn't have my hair tied up in a comb but, rather, had it done in the Western style; I was a tall woman and not too fat. And precisely because it was Rohan's daughter who wore the apron, its effect was as great as it could be. Wearing it had been my husband's suggestion. A kimono that covers a callow heart is powerful indeed. Or, to put it another way, a kimono is a thing that manipulates a person's heart. The work clothes were my uniform. They made me devoted to and proud of my work. My apron was a shield against every type of arrow, a shield protecting me from all life's troubles, a barrier that hid my anguish.

The previous year, the *Asahi shinbun* had run an article about me on the society page, in its end-of-the-year humor column: "Heavy drinker Dr. Rohan's Little Girl Opens Sake Shop. From Woman of the House to

Entrepreneur of the Streets." It was a light comic piece, and the reporter's writing was not clever, so there was no reason to expect people to take it seriously, but I sensed in everyone around me a special courtesy. My husband said we should give the reporter a gift, and so we had the errand boy take him a drink, though I thought the gesture was pointless. When the errand boy returned, he sullenly mumbled to me what the reporter had said: "I'm not to be taken so lightly, you know. After all, I'm an Asahi reporter. You'd better not ignore that!" I've forgotten this reporter's name and everything about him, but I remember him fondly. How full of life he seemed to me then; how pitiful to think of my dispirited husband. But time passed, and my work clothes and apron put a lid over my heart and my feelings.

There was so little time to make deliveries that I was exhausted when I reached my destination and still I was late. On the way home, too, I was frantic and irritated. I had to carry the five empty bottles, the day's proceeds were meager, and it was painful to spend money on a bus. But I had no choice. The smell of fermented sake wafted up, and the shaking at the back of the bus was terrible. A small sake business often requires work in the evening, and as I sat on the speeding bus, I thought of my husband, lazily writing receipts or sticking on labels, and of the errand boy, who, if I took my eyes off him, became a bumbling fool. My feet felt as if they wanted to run off somewhere.

The bus passed Hibiya and was very near Tsukiji. The many edges of the roofs on the Shinbashi side glittered brightly, though around them there was increasing darkness, the sun having disappeared from my sight or having set already. On the Kyobashi side, there was only a broad expanse of brightness. Sukiyabashi: A streak of water, water lit by the setting sun, distant, far away, hometown water, the Sumida River. Nostalgia seemed to run with the water and flow into my chest. One wave, a thousand waves— in the thick and quiet afterglow, the radiant, murmuring shallows seemed to be moving in all directions in the area of the temple. Suddenly I gasped, for before my eyes the letters ROHAN shuddered and disappeared. A stroke! The *Asahi shinbun*. In a daze I rushed back home. An intersection.

I stood to the side of the police box. The belt of lighted letters flowed dimly by, but I couldn't read it. The letters ROHAN waved by once again and disappeared. I stared ahead, thinking only that the stroke must have been fatal. Nauseated, I pressed the base of my tongue down to keep from getting sick, but I could taste the bitter bile in my mouth. I put down the empty bottles. I went to the back of the police box. The stench of urine assaulted me. In my pain, my nose dripped and my eyes teared. My handkerchief was stained brown. When I looked up again, I read, "Our Nation's First Recipient of the Medal of Culture." Once more, ROHAN passed by. Shining quietly.

As I looked at the sky it changed from rose to light purple. I could endure the apron no longer, so I folded it in three and jammed it tightly under my belt. I took up the empty bottles in both hands. Long threads of willow were darkening before my eyes. Sadness seemed to collect around me, and my head throbbed with pain. I quickly walked home. As I expected, orders had come in, but the sake had run out. My husband, already completely absorbed in other matters, of course did not know the news. He said nothing to me about the award, and I said nothing to him. I ran off to Shingawa to pick up some supplies.

Unless there was a special order, the wholesaler bolted the front door of the warehouse and the main entrance to the store before sunset. When the counter clerks had gone home, all that remained were the employees who lodged on the second floor of the store and were known for their abundant youthful vigor. The atmosphere was full of male energy, of men playing go and shogi, talking, and eating. They greeted me as I rushed in, some standing up, some merely shifting to acknowledge me. They had been taught to speak politely and graciously. "Our congratulations to the master. A truly glorious achievement. The master from Koishikawa is truly magnificent. Please accept our sincere congratulations."

These men, far removed from the world of letters, immersed in their daily work, expressed their joy simply. They did not know what was so glorious about Master Rohan or what was so glorious about the award. And I was not far from them in that way. If I hadn't known him, I would have found it hard to say who Rohan was or what the glory was. But their congratulations made me happy, and I wanted somehow to offer them something in return. I wanted to treat them to noodles, I wanted to buy them cakes. Above all, I wanted to let go of myself a bit and celebrate my father's success with these men, who had such a light, easy way about them. But all I had in my wallet was the small change I had collected at Horinouchi, plus a bit more money and a packet of tickets for the bus. Well, never mind. Hadn't I just the day before already ceased being the wise and good wife? I couldn't even put together three proper meals.

A young man stood up, grabbed hold of the keys to the warehouse, and stepped outside. I could hear the roar of an engine being started on a motorbike. What he was doing for me now was on his own time. "Shall we ride together?" We both knew that the cushions in the back and the front were equally dirty, and I was pleased by his courtesy in turning them over.

My muscles were warm but my skin was cold as we cut through the wind. There was a star.

That night I grew weak and was unable to visit Koishikawa; only my feelings continued to race. Now that my father lived apart from his wife, his home and his appearance tended to be neglected. There were probably crowds of journalists and visitors, and there probably weren't enough teacups and sitting cushions. The young maids who work in a wifeless house may be used to it, but they can't be expected to manage that much. The poor girls—they were probably frantic.

Had the award merely been announced? Or had he already received it? He would certainly have been required to wear appropriate attire—what about that? Had a matching hat and shoes been found? While I knew there was no point daydreaming like this, I found myself considering a thousand such things and in the end felt too much anxiety to look forward to congratulating him the next day. Hadn't my feelings of joy and celebration been completely used up a few hours before, when I was chatting with the men in the warehouse? This thought made me sad again. How impoverished my heart was. Isn't one taught that one should make another's happiness one's own? Is there such a thing as a child who does not wish for her father's fame? We were just a father and a daughter—what kind of child was I? It was as if I were at the bottom of a pitch-black valley, gazing up at the image of a father off in the distance, obscured by mist.

When I was very young, I sat across a sake table and heard the following story from my father. When a lion cub grew up, its father would test it by kicking it off a steep cliff. A brave cub, when it realized it had fallen, would kick its feet in the air and spring up again. There were cubs who landed lightly, stretched their legs and looked about them, then gradually scooted up to the top without a struggle and there were cubs who would grope their way along rocky paths. Rank was established in this way. To the cub who would not make its own way but shrieked and cried convulsively, the lion would say: "Go off and be eaten!" I was raised on the story of this cub, and I often cried when I heard it. I didn't know that I would become like that pathetic cub and feel compassion for the weak out of sympathy with it.

"If I had been the lion, of course I would have felt sorry for the cub. But lions have no patience for weakness, so nothing could be done."

Every time Father repeated the story to me, I chafed at that detestable lion, the king of the beasts and parent of the cub, who could tell its own child to "go off and be eaten." Once, just before Father was about to speak, I shouted at him to "go off and be eaten." I had hoped to howl at him all my resentment of the strong and my compassion for the weak. Father laughed, but my eyes were filled with tears. After that he didn't tell the story often. The laughable words I had thrown at him were the exact words of the father lion. But for a long time I didn't notice, and the words "go off and be eaten" had a certain exhilarating feeling to them. Years later Father was retelling this story to his little granddaughter. Sitting at their sides, I listened, thinking about how greatly he had toned the story down. He didn't say, "Go off and be eaten," but said instead, "Another animal might come by and eat you up." A grandchild was different from a child.

"When it's eaten, then what?"

"Then it dies."

"When it dies, then what?"

"Then it goes away."

"If it goes away, then what?"

"That's the end."

After a moment the grandchild said, just as if she were an adult, "How awful!" People's minds are funny: just at that moment I remembered the words I had yelled at my father years before. I felt ashamed and embarrassed.

I have nothing of my father's powerful learning and understand nothing about his art. When it comes to questions of fate, free will, the great complexity of human character, again I know nothing. But although I know little of these things, I have never been so foolish as to fear him because he is "a lion of the literary world." The only thing linking us was the flow of feelings between parent and child. But if I were to try to express these childhood feelings—warped in that peculiar way children's feelings are—I would have to say that there was truly something of the beast about Father, something in him that wanted to test me, to kick me down and tell me to go off to be eaten. Whenever I thought of this, my chest would constrict.

My husband and my child slept peacefully on the three mats arranged one next to the other. But in the darkness, my nerves were frayed. What is a person who surpasses hundreds of thousands of others? What is the fate of a child, so much like those hundreds of thousands, who is connected to such a father? My pillow grew damp with tears. The tears comforted me, and I fell asleep crying.

When morning came my feelings revived. In my second year of elementary school I had been presented with a new mother, and because my family hadn't given much thought to how I might respond, I was terribly wounded by the children at school, who first planted in me the awful idea of having a "stepmother." I had learned my lesson, and I didn't want to see my daughter battered about by Rohan and by the medal and have her gentle disposition—she was in her second year of school, as I had been—ruined by conceit and vanity. After telling her in a general way what had happened, I asked her, before explaining any more, "How does Tamako feel about it?"

She replied, "Is Grandpa happy about it?"

I felt choked. She had no real sense of the award and was unaware that her mother was having trouble answering her.

"If Grandpa is happy, Tamako is happy. If Grandpa doesn't like it, neither does Tamako!" She danced up the steps of the store on her delicate legs, her rucksack jiggling as she went. I relied on those feelings of a child.

That afternoon I went to Koishikawa to pay my first visit to my family home in a long time. Although nothing had come between parent and child, everything seemed to have turned sour, all the more so because we had neglected to write or call, and discomfort about every little thing— about money, about obligations, about feelings—had piled up in direct proportion to our intimacy. Father cared for me, but at the same time he kept his distance, and I could not fail to notice his aloofness. My fear of him made me have to steel myself before every encounter. Father was a strange man. With the same whip he cracked, he would suddenly point out and describe the beauty of a flower or of the clouds. With the very knife he used to dissect, he would serve up some delicious delicacy. Nobody else around me had that skill. Father had the power to captivate me. I felt I wanted to blush and wag my tail but also to resist him to the very end, and I felt humbled by his love for me.

A black car was stopped at the entrance to the house. Fearing people's eyes, I entered through the kitchen door and took off my sailcloth apron. Large barrels of sake and bottles were sitting in rows in the kitchen. Seafood was heaped splendidly in large and small bowls and in new bamboo baskets; there was colorful fresh produce from the fields. I had known to expect such splendor, but my heart shrank before all these glorious gifts. I quietly put down the bottle of sake I had brought as a gesture of congratulation. Everything around me had been unwrapped, and there wasn't a maid to be seen. The sitting room was in even greater disarray. Congratulatory letters written on fine paper in black formal script lay in piles, there were business cards and other letters here and there, various objects were stacked high as a mountain on top of the tea cabinet and were sticking out of drawers, and bowls had been set down everywhere, right on the tatami. Father's sitting cushion had been disturbed and was sticking out at an angle; someone's handkerchief lay on it untidily. I sat and waited. Loud footsteps descended from the second floor, passed the entranceway and a small room, and went on to the kitchen without stopping where I sat. I called out.

She appeared and said, without bowing in the slightest, "Oh. So you've decided to come?" She stood as she was and didn't offer a polite greeting. I saw that she was neatly dressed and heavily made up. "It's certainly a happy occasion for Father, isn't it?" I said, attempting to draw her in.

"Yes, so busy . . ." she replied, as she withdrew to the kitchen, from which I could hear the rattle of drawers opening and closing and of tea being made.

I retreated to the kitchen. "Who was that guest?" I asked. The fish that had been there when I entered had all disappeared, except for one box.

"I don't really know," was the reply.

What could be happening? It all seemed so strange. I had a disturbing feeling. There was nothing to do but retrace my steps and wait in the sitting room again. I was ashamed. It seemed new guests had come, and the previous ones had left. Dressed as usual in a loosely fitting kimono, the woman went back and forth before me busily, flashing something red as she went by. At the very least, I thought, I was glad to have come alone, without my daughter.

Father descended and, greeting the guests, quickly made his way to the table at the center of the room. I wiped off Father's cushion and set it properly. He waited a moment for my words of congratulation and said, "Have you been well?" In this one word I felt the warmth of a hot spring. I felt myself unravel and relent. I noticed how exhausted he looked.

"You must be exhausted by all the guests."

"Yes. In any case, everyone here has been working as if possessed and everything's a complete mess. They seem to think I have an obligation to meet with every single person."

He told me to wait a moment—he'd soon be done—and I turned my back to him and excused myself. Father ordered someone to give me some fish. I took home the single box that had remained untouched from before. The head of the halibut was scowling at me.

The child seemed very pleased. She talked about school as she ate the fish from her grandfather. "The teacher talked about the award. Everybody was asking the teacher if my grandfather was really such an important man, so she told them he was. Everyone said they wanted to see the medal." How innocent these children were!

The next day I took the child along. There was pomade in Father's beard. The "Mandarin Crest" sounded much less imposing than the Medal of Culture. The grandfather pinned the medal on his granddaughter's white blouse. The child began to giggle. I thanked him for the fish.

Father asked the child, "Was the sea bream delicious?"

The daughter, who didn't know the difference between bream and halibut, answered, "It was delicious."

It had indeed been top-quality fish. I promised myself never to forget that halibut or the despicable nature of a woman who lived off such gifts from her father.

Neither my husband nor I had much money. Even if we were careful, we could only barely get by. The following month, Aunt Nobuko held a celebration banquet for the entire family at her home. The pawnbroker wouldn't give me enough to afford anything more than a faded striped kimono. One of my young cousins said to me, "Why are you wearing an outfit like that?" An open confrontation was far preferable to a silent frown. In the midst of the piano music and the flowers and the cushions resembling flowers and the food and the kindness of guests, I kept my place, far away from my father's seat.

In June a ceremony was hosted in Tokyo by my father's colleagues and publishers—Koizumi Shinzō, Shibuzawa Keizō, Saitō Mokichi, Iwanami Booksellers, Chūō kōronsha, Keizosha, and others—at the Tokyo Kaikan. Kobayashi-san of Iwanami invited my husband and me repeatedly. He even came by that morning, and said, "*Sensei* will be lonely all by himself." I didn't give in to compassion. But when he left I listened, disconsolate, to his departing steps. I bit my lip and wondered why my feelings about the medal had to be so empty and forlorn.

That night Father said in his speech that art doesn't necessarily require fortunate circumstances. I felt that this father who could remain so self-possessed amidst all the acclaim and excitement was a magnificent man, and that his magnificence was a lonely magnificence.

The father wears his award and the daughter her apron—that's what Higuchi Ichiyō's nephew Higuchi Etsu said to me. I laughed loudly, not wanting to show my weakness, on the surface at least, but that apron had an unyielding fierceness about it, and it chafed my palm and my heart. The medal itself somehow managed to survive the wartime fires, and the words that I put down now provide the solace of tears. The feel of that canvas apron on my body sometimes comes back to me with a living freshness that wraps me in a tight embrace.

Hair

It was a long relationship. But she died, it ended, and I alone remained. A strange feeling—vacant, as if something had slipped out from inside me. A parent is expected to die first, but for some reason I took her death hard. Why was it she who died first? Why did I remain behind? She had always been a strong person, able to do things I couldn't—how could she have succumbed so easily? I found it hard to believe; it would not sink in. Perhaps that was because for many years we had lived apart and had had few opportunities to be together, so that when she died, there was nothing of the sadness that normally accompanies death, only a feeling of distance. It was similar to some other feeling, one I knew well but couldn't manage to place for several days until I realized: yes, it was the snow, the snow sliding off the eaves; it was a feeling very much like that.

Her personal belongings were moved from her place to mine. As a daughter unrelated by blood and a mother related only through marriage, we had known similar sorrows. If we had merely hated and resented each other, that would have been bearable: in moments of resentment and hatred, love, too, may mingle, and after all, relationships can be difficult. But my mother and I shared essentially the same personality, and we had spent many years raising each other. We came to admire each other's assertiveness and even to resemble each other. Yet Mother opposed me with the profound, hidden tenacity of an adult, and I flaunted the arrogance of youth. The discord that grew out of our similarity repeated itself endlessly. Had we been strangers, the combination might have worked better.

But the discord and antipathy between mother and child, which seemed to spring from something deep-seated and abstract, were actually spurred by trivial everyday events and feelings. And so, each of my mother's stained and battered household implements—which I had once been accustomed to seeing daily but which I now saw for the first time in a long while— spoke of old wounds and revived the past. The bulkiness of the open chest of drawers brought to mind the stubbornness of my mother, sitting sullenly, in a foul mood, refusing to eat; the glint of the uncovered mirror was my mother's habit of casting a sharp glance as she rose to leave a room.

An unusually large *tabi* now revealed itself, bringing to life Mother's misery at having to wear three layers of socks to ease the anguish of neuralgia. When I looked at the teeth of a comb blackened by dye, I thought of the beauty of her hair, in which she took such pride. "Parent and child," "existence"—their deep-rootedness, their persistence had permeated these objects. I felt a pang, as if someone had carelessly poked at old wounds. But my sadness at her death, by contrast, was shallow. The business of taking care of this rubbish was unpleasant indeed.

A red pincushion remained. It was handmade, of course, shaped like a slightly irregular paper container. Mother was skilled with her hands, but for some reason she never used Japanese-style pin boxes, always preferring this more portable type. Unbeknownst to anyone else, the red pincushion lost its proper place and settled among my own shabby sewing utensils. I had a sense of fastidiousness about these things, but my family, unaware of the history of the pincushion, treated it as if it were a dead and useless object. Four years had quickly passed since that time.

"Mother, come here and take a look. Look at this."

There was a certain urgency in my daughter's voice, so I put aside the wash. In her fingers she held a mysterious object that glistened in the winter sun. From where she sat on the veranda, facing the screen, she thrust it toward me to show it to me all the more quickly.

"What is it?"

I looked. It was something quite distasteful, something that one couldn't quite call hair but that wasn't exactly pins either. Pins were protruding from a ball of infinitely intertwined hairs. I sat down slowly and stared.

"I undid it to wrap it more tightly, but look at it—it's disgusting. What should I do?"

Indeed, scraps of red lay scattered about. I looked at the expression in my daughter's eyes, which seemed to plead for forgiveness.

"If you go like this, it seems to cry."

Pressed with a sewing instrument, the clump gave off a faint squeak. In turn, a loud creaking seemed about to emanate from inside my head, and to keep my daughter from noticing it, I pressed my hands to my temples. The stiffness traced a path between my temples and settled in.

"How old is this pincushion? I wonder . . ."

I was silent. Over the thirty—or was it closer to forty?—years since my mother married into our family to become my stepmother (and to be referred to by others as a second wife), I had come to know this cushion intimately. Broken pins, bent pins, pins for cotton and silk, futon stitchers, American needles: the cushion had suffered all these, but the pins, embedded in red, still held the charm of childhood. And yet . . .

"I'll take care of this. You needn't bother anymore."

Not waiting to see what would happen, Tamako rose and went to the next room.

Although I was as careful with the needles as if they were poisonous, my fingers fell victim to my fiercely pounding heart and I pricked them several times. No matter how often I pricked them, I persisted in pulling the needles out; no matter how often I pulled, the ball only stiffened more at the core. The one needle that was thrust into my own core—the needle of being a stepdaughter—was surely quivering. Hairs poked out demurely, reluctantly, as if they meant to remain in hiding, and they seemed all but devoured by the needles; yet the needles seemed endlessly wrapped in hair.

I had forgotten the half-done wash, along with everything else. Slowly but without fear, I tried clenching and releasing the ball, which now looked as though it had been reduced solely to hair, and I felt satisfied. My calm made the task of loosening and unraveling the ball easier, and after a time it began to give way. Just then, for the first time, I realized that it might be my mother's hair. Once again feelings rose in my quiet chest. I pulled at the hair, and it made me feel its resistance; then it snapped back, and two or three long strands appeared, one after the other.

Mother's hair was worthy of pride. In abundance, length, color, and shine it was unsurpassable. Ironically, however, it had behaved contrary to the will of its owner. Thick and strong, it could not be done up in the delicate style she desired. As Mother aged and faded, how often was I forced to pick out her dandruff, to help her pull out gray hairs, to dye her hair? Each time Mother would become irritated and lose her temper, and I would get angry. It was the peculiar nature of her hair that each strand was tightly twisted and curved.

Before I realized it, the sun's rays had crossed my lap, and I felt relieved.

Does fallen hair have no age? One would not have believed that for over thirty years this hair had been separated from a living body and pressed into a ball. Although it had developed a slight kink, one would have taken it for hair that had just been pulled from someone's head. It recalled the abundance and texture of innumerable, beautifully brushed strands arranged with a boxwood comb, the excess flowing out from under the hands piling it in bundles.

Suddenly I felt a shock. A hair seemed to move. The wind? I gazed at it. It definitely moved. Glistening in the sun, it seemed to float up ever so slightly and curve. I pulled out another hair from inside the ball, and just as I placed it on a piece of white paper, it took in the sun and, like a dream, gently wafted up, as I thought it might. For a second it looked like a young girl stretching herself: tightly curled up beside a hibachi or a chest of drawers, deeply asleep for the briefest moment, then suddenly awake, lifting her head, looking about, rubbing her back as she wriggles across the tatami—her chest and hips raised slightly, the line from her toes to her fingers stretched taut, a fast pulse of pleasure racing through her, her energy subsiding, and her chest quieting to its original, gentle calm. This was the bewitching figure conjured by the curved hair as it straightened itself out.

The sleeping figure of my young mother, that figure of her behind the rattan blinds in summertime, where she often slept—do I recall that she wore a *yukata* with a pattern of sparrows and bamboo?

She planted her hands on the tatami and rose. Facing away from me, she put her hands in her hair and glanced back at me with a smile.

She looked at me with the face she wore in happy times. "I'm so glad . . . I'm no longer a stepmother." This is what she said. No—this is what I seem to have heard. No—not that either: this is what I had her say. But her voice truly fell from above—truly.

Tamako, in her white cardigan, collected the countless needles in a small glass bottle, and poured in some pungent oil. "Should we bury it or throw it away?"

I warmed myself in the winter sun, but only my body; my feelings had been cleanly stripped away.

"What should we do with the hair?"

"What should we do?"

I hesitated but decided to burn the ball when the fire under the bath was at its peak, in the way we normally disposed of things. There is a certain dignity and power in the roaring of a flame. I wanted to let the hair wither under this dignity, hidden from all eyes, and return to nothingness. This is what I did. But the needles still remain, just as they were, in my needle box.

Without a doubt, Mother smiled and broke loose of the chains of being a stepmother. I, too, should long ago have been freed of being a stepdaughter. When one thinks of it, ours was a relationship that seemed both long and short. The relationship between parent and child lasts vastly longer after they have been separated by death than during their time together alive.

The Black Hems

The sixteen-year-old was stiff with strain. It was Chiyo's first occasion to venture out into public, to be among other people, in place of her mother. She was to attend her uncle's funeral as her mother's surrogate, and she intended to perform her services in a manner befitting an adult. From the moment she left the train, she was nervous. The tension made her lean back and thrust her chest forward as she walked toward the temple.

She wore a sober kimono unsuited to a girl her age and new *tabi*. She had wrapped black strips of cloth around the thongs of her sandals to eliminate as much color as possible from what she wore, but even having done this, she felt ashamed at not wearing proper mourning attire.

"You're still a student, so even if you're not perfectly dressed this will be fine."

The independent-minded daughter of a single parent, Chiyo had accepted her mother's impatient assurances and set out from the house. But after leaving she realized that her odd clothing was inappropriate after all.

She approached the gate to the temple and stopped short. It seemed that an earlier funeral had not yet concluded. An imposing curtain hung along the pebbled pavement, and tables covered in white stretched in a long row. Three men in striped trousers but no jackets were standing about, doing nothing in particular. In front of the entrance to the main hall, three workers fumbled with the clusters of real and artificial flowers arranged in all directions. The hushed temple lay scorched under the sun of a late-July drought, and there was no sign of movement. The ceremony was to be at two, and it was now a little after eleven. Chiyo had figured that it would take a great deal of time to help prepare the funeral bier, but she had not anticipated another funeral ceremony in the morning. She was unsure what to do and chagrined at having come too early. Suddenly she looked up and noticed a sign inside the curtain: "The Ceremony of the Funeral of the Deceased Mr. —" She realized that the present funeral was that not of another family but of her own. But would her own family really have arranged things in such grand style? Chiyo stood there blushing, embarrassed that her uncle's funeral was more elaborate than she had expected. She felt betrayed by her stupid assumption that things would be arranged a certain way.

She was even more humiliated because the three men by the curtain were staring at her, at the little girl standing there by herself, turning bright red. The reception table where the three men stood seemed to Chiyo a barrier gate she could not easily pass through, but awkwardly her feet began to move in their direction. She had utterly lost her poise.

"Today is indeed a sad occasion for all. Both mother and I would have been honored to attend today, but because of her ailment she is indisposed, and I have come in her stead to help in the kitchen or in whatever way I can. Also . . . I am truly ashamed that I have not come in proper mourning attire. Please be kind enough to forgive my everyday clothes."

Although she realized that sweat was pouring down her face, she felt she would fall apart if she wiped it. The atmosphere grew tense. She struggled hard to regain her composure, but the men merely stared at her unblinkingly, without responding, and everyone became ill at ease.

Suddenly a handsome man appeared from the side, bowing low. "I am deeply moved by your sincere expression of condolence. There is still time, so please make yourself comfortable over there. I'll show you the way."

He wore a stiff pleated skirt, through which one could see layers of white on cool black Akashi silk. As he turned toward the reception table, he exclaimed, "Damn it," and in an instant his carefully composed facial expression collapsed entirely, and he became a mere awkward youth, easy to approach.

"I forgot to ask your name."

Chiyo, too, now relaxed.

"I am Chiyo, from Ushigome."

"Ushigome? Uncle Jiro's Ushigome?"

"That's right."

"Oh, is that so?" He was taken aback. "If that's the case, you didn't have to bother with such a formal greeting."

"It came out automatically, exactly as Mother taught me."

"As a matter of fact, I had some help myself last night about how to offer proper condolences, but you're much better than I am. I was so overwhelmed by your words that I blurted out those inappropriate words." He left her at the entrance, and as she arranged his sandals, she wondered who this man was who had behaved so familiarly, and she realized she hadn't asked his name.

Finally, Sakai, who was married to Chiyo's uncle's oldest daughter, drove up. Chiyo, alone in the spacious waiting room, intended to greet him especially politely but, in the end, could say nothing but exactly what her mother had taught her: it was as if she possessed no words of her own. But Sakai answered her with perfect formality, and Chiyo felt satisfied that she had said well everything she had to say. Sakai was the heir of a prosperous provincial family, who had entrusted his affairs to his healthy father and come to Tokyo to live and work. It seemed that he was more intimate with his father-in-law than with his real father. A man of insight and taste, a hard worker, sincere in his dealings with people, he was the best of the men who had married into the family—or, to put it differently, the most highly regarded of all the nieces and nephews related by blood or marriage. That day he was in charge of the funeral.

"Chiyo-san, how can you help? Excuse me for asking, but what can you do?"

Chiyo was nonplussed. There was nothing in particular she could do. "If it's just pouring tea, I think I can manage."

"Well, let's have you do that." With a sigh of relief, Chiyo went off to be among the women.

The relatives had begun to assemble early, and Chiyo became busy pouring tea, although, again and again, the tea she had so troubled to serve went to waste. A teacup set out for a guest who had just arrived would be taken up for a moment and then placed down elsewhere. People moved around exchanging greetings without stopping in one place, and the tea-cups got in the way, as if mischievously. They got knocked around and overturned, and finally one couldn't tell whose cup was whose. Some even went untouched, dust settling on them. Chiyo couldn't help but think the problem was her awkwardness and lack of skill, and she was ashamed of her efforts.

Wanting to do something to dispel that feeling, she sat staring at her lap until she realized that she needed to time her service of the tea. As long as she timed things well, people quickly put their cups to their lips, and some even returned their empty cups and said, "Thank you so much, thank you for your trouble." That made Chiyo happy.

Sakai became busier as the time passed and more people arrived. He was always talking to someone or being talked to; occasionally he consulted with two or three people at the same time. Activity collected around the young man from four corners and extended out from him in four directions. So incessant was it that he was almost to be pitied. The man from earlier, at the reception table, referred to Sakai as Uncle, and Sakai addressed him as Ko, in a superior way that seemed to make him bristle. Chiyo thought that Sakai might be the person who most needed some tea.

"Delicious. Another cup." Spoken to kindly, Chiyo suddenly grasped the essence of working—that it involved discovering the place where one could be of service. Gradually her spirits lifted.

The hearse arrived at the main hall. The principal mourners and close relatives streamed into the waiting room. In the stifling heat, confusion and agitation made the room seem like a whirlpool. Even Sakai was swallowed up by it, so of course the inexperienced Chiyo was absorbed as well. She forgot that she was at a funeral, and she forgot the feeling of sorrow. She continued doing the one thing a fool like her had learned to do—keeping the hot water flowing and devoting herself to offering tea to quench people's thirst. She hadn't noticed that at some point she had become the axis around which all the other women serving tea were spinning.

There was an announcement summoning the mourners to be seated in the main hall. Chiyo changed from chief tea pourer to the niece she really was and lined up with the other female relatives her age. The unmarried among them, as if by agreement, were wearing purple kimonos with white obi that attractively complemented the customary black kimonos worn by the adults. In the midst of this elegance Chiyo remained peaceful, undisturbed by the inferiority she had been prepared to feel about her kimono, worried only by the stains on her *tabi* and by the perspiration on her face. She felt at ease knowing she had been able to accomplish her task, and the objects around her looked pleasing: the flowers and birds painted on the ceiling, the cypress-colored canopy, the dark inner chamber, the coffin covered in gold brocade, the Buddhist altar with the image of the deceased on it. There was even a note from the imperial household, and there were piles of offerings, large *masakaki* branches—one, two, three of them— profusions of flowers, and mourners overflowing from the seats. At long last, the sadness of the funeral and the feeling of separation seemed to drift in, intensified by the sound of the boys' choir chanting sutras. Sobs could be heard, and the place was awash in tears. Although Chiyo should have been among the most emotional, she looked downward and did not shed a tear. This funeral was different from those she had known, and understanding this seemed to be the final act of love and esteem for her uncle.

The ceremony ended, and Chiyo and Ko stayed to the very end to help. The evening breeze seemed to blow through their bodies, strained from working hard for seven or eight hours.

"You've been very diligent. Thank you." They parted, one to the right, one to the left, and she never learned Ko's family name.

Late in autumn, after the hundred days of mourning had passed, a letter came from Sakai Keiko. It was an invitation to a gathering of those who had worked especially hard at the funeral. All the guests were members of the Sakai household—people from Tokyo, Ko, and even one of the women who had served tea were there. It was clear that the ones who had done the real work at the funeral were not the relatives of the chief mourners but Sakai's maternal relatives. They reintroduced themselves to one another. Just as Chiyo had thought, Ko's family name was Sakai. He had just graduated from school and begun a career, and, like Chiyo, he had been helping at a funeral for the first time.

"You really surprised me. How can I put it? It's just that you had . . . you had an incredible way of doing things—you were so poised. Anyway, everyone was very surprised, and the answer I'd worked so hard to memorize disappeared before I could get it out."

Although she liked his exaggerated, energetic, friendly way of speaking, she wanted to tell him to stop talking about that time. She laughed with him, but she was a bit annoyed. Ko wouldn't stop.

"There were all those people there, and even some men in everyday clothes, but there was nobody else who apologized for what they were wearing. Next time I wear a casual jacket or informal kimono to a funeral, I'll remember your words: 'I have not come in proper mourning attire.' You were just magnificent, Chiyo. I really admired you. I was wearing borrowed clothes, too—my uncle's—so I was touched."

"No, please. Those were words my mother taught me. If they were dignified words, it's because Mother is dignified. If I told her how much she's been praised, she'd be overjoyed."

Whether on purpose or just naturally, Ko seemed to create an atmosphere of gaiety at the gathering. Chiyo might have let her mind wander and ignore his remarks, but because she herself was being talked about she listened intently. His frankness came out in a light, easy manner. The sake began to affect him, and he did a merciless imitation of Chiyo's gestures and voice. Finally Sakai told him he had gone too far, and he became quiet immediately, but soon after he grew boisterous again, as if to prove that he could control his alcohol.

For a daughter accustomed to eating alone with her mother, the gathering, with its animated goings-on, was memorable. Chiyo was happy to be seated between the hosts, and she enjoyed the many dishes served, but what pleased her most was the warm atmosphere enveloping her—the only outsider in the group—as if she were the daughter of every person there.

"It's really nothing at all, but Sakai says he'd like to give you a memento to commemorate your meeting." It was chilly in the hallway leading to the host couple's room, and the night seemed to have grown considerably darker. There was no scroll hanging in the *tokonoma,* just a planted yellow chrysanthemum.

"Ko says some silly things. Please don't let him bother you. He's not a very serious person. . . . Everyone in my family feels that your behavior was admirable, and we're all very grateful that you worked so generously for us."

Such a sincere sentiment and manner—could she only experience this now, for a few brief moments? Chiyo felt that when she looked back on this day it would be a good memory from her youth.

"And so, well, to put it another way, perhaps we can call this a memento of Chiyo-san's sixteenth year."

The gift was a faceted silver-plated makeup bowl, with her initials carved on the cover. Apparently it had been Keiko's idea. Somehow Chiyo felt that her uncle's funeral, though it had left its mark on her, was now completely over.

But it wasn't that there were no more funerals; indeed, Chiyo's connection to funerals was just beginning. Her paternal and maternal aunts, her uncles, grandparents, and other relatives numbered close to fifty, and counting those who had married into the family, along with their children, there were a great many more, so something was always happening somewhere. She could get away with not attending celebrations, but on unhappy occasions peoples' feelings were involved, and they had to be respected. In the spring of the New Year—the celebration of the Seven Spring Herbs had only just passed—her paternal grandmother lost her husband. Until now, Chiyo's mother had seen to such duties and obligations, but Chiyo, who had passed her test as her mother's representative at her uncle's funeral, was sent to attend the wake.

"So we meet again. That was quick."

"That was quick" sounded strange. The Sakais had just returned to their hometown for the New Year visit, and Ko was there to represent them. Seemingly dissatisfied with just offering condolences, he asked if he could help Chiyo with the work, then diligently devoted himself to every task at hand. Naturally the entire family of the deceased grandfather was there, but the grandmother and her branch of the family dominated, perhaps because she was so steady and strong amidst all the commotion. Her strength was no trivial matter, for it was clearly reflected in the people working under her. A subtle shadow had formed in the room: there was a hint of dissatisfaction on the husband's side of the family.

Ko whispered in Chiyo's ear. "If we don't act modest and flatter them, things will turn out bad." At eight o'clock he whispered to her again, "It might be better for us to leave soon. If we say formal good-byes, we'll get stuck here, and that won't do. Go tell those young people over there that you're leaving, as simply as possible." He spoke like an adult. Although only half a year had passed since that other time, his way of speaking had changed drastically; he had become more at ease with himself. Chiyo was so surprised she couldn't keep up with him. He seemed to want to protect her, and it seemed a good idea to do what he said, but when she looked at Ko, now so matured, she remembered Sakai's words: "Your behavior was admirable . . . a memento of Chiyo-san's sixteenth year." Chiyo stayed until ten, just as her mother had told her to, said goodbye to her grandmother, and left. At this funeral she no longer thought of the reception table as a barrier, nor did she apologize for her everyday clothes. Ko, too, had become closer with her side of the family, and people jokingly told him they would be happy to have him stand in for Sakai the next time.

A third misfortune made the joke come true. It was as if a special period of tragedy had begun for the family. This time it was the death of the eldest brother of the main house, but because of the age difference, he was more like an uncle than like a cousin to Chiyo, and they had not been close. The experience of assisting at two successive funerals for cousins with whom she was not particularly close and whose deaths caused her little distress gave Chiyo an understanding of the role of a woman at an ordinary funeral. While serving tea, Chiyo had quickly learned the practical aspects of the funeral ceremony—the way one decided on the arrangements with the spouse and family, handled the condolence callers and the kitchen helpers, or figured out the amount of food necessary. Although none of the tasks was particularly hard, they required considerable energy and expense because no procedure had been agreed on. When Chiyo asked, "Can't something be done about this?" Ko laughed and said, "Just go try asking one of them that. They'll tell you to stop talking like you're at a girls' school graduation. If you ask the older people, you're almost sure to be ignored."

Had it not been for misfortune she, as her mother's representative, and Ko, as Sakai's, would never have met. When Chiyo graduated from school, she said to her mother, "From now on I'll be making more and more condolence calls, so instead of a graduation gift couldn't you get me a formal mourning kimono?"

"What are you saying? That's not something you have made without a specific occasion in mind. I've never heard of such a thing . . . instead of a graduation gift!"

Mother and daughter fought only briefly before the mother gave in. She asked Chiyo to have the kimono be purple, if not white, but Chiyo resisted and stubbornly requested good black material because she intended to wear it her whole life. The mother was regretful: "Are you listening to me? I am not responsible for this."

Unfortunately, the new outfit seemed to have been made in anticipation of the death of Sakai's younger brother. Chiyo's mother knew he had come to Tokyo for medical treatment and had been living in the suburbs. When she heard the news, she reminded Chiyo of her superstition. "You see what you've done? It's as if you've called this terrible thing upon him." Chiyo pretended not to hear and ran her hand across the shiny black kimono. There were two layers, and they fit snugly. Even with mourning garb, there was the joy that comes with newness.

Although her mother objected to the outfit, she said, "Whatever one wears one must do so when young. It's strange to say this suits you or is pretty, but it really is awfully nice." The silk gave off a dry rustle as she rubbed it.

Ko, who for a long time had been wearing his own formal suit, teased her, saying, "My, Chiyo-san, you're not going to greet me by saying you've had formal wear made for you, are you? In black you look all the more intelligent." He spoke to her as he always did.

The makeshift funeral—the formal ceremony was to be performed in the deceased's home village—was a sad affair. As if to combat the sadness, Chiyo worked as hard as she could, under Keiko's direction. She had only met the deceased five or six times, and very briefly, but for some reason this ceremony, more than any other she had assisted at, left her with a feeling of sorrow that slowly penetrated her heart. Could the sorrow Sakai felt for his sickly younger brother have reached Chiyo as well? Or was it that the dead man's misfortune itself was painful to her? The sadness of the funeral could be understood in various ways, even by this young girl of limited experience.

A week later, two postcards of winter scenes came from Ko one after the other. Chiyo had never received mail. "A ceremony in the morning. Many elders of the family are here, and they're very strict about customs; I feel I'm going to suffocate. And these country women, whom I haven't seen in a long time, are so slow and interfere so much I can't stand it. The cousin who is working with me is the worst of all, and I feel like this is going to drag on forever. Far from helping with the ceremony, she's just a nuisance. If it's going to be like this, I'd be much better off alone. It's wrong of me to be thinking of you here, but I must tell you how happy I would be to be in Tokyo now, receiving your kind help. I imagine we will meet up again sometime in the future, and when we do I feel I must express to you my deepest gratitude."

But before they had a chance to meet again at another funeral, Chiyo heard from Keiko of Ko's marriage. She wondered with amusement if he had worn that formal suit he always wore. Apparently her mother had sent him a gift.

Chiyo, for her part, had work to do. Even her mother, who worried that women who worked too much missed their chances to marry, became accustomed to a regular income and could no longer tell her daughter to quit. Spring passed and autumn came, and after a year, another year went by. Chiyo's marriage was put off later and later, leaving a sadly fresh girl behind. When a woman passes age twenty-five, her internal beauty and glow increase, but youth vanishes from the lines of her shoulders and back. Age sneaks in from places the mirror doesn't show, and decay begins to spread from unnoticed corners.

A black kimono now seems most becoming. Every time Chiyo wore her mourning garb, she shone with beauty. The artless, natural appearance of sadness had its effects: in her words of condolence and in her burning of incense she had acquired experience, and she came to be known as the woman of the double-layered black kimono, distinct from all the other women. At times she even looked more like a mourner than the chief mourner herself. At work she was called the Black Princess, and she was always the one sent to make arrangements when something needed to be taken care of. Wherever she went she was helpful. At funeral ceremonies, in particular, she left an impression on people in even the smallest matters, and that impression later deepened into an opportunity for establishing personal relationships. The gossip, however, was annoying. "How nice to be that kind of woman. You get by with one mourning outfit as your entire dowry. If you go to just one funeral, somebody flirts with you, and if that turns into marriage, you've earned your room and board for life."

Chiyo, ever fastidious, ignored the gossip and seemed to grow more determined. Keiko was sorry about this and let a comment slip in the course of conversation.

"There was a time when Ko wanted to marry you, but my husband was vehemently opposed. He disliked Ko's frivolness and said Ko wasn't good enough for you and would only bring you unhappiness. He wouldn't have interfered if the two of you had decided to go ahead with it, but he refused to act as go-between. But Ko is doing very well now. He's the head of a department at his company, and he's making money from a business he started in his spare time. I feel bad that you didn't get together."

Chiyo was forced to listen, but she felt hardly anything at all about herself personally; instead, she felt angry at Sakai for objecting to the match and doubtful about Ko for being so susceptible to what Sakai said.

"I haven't seen him in a while. Not seeing him means there haven't been any funerals in a while."

"That's true, but you might be seeing him soon. Eiko's doing very poorly." Eiko was Keiko's youngest sister. She had married into the Sakai family, but since marrying she was always ill; whenever Chiyo visited her she was sleeping restlessly in a room with round windows.

When Chiyo finally saw Ko, he had grown stout and had developed the exaggerated swagger of a gentleman of means. What hadn't changed was his old gabbiness and charm.

"This is not the place to say it, but there are many things I want to congratulate you for. You've married, had two children, become a department head, done well with your business—that's five things right there to congratulate you for."

"You really do know everything, don't you?" His white teeth gleamed as he smiled.

"That's right, I know everything—big and small, bad and good, everything." It was just for the briefest of moments, but she felt something like panic. It was just a moment, too short for her to be sure.

"Really?" Ko's look was intent, almost shamelessly so. "You probably don't know—I've been unhappy."

"You? Unhappy?"

"Yes. These days I'm somehow restless, unsettled, and that's making me unhappy. I'm fed up with things. I can't stand it anymore."

"That's because you've been too fortunate. Aren't you saying you're fed up with being satisfied? What a luxury."

"Don't be sarcastic. You've always had that habit. You once even told me I had a natural talent for sugarcoating things." That was something even Chiyo remembered having said. She said he was good at noticing people's faults, crushing them as small as possible, covering them with a thick sugar coating, trimming them neatly, and merrily serving them up.

"In any case, you're the one who said 'Forgive me for not wearing a mourning kimono.' I'll never match you at that." Here it comes again, Chiyo thought, as she stood up and moved away. Keiko confided to her that her husband was extremely upset about Ko and disturbed that Ko was not keeping in touch.

But Ko, in his usual diligent way, performed all the tasks of the funeral ceremony with great skill and seemed to be suppressing the self-satisfaction of a man on the road to success.

"Chiyo-san, hasn't there been something recently to congratulate you for?" he asked. How perceptive he was. She hadn't even told her mother, but just the day before, she had decided in her heart to get married.

At first, Chiyo's married life was paradise, but in the end it was a dismal failure. With enormous appetite she had devoured the happiness of her new marriage, a happiness she had denied herself through the long unmarried years. Her husband was good-natured but weak-willed, and, having received a small inheritance from his parents, he lacked the energy for getting on in the world. After two years, about the time their child was born, things went awry for his supposedly superior wife. Love faded for both of them, leaving only a lingering regret, which kept their love from dissipating completely, and all they could do was bicker. Then the family finances suffered, and life pressed down on them.

But when this happened, Chiyo's character asserted itself gallantly. Alone, Chiyo devoted herself to recovering the losses, and, ashamed of her ruin, she stopped communicating with her relatives and friends. For ten years she was completely cut off from everyone. The couple's discord, despair, and poverty made their life for those ten years seem like being encircled in a stockade, and the only memento of the past that remained in the midst of their straitened circumstances was her mourning kimono. Even at a used-clothing store, it would have had no value. Often Chiyo thought of turning it into a cloak. Having escaped being cut up and used as a cloak, however, the mourning kimono finally draped Chiyo's shoulders for the first time in many years on her husband's death. Their dark married life, which she had not been able to sever, ended naturally then, and she wore the mourning kimono thinking that this black curtain might bring it to a clearer close. And yet for some reason she broke down, and the tears poured down her face as they never had before.

Her mother—whose complaints had continued to increase—lamented her daughter's decline: "You're wearing the same funeral kimono as always, but you have none of your former glow."

A year later, the kimono was of use again, when the famous doctor who had checked her husband's pulse at his death died. Her husband had had an unusual disease with a long German name and had received the doctor's finest care before leaving this world, so Chiyo was deeply grateful to him. The doctor's funeral was held in the research lab of his university. On the dark, forestlike campus, the crowd of mourners filed through the trees, circled around the edge of the pond, and continued up to the sidewalk of the building. It was a hushed, impressive funeral procession. When, after burning her incense, Chiyo left to catch her train, she saw Ko standing outside. He was wearing a brand-new formal suit and was accompanied by a personal chauffeur.

"I noticed you so I waited." Since he didn't once mention her life these last years, she realized he must already know everything.

"You and I had only one enjoyable time together," he said during their few minutes together as he drove her home. "After Aunt Keiko's father died, there was that banquet at Sakai-san's house. That was the only time. In those days, funerals were somehow interesting things—having nothing to do with me personally."

With her meager means, a senile mother, a child, an ever-diminishing sense of purpose, and the increasing prospect of defeat in the war, Chiyo had less and less reason to go on. The days went by, empty and fleeting. Soon the air raids came, and everything was scorched to ashes. Those who managed to survive waited in fear of dying in the flames, but could not relinquish their attachment to life. The feeling was horrible.

A siren screamed just as dawn broke one day, yet amidst all the noise she heard Ko's voice calling to her. Sakai had been injured, he said, and Chiyo must go with him immediately. Sakai had taken temporary refuge in the next district but had decided two nights before that it was safer to return to his home village the following day. The news that he had been caught in an air raid had just come.

Ko asked Chiyo to ride with him. She noticed that his car was a military vehicle and that he was wearing the yellow uniform of the civilian army. The figure of Ko in such an outfit, leaning over the driver's seat and barking orders, seemed to her pitiful.

The village by the sea was a heap of smoldering cinders. Sakai was being attended to in a former lumber warehouse on the outskirts of town. He lay on the bare wooden floor with no futon under him and only a military blanket over him. Keiko was grasping his hand. Chiyo and Ko made it there in time to witness him take his last breath. The scene was profoundly sad. His proud nose was chiseled on his miraculously untouched face, and his thick, placid eyebrows, always steady, had been singed.

Ko worked as if possessed, and although everything was a shambles, he managed to do all that was required in this most common of events. There was, of course, no wake, nor were any of the other ceremonies observed. Even the offerings to the deceased had to come out of rations. As there were many pine trees in the area, the mourners made do with cones instead of flowers: that was the sole way of comforting the deceased. Because burial was the regional custom, there was only one crematorium in the area, and it was far away, in the mountains.

The deceased, Keiko, and the rest traveled by truck to the crematorium, where they were met by a wild-haired old woman.

"You men carry the coffin and put it into the oven."

Chiyo joined the men of the Sakai family, who had been there two or three times before, and, with the strength of a man, took up a corner of the casket. Her pain was pleasurable. Nobody else lived there but the wild-haired woman, and Keiko and the rest waited uneasily on the veranda of her house. The pines whistled, the sun began to set, and after a long wait the woman said, "The ashes are ready." She pulled the iron tray out of the oven with a clatter and rested it on a handcart, then roughly took it through the darkness out into the open. Flames too large to be called embers drew the fresh breeze and came together in a blaze: the scene resembled the screens depicting hell, with the old witch-hag pulling the carriages of fire. Ko said something to her. The hag turned her red face to him and barked, "Don't be a fool. I'm doing this out of kindness to you. Without a fire, do you think the women could see their way? I could, but then I'm used to it."

After making a token gesture of gathering the bones, Keiko became faint, and people helped her away. Only Ko and Chiyo remained. The thick, wirelike chopsticks heated up quickly, and it was hard to pile up the bones rapidly enough. The woman watched them from where she sat at the base of a tree and laughed to herself.

"Hee hee hee hee. This gentleman and this lady are not married, are they? I can smell it."

Ko cast a sidelong glance at Chiyo, who had stiffened and put down the chopsticks, and, with his face like a red demon's in the flickering flames, calmly continued gathering the bones. The woman brushed together the embers that remained and placed them in the urn. As she splashed water over them, white smoke rose with a hiss. Ko brusquely marched up to her. "I'll give you as much as you want. How much extra do you want?" Chiyo ground her back teeth and tried to listen to the wind whistling high in the tree tops in the darkness behind her, but she couldn't keep her eyes off Ko's back.

After returning from the seaside, Chiyo took to her bed for a time. Though there was really nothing wrong with her, she couldn't sleep and had no appetite. She tried not to think about it, but the crematorium haunted her; the stench lingered in her nose. A note came from Keiko saying she had returned to her husband's village in the provinces. The New Year began, Hiroshima was destroyed, and the war ended. On the very day it did, Chiyo was the lead mourner at a funeral in her own house, which had survived the flames. She was sending her mother off. She hoped Ko might come, but only the neighborhood people had been informed of the funeral. Although she had a summer mourning kimono, she thought it sufficient to wear her black cotton trousers, say a brief prayer, offer strong incense, and perform both her country's funeral and her mother's at the same time.

When the three years of mourning for Sakai had passed, Keiko came up to Tokyo.

"Have you heard about Ko? Something terrible has happened. He's disappeared." The reasons Sakai had shunned Ko in his later years had become clear after the war. Ko had committed a number of crimes. "The more you hear, the worse the things he plotted seem. After all, you remember how extravagantly he used to live."

Sensing he had come to the end and fearing arrest, Ko had hidden himself here and there until he had finally come to a cliff on the seacoast, very near his family's home, and disappeared. Ko knew how to drive, but where had he got the car and why had he driven it there? That Ko had been in the car was certain; the townspeople who discovered it found it with its front wheels just over the edge of the cliff, and there were marks showing undeniably that he had jammed on the brakes. Where had the man gone who had so narrowly escaped death? Chiyo listened to the story and could feel the car as it screeched to a halt. The police and the Sakai family, concluding that he had probably committed suicide by throwing himself into the sea, continued to search at great expense; he remained missing, though, his body nowhere to be found. What he might have done after stopping the car was easier to imagine than the crimes he had committed. Chiyo felt as if a wave of fear and sadness were coiled around her.

"So there hasn't even been a funeral," said Keiko.

Chiyo's last and eldest uncle passed away. The day of the funeral, Chiyo began preparing herself forty minutes ahead of time—ten minutes to wash her face, brush her hair, and change her clothes, twenty minutes to relax on the way, leaving ten minutes when she arrived. The forty minutes was plenty of time, more than she usually needed. The days when she might have vainly gazed into the mirror had slipped away, she didn't know when, so she had no strong feelings about how her face or hair should look. The mirror showed a thin, uninteresting silhouette, and, looking at that reflection, Chiyo dressed herself with no particular interest. Even had there been a cushion to sit on, she would merely have knelt in front of the mirror, as was her habit.

She ran her hand over the black layers of kimono covering her white undergarments, tied a waist cord, adjusted the collar, tightly secured the undersash and obi, and fastened herself with a single braided black cord. Her funeral self was now complete. She was so accustomed to wearing this outfit that she dressed herself more by relying on the feel of it over every part of her body than by looking in the mirror. But even so, she bent down to look at the area of her chest and twisted around to see the crookedness of the line down her back. When, satisfied, she started to rise, her hems hung down to reveal a vague discoloration on the white of her crisp new *tabi*. The hems had worn completely through, and in some places their lining was soiled gray and hung down like a sagging bridge. The housekeeper, realizing she was in for a scolding, spoke up quickly, as if defending herself from the sharp gusts of a harsh wind.

"I just noticed it as I was preparing it for you. . . . Fuki-san has been taking care of your clothes, so I had no idea. I had no time to fix it. I just didn't know what to do. . . ."

The old woman was right about the hem's needing fixing: there was no way Chiyo could go out looking like she did.

"How many minutes are left?"

"Excuse me?"

"The time! How much time?"

"I see. Shall I go look in the sitting room?"

The bothersome old lady. Prod her and there was no response. But Chiyo had given herself only ten minutes to prepare, so she knew the time without asking.

"Never mind. Scissors, get me the scissors. Can I do it in three minutes?"

"Excuse me? Do what?"

"Scissors! Hurry!"

"There, in the drawer of the mirror stand."

"Not these! These are nail clippers. I need the shears."

"Excuse me? You're going to cut it?"

"Just get me the sewing box." As Chiyo spoke, she undid the braided cord and obi, and now, dressed only in her white undergarments, she tossed both sleeves of the kimono in the air, so it looked like a bat flying up, and threw it down on the tatami. She opened the scissors wide as she cut into the hems.

"You're being so rough."

The cloth made a sound, as if resisting. "There's nothing else to do." As she got to the side seam, the scissors hesitated, the cloth resisted, and as she continued, the sound of the cutting, too, seemed like a protest. Unmoved, Chiyo put more force into her thumb.

"Don't sit there staring into space! Thread a needle with black thread. There's no time left!"

White silk now protruded below the hems, whose lopped-off edges coiled on the mat like a long, dead snake. Irritated, Chiyo grabbed the thread from the old woman, who was scurrying about nervously, but Chiyo couldn't thread the needle without her glasses. Although she didn't look angry, she snatched them up. With quick basting stitches, Chiyo made rough seams sufficient to bring the front and back together. The old double-layered kimono gave off a final murmur of protest.

How much time had passed? But there was no point worrying about how long she had taken. It had probably been about three minutes. When she draped the kimono over her shoulders and straightened the front, the warmth passed through her *tabi* to her feet. "I'm a bit late, so please call a car."

After making the call, the old woman sat down solidly on her heels.

"Is something wrong?" Her eyes seemed to swell. "What's wrong?"

Chiyo knelt and looked into the old woman's eyes, and it was clear that the old woman was crying.

"It's nothing. But suddenly . . . well, I felt something in my chest."

"What was it?"

"You're about to leave. Perhaps we can talk about it later."

Tying her obi, Chiyo said, "I don't know what's going on, but if you put it off until I come back, won't it bother me the whole time? Did I do something I should worry about?"

"It's nothing, really, but Madam, please have a new mourning kimono made."

"Why should I?"

"I can't tell you how I felt when I saw you cutting it up. To do what you did to a kimono—I couldn't imagine doing it myself." The old woman fumbled with the black snake, its bowels dangling out, and dragged her hands across it. "They say it's bad luck to have a mourning kimono made with no specific occasion in mind, and when I thought that I might be the reason for your making a new kimono, a feeling welled up in me and the tears began to flow. Madam, please take care of everything when the time comes."

The old woman's feelings were perhaps justified. She was old, and the sight of a woman in her fifties in her white undergarments, brandishing shears and cutting the hems of a black mourning kimono . . . the old woman's brittle nerves probably couldn't stand it. In her hurry to be on time for the funeral, Chiyo had wound up showing a living person the specter of her own funeral. It was at times like this that the intensity of a woman living alone revealed itself.

"You're right. Maybe I should have a new one made. But why don't we promise to put off both your funeral and mine for a while?"

She grabbed her handbag as if kidnapping it and went out to the car. She could see the old woman's bowed head. The wide car windows let in an abundance of sunlight. How troubling a woman's kimono was. A man could have formal clothes made for happy occasions as well. Yes, he would be the perfect person to see just now. . . .

Ko . . . he had owned a fine formal suit. But what had happened to it?

Now that she looked at her mourning kimono carefully, she could see it was badly worn. Should she have a new one made? Where would she wear it? After she had seen off her uncle today, there would be nobody left of the older generation. There were plenty of cousins, but they were all quite young. A distant relative perhaps? There were many distant relatives. And yet, now that she counted, there was nobody left for her to see off. She had seen them all off, and she realized that indeed she was seeing off the last of the line today. That was the truth—she had finally seen them all off. How many more years could this mourning kimono last? To make do, she had been rough with it today, but if she mended it better and wore it more carefully, it might last even after she died. Are the life of a mourning kimono and that of a woman the same?

No, you should make a new one. There's still one important event left. You should go to your own funeral in a brand-new one. Ko could have made a joke like that. There's nobody who will come to my funeral, but perhaps, might it be possible, that he, Ko, would appear? What would he look like? Would he be joking, as usual? I'd be happy if he were serious. Then, and only then, I'd be able to accept him entirely. Only bad things were said about him, but they were all things between him and other people. However bad he was to others, I don't remember ever being mistreated by him. He's my friend, my funeral friend.

The car entered the residential area, and even in the city the early summer breeze was pleasant. Chiyo felt light, felt that she wanted her funeral friend to remain a good friend. They had been a man and a woman who met at various places, and only in times of misfortune, to work together as partners for two or three days. They were friends who said goodbye when their job was done and then disappeared from each other's lives. I am the only one left, she thought. Riding in the car, Chiyo recalled all the years from the tender age of sixteen to now . . . a man and a woman meeting only at funerals—perhaps her experience was that of a whole generation of Japanese women.

"Ma'am, we're on time. You still have two minutes."

"Thank you very much. You may go." She quickly wrapped some money in paper and gave it to the driver. "This is for cigarettes." But she felt that being on time no longer mattered. As she entered the open gate, she met the son of a cousin, who was standing at the mourner's register.

"Am I on time?"

"What?"

"Don't be so absentminded. It's time, isn't it?"

"Oh, time." His cuffs were immaculate under his dark blue sleeves. "Yes,

Aunt, you're just on time, as always. I've been trying to get everything ready on time, to get it all done on time. That's all I've been doing, so, when you suddenly asked me if you were on time, I was startled. I thought I was having a strange hallucination, that you, too, were telling me to get something ready on time."

The boy put his hands on his waist, stretched his upper body, and took a deep breath. "It's my first time to help at a funeral—funerals are full of things that have to be done on time, aren't they? Everything has to be on time. That's not exactly what I mean. Funerals are full of things that aren't on time. That's right, full of things not on time. Isn't that so, Aunt?"

Ah, how young this child is, Chiyo almost said. They were standing at the entrance to the kitchen, and there was a sound of water and dishes at their backs, but around the boy an aura of carefree youth, unburdened by household chores, shone like a beam.

Through the layers of green leaves deep inside the garden, a balmy summer breeze drifted in with a glimmer. The air passed through Chiyo's hastily mended black hems. She felt that a calm—a funereal calm, the calm of a person's having died—had begun to settle under the roof of the house.

Dolls

It is said that the female dolls that every family exhibits during the Doll Festival are made to look like the reigning empress, but is this true? The dolls usually come in sets of fifteen, and the twelve arrayed on the top tiers of the display—the emperor and empress, three ladies-in-waiting, five musicians, the ministers of the right and the left—are presented as the most beautiful men and women conceivable. Only the three attendants arranged on the bottom tier—the lowest in social class—resemble ordinary people. Compared to the faces of the twelve elegant dolls, their faces are imperfect, almost comical. A face that is slightly ugly seems familiar to us, and a somewhat vulgar expression makes us feel truly alive and at ease. The other twelve dolls are crafted too precisely and too perfectly. In short, it is as though the charmingly ugly dolls were added to the set to create a harmony of disharmony. Nevertheless, if a nose was too flat or a forehead projected too much or an expression seemed too homely, a doll would, presumably, not be well received. It is human to want to make everything beautifully and well, so it is interesting that the three ordinary dolls, though delicately made, are part of this group.

We can understand how artisans came to portray such humble people, who exist in great numbers everywhere, and how they produced such an animated effect. But it is mysterious to me how the visage of a distant empress, higher above us than the clouds, is transferred to the face of a doll. The custom of displaying dolls occurs as far back as *The Tale of Genji,* and I hear that our practice of setting them up on the third day of the third month goes back centuries, to the Muromachi era. Yet when I once asked whether doll makers of the past might have seen the empress up close, one person hypothesized that the model was not the empress herself but the first lady of the Tokugawa family, because the Tokugawas were more important than the imperial family. In any case, she would have been the premier lady of an isolated Japan, a woman shielded behind fences. It is not likely that her august visage could have been reproduced in an age without photographs.

Having said this, however, I have to admit that, when someone points out that a doll resembles the empress, I have to agree. The doll of my own childhood resembled the Meiji empress. She had a slender face with eyes gently raised at the corners, a stiff face, to tell the truth. My daughter's dolls were made in 1930 or 1931, and perhaps I imagine it, but they somehow resembled the reigning Showa empress. The area around the eyes and cheeks, the line of the jaw were like hers. The features of my daughter's dolls, too, are plumper and softer than my dolls'. I've never heard anything similar about the features of the male dolls. No one claims that they are modeled on the Meiji emperor or the emperor of today. They simply represent the essence of masculine beauty.

I recently saw the film *Roman Holiday,* and what first struck me about the up-and-coming Miss Hepburn was that hers was a face from days gone by. I didn't know why what young people see as a new face seemed to me a face from the past. But when the movie ended, I suddenly realized that yes, the makeup at the corners of those eyes made her look like the Meiji empress. Movies are today's tales of princesses, and I had thought of the photograph of the empress taken fifty years earlier. Miss Hepburn's makeup artist most certainly did not consult the beautiful face of the Meiji empress, but perhaps in attempting to convey refined, imperturbable dignity, he hit upon the idea of using eye shadow to create almond-shaped eyes. I may have discovered the similarity to the Meiji empress by coincidence, but it seems to me that ideal beauty transcends time and national boundaries. People always pursue beauty. The Meiji empress was exquisite, and I can well imagine that she might have been the model for a doll. After the Meiji era, photographs became common, and a doll maker could, in any event, have glimpsed the empress through the window of her palanquin if he had slipped in among her attendants along the route during an imperial visit or the like.

Women are much younger than men when they become parents. Unless she is unusually serene, a woman is exhilarated when she has her first child. With the energy of youth she persists in her headlong way of doing things and ends up making old people tremble. I, too, in the happiness of having a child, wanted to express limitless love. The expression of love between child and parent after the child becomes an adult and the signs of affection and romance between men and women, between married people, are checked in front of other people, but we tend to expect the love for a young child— the affection itself and the expression of it—to be unabashedly free. This way of thinking informs most everyday things, especially annual obser- vances, in which young mothers express their affection single-mindedly, with little thought for others. I'm embarrassed to say it, but I, too, was like that. I felt that as silly an occasion as my daughter's first Doll Festival was somehow a great event, and I wanted to arrange things as perfectly as possible. That's easy to wish, but given my character, wanting to do something always means doing it, and I tended not to be able to separate desire and action.

The Jikkendana was still in business then, so I went there, as well as to all the other department stores, hunting for dolls to display. I made foolish purchases, well beyond my means, but I was vain, and I was obsessed with doing things just so. Although I realized I had done more than was reasonable, I felt justified. With the dolls taken care of, my desires expanded all the more: I wanted a child's small cushion, an especially nice little table and bowls, and lacquer trays. If I could get all these, I would decorate the dolls' platform and the curtain stand. Otherwise the noble faces and splendid clothes of the dolls I had taken so much trouble with would somehow seem naked and plain, and that wouldn't do. I wanted to create shadows there, to hang up a curtain, but ready-made curtains with family crests seemed too common. I imagined the effect of skillfully dyed cherry blossoms on a light green background, and it came to seem that to not have a curtain like that would show my lack of ingenuity. The dyer was sent for, and even though I knew it would be difficult for him to finish in time, I asked him to make a fine curtain of crepe.

The desire to do all I could pulsated through me. On the ceiling I had silk peach flowers, by the edge of the sliding doors I had masses of mustard flowers, on the platform I had a glistening new crimson rug. The food was arranged as well. I carefully wrote out the menu on red-trimmed paper. There were only three guests—my husband's mother and my parents, the grandparents of the child. My preparations were completed, and all that was left was to wait until the following morning. But the dyer had not yet arrived. It was already evening when I called about my order, but I was told that the master and his wife had gone out in the afternoon and had not yet returned. I pressed to speak to someone who knew what was happening, but the person on the phone was evasive and said everyone was out of the house. In the doll display, which was charming down to the last detail, only the space for the curtain yawned mockingly, as though it were a large mouth, and inside that mouth the red and blue beaded-glass headpieces of the female dolls flickered, irritating me beyond endurance. When nine o'clock passed, I could wait no longer. Perhaps the dying wouldn't be done on time. I thought of the emergency measures I might have to take in the morning: I could send the boy out and have him buy an ordinary ready-made curtain, or I could make do with some scrap of cloth lying about the house. It was clear I had no choice but to somehow manage without what I so dearly wanted. The atmosphere in the house became brooding and unpleasant, and even the young nursemaid, who had been playful in the afternoon, was gloomy when she quietly rose to go lock the gate. I had poured ashes over the hot coals in the hibachi and taken off my *tabi* when there was a loud knocking. Although we had already abandoned hope, the young woman and I looked at each other, startled.

"If it pleases you, I have come with your order." The peculiar, old-fashioned speech of the dyer made it hard to be suspicious, but in the light of the entryway, the man on the bicycle looked quite unusual. There was an ungroomed black beard around his mouth, and a small nose sat firmly on his haggard face. The expression in his eyes was so grim I couldn't even ask what the matter was; his utter exhaustion was obvious. As he passed through to the sitting room, he made lengthy apologies for his lateness.

"It was a rush job, but the dye has come out quite well. Would you please inspect it to make sure?" In a flash, cherry blossoms scattered on to the tatami, sparkling brilliantly, but somehow his hollow tone strained my patience. I had felt annoyed at him all afternoon.

"What happened? Something must have happened for you to be this late."

The dyer looked at me sternly, said yes, and fell silent.

The dyer worked with his wife, who was a seamstress. She was very skillful and strong-minded and didn't take on apprentices. But she did look after a fair number of girls whom she thought she could set up as professional seamstresses one day. The couple were not the typical Tokyo man and Kyoto woman but the reverse, a Tokyo woman and a Kyoto man, and they got along well, although neither would give in to the other at work. The day before, their daughter had been sluggish since early morning, and the wife, finishing a quick sewing job and giving a sewing lesson, said she couldn't look after her. A fight erupted. The husband lost the argument and felt belittled. He took the child out to urinate, but no matter how he tried to humor her, she would not stop wailing. "You're always spoiling her, so she's a spoiled brat at times like this, too," he yelled at his wife. Without meaning to, he deflected his anger to the child and gave her a slap on her bare buttocks. All night long the child moaned, and in the morning she grew feverish. They hugged her and carried her on their backs, but she continued to wail. She was just big enough to stand while holding on to something but, of course, couldn't speak yet. When the doctor came around noon, they were shocked to find that the husband's open hand had left clear red marks on the baby's little behind. The doctor gave the chilling diagnosis: "A needle." The father had unluckily hit the child where a needle was stuck in her body and had driven it farther in. With a great commotion the assistants helped prepare to move the child to the hospital. The strong-minded wife broke down and was no help at all. The husband, usually easily handled by his wife, had said to her at the end of their fight, "All you need to do is be careful with the needles until the child grows up, and I'll put up with all your complaints." The operation took place as soon as the little girl entered the hospital. A short, thick needle for cotton was biting into her hipbone, its head broken off. The bone had been scraped.

"I kept putting my ear to the door of the operating room, but I couldn't hear a thing. I'm sure that's because everything went well, and that's why. . . ." The charcoal that had been added to the hibachi glowed, and a burning smell drifted up. My body tensed as I listened to the story.

It was March, but only the beginning of the month. The bicycle light wove through the alleys, and the dyer disappeared. When people say that frost is coming on or ice is forming, is it weather like this that they mean? In that brief moment by myself, as I saw the dyer off, the lingering winter weighed on my stiffened shoulders. The coldness seemed heavy, and I felt that a corner had crumbled off my joy. I had been looking forward to having my parents come to the Doll Festival the following morning.

The next day the three old people enjoyed half a day of celebration. They noticed the trouble I had taken, and they all praised me. It was as if they were giving me a report card with high marks. They found the curtain especially beautiful. I looked at my daughter and thought of the operation on the dyer's child, and somehow their praise pricked me. I left the child's story untold.

The day after, I got a phone call from my father's house. Naturally it was to thank me for the invitation, but it was also to tell me to come see him— that was the message from my father. I couldn't guess what I was wanted for, but I felt deep down that I would be scolded. Father was unusually genial, first thanking me for the day before and expressing his appreciation for my efforts. "Was that all your own work? Or did you do it together with your husband?"

"He's the one who suggested inviting you, but I did everything else."

"Was the buying of the dolls also your doing?"

"Yes."

"Your husband had nothing to say about it?"

I had no way of answering. I had gone way over our budget, and my husband was feeling pinched. Father seemed to have guessed.

"Everything was done too thoroughly and perfectly. It's good to do the best you can when you have guests, but it seems to me that's not quite the way to use your energy. I wanted to talk to you about that. Of course, a woman who can't get things done lacks something. But a woman who exhausts herself and finds that she has nothing left, only emptiness, lacks something as well. Fortunately, you seem to have the strength to accomplish a great deal, but when you have exhausted yourself, what remains? You insisted that it was all for the child, but for all your efforts, what was left for the child? Everyone is allotted a portion of good fortune, but I think there is a limit. When a parent uses everything up so recklessly, shouldn't she fear for her child's future? Luxury is not in the availability of things but in their use. What you did was inappropriate for your child, and in my opinion, you even took something away from her. Your mother-in-law is a very proper woman, so she sincerely appreciated your skill, but what she considers skill, I consider a foolish way of using everything up. At the very least, I wanted to clarify my feelings on the matter."

Father's words were gentle. He said "exhausted yourself" when he wanted to say "wasted your time and money," and he disguised his true feelings by not saying "overdoing it" but saying instead "doing the best you can." But his words hit a painful spot. His logic found its way into me, and as it did, I experienced something akin to the heaviness and crumbling I had felt at the gate when I saw the dyer off. And yet, emotionally, I could not give in so easily. Although I had had to squeeze out every bit, the money hadn't been borrowed; and to receive complaints after using my own money, my own energy, my own body, to host a celebration did not seem right. His "took something away from her"—what worse could one say? The unfairness seemed plain to me. My father's tone also implied that I had better hurry to my mother-in-law's home and apologize for my clumsy way of overdoing things. Although I didn't accept what he had said, I went to see her.

The train ride helped. As the train shook its way through the afternoon city, the long, straight line of the passengers' indifferent faces mysteriously soothed me. It was as tranquil as a field of onion flowers in a gentle breeze. I sat there thinking, feeling as if blue skies were clearing above my head. What hurt most, after all, was being told that I had a parent's selfish desire to spend money on herself while claiming it was for the child. The phrase "using everything up" also hurt. My need to achieve more than was necessary had bothered my father. The benign impulse to do the best I could had wound up becoming a stubborn compulsion. But some things can't be helped, no matter what we say. If I were to place my husband in the onion field before me, I would see nothing but a delicate, tender bald head. He was a small person, and his financial means were as slender as a leek. My daughter and I depended on that slender support. That was our situation, but it wasn't worth lamenting. What seemed lamentable now were the too beautiful, too large dolls I had set up. My love for my husband, my love for my child rose up in me. Why did I do such a thing? That a small effort ended in vanity and need bothered me despite myself. If I peeled one more layer of that disturbing feeling, I would find a pleasurable pride in having imposed my will. If I looked still further, I would surely find a stock of ancient resentment toward my father.

"But Father, when you were young and had your first child, didn't you, too, make a big fuss? All the dolls that Sister had are proof, aren't they? How was it with your second child, me? There weren't any serving girls or musicians, were there? Only a wooden emperor and empress. I was treated as a less important child. Weren't you selfish, too? The reason I was so adamant about overdoing things was that I didn't want Tamako to have such pitiful dolls." My feelings streamed out and stagnated in pools.

My mother-in-law was ten years older than my father. She said, "The truth is, after I returned home that day I had a strange feeling I wanted to describe but couldn't find words for. Your father scolded you for overdoing things. As for me, I wanted you to leave me something for later."

My mother-in-law said that with everything prepared down to the last detail, there was no room for her spirit to enter. If something had been lacking, she might have had the joy of buying it for her grandchild the following year, and she was dismayed that no such joy was possible. She felt that shortcomings provided a better basis for intimacy than perfection did. She couldn't scold someone for not lacking anything; it wasn't right to criticize a daughter-in-law whose heart and hand reached into every corner—indeed, it was something to brag about. But in all honesty, she thought it might have been nice if two or three spaces had been left unfilled for her. Being able to do things well showed skill, but leaving nothing undone brought loneliness.

In her words I heard the honest feelings of an older woman, not just a mother-in-law and a grandmother. Father's words were direct; they said everything that needed to be said, and they convinced the listener, but they also aroused resentment. In my mother-in-law's tone was an intimacy derived from her endless desire to confide her sadness.

In the three years of my marriage to her son, she had praised me for having no faults, which made me feel secure, but now, at this late point, I realized that each time she praised me she endured a loneliness she couldn't articulate to her perfectionist daughter-in-law. As if I had briefly glimpsed my own future in another woman, I yielded to the understanding that was growing in me. The hard feelings I had toward my father softened as I talked with my mother-in-law. When they softened, I quickly lost hold of myself again.

"But what about the dolls I received, Mother?"

She suppressed a smile.

"Well, I understand your complaint, but you should stop letting your bitterness determine your behavior toward Tamako. With your temperament you'll do the same thing with a second and a third child as you did with Tamako. Suppose you had five or six girls? What do you think will happen then?"

I was taken aback. It was utterly stupid of me not to have thought of a second or third daughter. I was flustered. "It's no use. I could never manage that much. Perhaps . . . one child would certainly wind up with only a wooden emperor and empress. There would certainly be a pitiful one like me."

My confusion was embarrassing, and in the end I laughed as my tears fell.

"And that's why you mustn't think of things in such a narrow way," Mother-in-Law concluded, with a smile.

Seven or eight years passed, I divorced my husband, and I took my daughter back to my father's house. Her set of dolls and the accessories were sent to us, along with such things as an empty old chest. Every March the dolls and the curtain stirred my feelings. The years flowed on. Air raids came one after the other, and Tokyo was turned completely inside out. It was not a time to display dolls. Sensing that this was the end, everyone felt compelled to behave in unexpected and unconventional ways. My daughter, a student, enlisted in the student relief organization. Naturally she understood that the dolls would not be brought out this year. And for that very reason, against all common sense, I set up the doll stand as in the past. As always, the twelve dolls sat there in modest grace and elegance while the three attendants smiled vulgarly. But they had all aged a great deal. One doesn't expect dolls to grow old, but their faces were shrunken and pale. The white of their foreheads and cheeks had become transparent, like a cocoon about to open. The once cool and serene black eyes had a look of middle-aged complacency, and they no longer shone.

One small special feature had made me choose these dolls in the first place. Only extremely high-quality dolls have separate fingers. On most dolls, a gap is cut between the thumb and the other four fingers, but on somewhat better dolls, the thumbs and pinkies are separate. Although my dolls were not the very best, the five fingers were distinct. Now the gently elongated slender fingers, perfect for holding a cedar fan, had lost their softness. The ornamental silver-leaf circles on the miniature writing shelf had rusted black, scars had disfigured the brush holder on the writing desk, the brush itself had been eaten by insects, and the handle sat unused. The corners of the go and shogi boards had been rubbed smooth and the pieces scattered. The strings of the koto and the samisen had come loose, the gold and silver lacquer of the flowered horse carriage had dimmed. The curtain, too, was no longer the same—its light green had faded, and the glittering flecks on the cherry blossoms had peeled. How sad that the dolls had grown old and that I, too, had grown old, while my daughter still retained the bloom of youth. It would soon be ten years since I first set up the dolls, but

I could not hope to use them another year. I parted from the dolls with feigned indifference.

In the middle of that March the downtown area was transformed into a field of flames, and people fled the city. By the time we reluctantly decided to escape to the country, trains, trucks, and other transportation had almost all been stopped, but with someone's help we managed to obtain two trucks. First and foremost, our goal was to save all the books and written materials.

My aged and weakened father, unable to choose which materials to evacuate, merely saw the boxes off as they were randomly taken away. Suddenly he turned to me and said, "You're not going to load Tamako's dolls?" His face was peaceful, without a hint of emotion, so I thought for a moment and answered, "We're going to leave them here."

Behind this response were folded the many years and months that had passed. What my father and mother-in-law had said, the dyer's story—these had become a part of me. Only a month or two earlier, in the midst of turmoil, I had gazed intently at the dolls' faces. "But since you mention it, let's ask Tamako as well."

"It would be better to add even one extra book," said Tamako.

Her grandfather replied gently, "Is that so?" And with that, the dolls disappeared forever.

Notes

Chapter 1: Creating a Persona

1. Many literary fathers in Japan produced literary daughters, including Mori Ōgai (1862–1922) and his daughter Mori Mari (1903–), Hirotsu Kazuo (1891–1968) and his daughter Hirotsu Momoko (1918–), Dazai Osamu (1909–1948) and his daughter Tsushima Yūko (1947–), Ueda Mannen and his daughter Enchi Fumiko (1905–), and Yoshimoto Takaaki (1924–) and his daughter Yoshimoto Banana (1964–). Although some of these second-generation writers began their careers writing about their fathers, none seems to have been as troubled by second-generation anxieties as Aya was.

2. In 1956 the film of *Flowing* won the Ministry of Education Award for the Arts; in the same year "The Black Hems" ("Kuroi suso") won the Yomiuri Literature Award, and *Flowing* the Shinchōsha Literature Award; in 1967 the novel *Battle* (*Tō*) won the Women's Literature Award. See "Nenpyō," in *Kōda Aya shū*, vol. 38 of *Shinchō Nihon bungaku* (Tokyo: Shinchōsha, 1973), pp. 330–337.

3. *Kōda Aya zenshū*, vol. 1 (Tokyo: Chūō Kōronsha, 1959), pp. 357–358. *KAZ* is hereafter cited in the text.

4. Jane Donahue Eberwein, *Emily Dickinson: Strategies of Limitation* (Amherst: University of Massachusetts Press, 1985), p. 57. Eberwein describes Dickinson in other words that apply to Aya's career: "The design of her life was a process of movement from her smallness, a haunting sense of primal inadequacy, to circumference or the ultimate boundary between the finite and the infinite, the known and the mysterious, the human and the divine" (16). Joyce Carol Oates

describes Dickinson in words that come uncannily close to describing Aya: "The presumed limitations of her sex and her social position allowed her the sanctity of . . . freedom. The routine of household tasks—numbing, or oddly comforting?—the cyclical nature of domestic employment, the sense that one has a place, a role, that is given by birth and not to be challenged: these provide an ideal foreground for the woman of genius to contemplate her art." "Soul at the White Heat," *Critical Inquiry* (Summer 1987): 814. Sandra Gilbert and Susan Gubar write that Elizabeth Barrett Browning made most of her finest poetry "out of her reconciliation to that graceful or passionate self-abnegation which, for a nineteenth-century woman, was necessity's highest virtue." *The Madwoman in the Attic* (New Haven: Yale University Press, 1979), p. 575. Judith Fryer quotes Edith Wharton in a similar vein: "I have often sighed to think . . . what a pitiful provision was made for the life of the imagination behind those uniform brown-stone facades, and then have concluded that . . . the creative mind thrives on a reduced diet." *Felicitous Space: The Imaginative Structures of Edith Wharton and Willa Cather* (Chapel Hill: University of North Carolina Press, 1986), p. 148; see also Patricia Mayer Spacks, *The Female Imagination* (New York: Avon Books, 1976), p. 267. Julia Kristeva's reading of Bakhtin is instructive as well: "Dialogue and ambivalence are borne out as the only approach that permits the writer to enter history by espousing an ambivalent ethics: negation as affirmation." *The Kristeva Reader,* ed. Toril Moi (New York: Columbia University Press, 1986), p. 41.

5. Dan Miron, *A Traveler Disguised: A Study in the Rise of Modern Yiddish Fiction in the Nineteenth Century* (New York: Schocken Books, 1973), pp. 79, 117.

6. Kōda Aya, "Daidokoro no oto" (Kitchen Sounds), *Shinchō* (July 1962): 17.

7. This notion of a social script is taken from Karl Joachim Weintraub, *The Value of the Individual Self and Circumstance in Autobiography* (Chicago: University of Chicago Press, 1978), pp. i–xv. Weintraub describes how available models of personality proscribe values and virtues, offering a script for life: "They proscribe for the individual certain substantive personality traits, certain values, virtues, and attitudes. They embody specific life-styles into which to fit the self. They offer man a script for his life, and only in the unprescribed interstitial spaces is there room for idiosyncrasy." See also John Paul Eakins, *Fiction in Autobiography: Studies in the Art of Self-Invention* (Princeton: Princeton University Press, 1985), p. 226, for a discussion of how writers use a standard social self to describe a personal self.

8. Houston Baker, Jr., describes the strategies that African American writers have used to turn oppressive social restrictions and aesthetic conventions into self-expressive art "to negotiate the dwarfing spaces and paternally aberrant arrangements of western slavery." *Blues, Ideology and Afro-American Literature* (Chicago: University of Chicago Press, 1984), p. 31.

9. *The Reversible World, Symbolic Inversion in Art and Society,* ed. Barbara Babcock (Ithaca: Cornell University Press, 1978), p. 14. According to Victor Turner, cultural performances are expressive acts in which people, often the most

sensitive, "become conscious . . . of the nature, texture, style, and given meanings of their own lives as members of a socio-cultural community" and "turn,
bend or reflect back on themselves, upon the relations, actions, symbols, meanings, codes, roles, statuses, social structures, ethical and legal rules, and other
socio-cultural components which make up their public selves." *Dramas, Fields,
and Metaphors: Symbolic Action in Human Society* (Ithaca: Cornell University
Press, 1974), pp. 22–59, esp. 22–24. See also Turner, *The Anthropology of
Performance* (New York: PAJ Publications, 1987). Aya's writing was an act of
power "by which reality is seized and dominated," to quote Richard Poirier
from another context. *A World Elsewhere: The Place of Style in American Literature* (Madison: University of Wisconsin Press, 1966), p. 83. Poirier sees American literature as a struggle between freedom of consciousness and artificial social
systems.

10. Komatsu Nobuhiko, "Hito to bungaku," in *Gendai bungaku taikei*, vol. 39
    (Tokyo: Chikuma Shobō, 1968), p. 49; Akiyama Shun, "Stairu no naritatsu
    saseru mono" (The Formation of Style), in *Gendai no joryū bungaku*, vol. 5
    (Tokyo: Mainichi shinbunsha, 1974), p. 344.

11. Akiyama, p. 343.

12. Okuno Takeo, *Joryū sakka ron* (Tokyo: Daisan Bunmeisha, 1974), p. 14. This is
    a common argument. Takeshi Kamei talks of Aya's old-fashioned, rambling,
    unintellectual Japanese in nostalgic tones, in "Bunsho to iu mono," *Gakutō*
    (1956); Isogai Hideo describes Aya's prose as proceeding according to pure
    feeling, not logic, in "*Nagareru*" (Flowing), *Kokubungaku* 4 (1968): 84–86;
    Yamada Michiyo says Aya's prose is guided by a feminine sensibility that knows
    with the body and not the mind, in "Kōda Aya no bungaku ni tsuite," *Tamamo* 9
    (1962): 70–77.

13. Takahashi Yoshitaka, "Kaisetsu," in *Kōda Aya shū*, vol. 59 of *Shinchōsha Nihon
    bungaku zenshū* (Tokyo: Shinchōsha, 1959), p. 247. Takahashi concurs with
    other critics that Aya thinks with her body instead of her mind, in "Kaisetsu," in
    Gendai Nihon bungakkan, vol. 40 (Tokyo: Bungei Shunjūsha, 1968), p. 488.

14. Hirabayashi Taiko, "Kōda Aya ron," in *Gunzō* (Tokyo: Kōdansha, 1959),
    p. 125.

15. Until the tenth century only women wrote literature at court. They used a
    phonetic script (*hiragana*) reserved exclusively for private affairs, whereas men
    wrote in scripts reserved for public life (phonetic *katakana* and Chinese charac-
    ters). Women dominated belles-lettres through the tenth and eleventh centuries,
    but already in the tenth century their works had taken a place within a male
    canon. About 935, Ki no Tsurayuki, the courtier, poet, and anthologizer of the
    imperial anthology *Kokinshū*, wrote a literary diary—a form that was primarily
    the province of women—with a first-person woman narrator. That he posed as a
    woman reflects the still-low social prestige of such writing. In this transitional
    period, writing poems in the native Japanese hiragana, instead of in Chinese
    characters, was becoming more acceptable. In the late Heian and early Kamakura
    periods the issue was further complicated when Heian women's writing was

canonized by male poets and scholars like Fujiwara Shūnzei (1114–1294) and his son Teika (1162–1241), who found an aesthetic of *aware* (ability to feel pathos) in *The Tale of Genji* and elevated this aesthetic to central critical status.

16. Catharine R. Stimpson, *Where the Meanings Are* (New York: Methuen, 1988), p. 156. Sandra Gilbert and Susan Gubar describe the "masculinist deprecation of female language" in the West, as well as the female response to it, which has been to seek out an alternative voice and language. Vol. 1 of *The War of the Words, No Man's Land: The Place of the Woman Writer in the Twentieth Century* (New Haven: Yale University Press, 1987), p. 268.

17. Sarah Orne Jewett, quoted in Nina Baym, *Woman's Fiction* (Ithaca: Cornell University Press, 1978), p. 15.

18. Gilbert and Gubar, *Madwoman,* p. 81; Mary Mason, "The Other Voice: Auto-biographies of Women Writers," in *Autobiography: Essays Theoretical and Critical,* ed. James Olney (Princeton: Princeton University Press, 1980), p. 234; Anne Stevenson, "Writing as a Woman," in *Women Writing and Writing about Women,* ed. Mary Jacobus (New York: Barnes and Noble, 1979), p. 146.

19. Quoted in Fryer, p. 148.

20. Discussions of modern Japanese women's literature usually devolve into bio-graphical descriptions of independent political women, such as Miyamoto Yuriko and Sata Ineko; or daringly sensual women, such as Uno Chiyo; or women informed by the native feminine aesthetic, most especially the aesthetic of the Heian court, such as Enchi Fumiko; or contemporary writers, such as Tsushima Yūko, who portray the "plight" of Japanese women today in so-ciologically accessible terms. The one full-length English-language study of Japanese women's writing focuses on its overtly political aspects. See Victoria Vernon, *Daughters of the Moon: Wish, Will, and Social Constraint in Fiction by Modern Japanese Women* (Berkeley: Institute of East Asian Studies, University of California at Berkeley, 1988). Anthologizers of Japanese women's writing in English share an interest in writers who battle repressive social norms. Noriko Mizuta Lippit and Kyoko Iriye Selden complain that Japanese critics have been interested only in issues of feminine psychology, mystery, motherhood, and eroticism; they themselves valorize women writers who fight for new identities and lives: "Most modern women writers pursue the fulfillment of self and the self-expression which they consider essential to attain identity." All these women writers seem to experience the problems of "modernity." *Stories by Contemporary Japanese Women Writers,* trans. Lippit and Selden (Armonk, N.Y.: M. E. Sharpe, 1982), p. xvii. There is little room for Aya in this scheme. Similarly, Yukiko Tanaka selects writers contemporary to Aya who imagine strong, independent women who shape their future in opposition to sexual oppression. *To Live and to Write: Selections by Japanese Women Writers, 1913–1938,* ed. Tanaka (Seattle: Seal Press, 1987), p. viii. Here, too, there seems to be no room for Aya.

21. See Richard Poirier, *The Renewal of Literature: Emersonian Reflections* (New York: Random House, 1987), pp. 152–153.

22. Robert C. Elliot, *The Literary Persona* (Chicago: University of Chicago Press, 1982), p. 95. Michael Holquist makes a similar point: "Individual consciousness never—even among the most wholly committed ideologues—fully replicates the structure of the society's public values." "The Politics of Representation," in *Allegory and Representation: Selected Papers from the English Institute, 1979–1980,* ed. Stephen J. Greenblatt (Baltimore: Johns Hopkins University Press, 1981), p. 179.

23. Turner, *Anthropology of Performance,* p. 22.

24. Kōda Aya, *Nagareru* (Flowing), in *Shinchō gendai bungaku,* vol. 34 (Tokyo: Shinchōsha, 1980), pp. 5, 18.

25. Edward Fowler, *The Rhetoric of Confession: Shishōsetsu in Early Twentieth-Century Japanese Fiction* (Berkeley: University of California Press, 1988), pp. 37–38. See also Noguchi Takehiko, *Kindai shōsetsu no gengo kūkan* (The Linguistic Space of the Modern Novel) (Tokyo: Fukubu Shoten, 1985); and Barbara Mito Reed, "Language, Narrative Structure, and the *Shōsetsu*" (Ph.D. diss., Princeton University, 1985), for a rehearsal of kindred arguments.

26. See Nakayama Masahiko, "Kyōko no gengo o kataru mono wa nani ka—*Genji Monogatari* to sono Furansugoyaku ni tsuite" (What Is It That Speaks the Language of Fiction?—Concerning the French Translation of *The Tale of Genji*), in *Hikakubunka zasshi* (Tokyo: Tokyo Institute of Technology, 1988), pp. 16–18.

Chapter 2: Mastering the Past

1. Walter Benjamin, *Illuminations,* ed. Hannah Arendt, trans. Harry Zohn (New York: Schocken Books, 1977), p. 94.

2. Chieko Mulhern, *Kōda Rohan* (Boston: Twayne, 1977), p. 20.

3. Shinoda Hajime, *Kōda Rohan no tame ni* (For Kōda Rohan) (Tokyo: Iwanami Shoten, 1984), pp. 37, 59.

4. *Masamune Hakuchō zenshū* (Tokyo: Fukutake Shoten, 1985), p. 152.

5. Shinoda, p. 26.

6. Ibid., pp. 5, 24.

7. Mulhern, pp. 7, 19.

8. Jean Strouse, *Alice James: A Biography* (Boston: Houghton Mifflin, 1980), pp. 319–326.

9. Benjamin, p. 94.

10. Okuno Takeo, *Joryū sakka ron* (On Women Writers) (Tokyo: Daisan Bunmeisha, 1974), p. 99. The cartoon appears in *Shōsetsu shinchō* (May 1957).

11. Noda Utaro suggested that she follow this approach to writing. "Sakka no taiwa" (Writer's Dialogue), in *Fūkei* (Tokyo: Bungei Shunjūsha, 1968), p. 208.

12. *Kōda Aya zenshū,* vol. 1 (Tokyo: Chūō Kōronsha, 1959), p. 352. *KAZ* is hereafter cited in the text.

13. Harold Bloom, *Map of Misreading* (New York: Oxford University Press, 1975), p. 68.

14. Shinoda, p. 24.

15. Shiotani San, *Kōda Rohan*, vol. 2 (Tokyo: Chūō Kōronsha, 1965), p. 390.

16. Ibid., 3: 9.

17. Ibid., 2: 386; 3: 75.

18. Ibid., 3: 226. Aya sold sake to writers like Izumi Kyōka and Satomi Ton.

19. Kobayashi Isamu, *Ogyuan kimonki* (Tokyo: Iwanami Shoten, 1980), p. 61.

20. Noda, p. 206.

Chapter 3: Lessons of the Father

1. Kōda Aya, "Kunshō" (The Medal), in *Kōda Aya zenshū,* vol. 7 (Tokyo: Chūō Kōronsha, 1959), pp. 3–15. *KAZ* is hereafter cited in the text. For my translation of "The Medal," see the Appendix.

2. When the literary critic Yamamoto Kenkichi asked Aya about her father's influence, Aya said: "I can't be sure about that, but I started [writing] without thinking, as if in a daze. *Shūkan asahi* [a weekly news magazine] told me to write a few pages—five or six—and for the first time I became aware that the number of pages could be limited. At first they allowed me to go about things in my own way, because I wasn't sure that I could write at all." "Taidan" (Conversation), in *Nihon gendai bungaku zenshū,* vol. 26 (Tokyo: Kōdansha, 1963), p. 4.

3. *Chu Hsi and Neo-Confucianism,* ed. Wing-tsit Chan (Honolulu: University of Hawaii Press, 1986), pp. 280–284.

4. Ito Jinsai, quoted in David Pollack, *The Fracture of Meaning* (Princeton: Princeton University Press, 1986), p. 200. On Rohan's style, see Awazu Norio, Buntai no hakken (The Discovery of Style) (Tokyo: Seidōsha, 1978), pp. 12–14.

5. Quoted in *Principles of Practicality: Essays in Neo-Confucian Practice and Learning,* ed. William T. de Bary and Irene Bloom (New York: Columbia University Press, 1979), p. 31.

6. *Chu Hsi and Neo-Confucianism,* p. 285.

7. Quoted in ibid., p. 231; brackets in original.

8. Quoted in Ch'en Ch'un, *Neo-Confucian Terms Explained: The* Pei Hsi tzu-i, trans. and ed. Wing-tsit Chan (New York: Columbia University Press, 1986), p. 112.

9. Quoted in ibid., p. 244.

10. "Futatsu no isu," p. 196.

11. Kōda Noriko, "Kōda Aya ni okeru miru to iu koto" (Vision in the Works of Kōda Aya), in *Kokubun Shirayuri* 8 (1977): 57–58. This short essay is perhaps the most intelligent analysis of Aya's work.

Chapter 4: War and Recovery

1. Saeki Shoichi, "Nihon o kangaeru—Sengo bungaku no renzoku to danzetsu" (Thinking of Japan: Continuity and Discontinuity in Postwar Literature), in *Shōwa hihyō taikei* (Tokyo: Banchō Shōin, 1966), p. 340. Others have drawn attention to the same oversight.

2. These issues are discussed in virtually all studies of postwar literature. The most idiosyncratic and interesting avoid schematic delineations of the hot postwar issues, but they also find little or no place for Aya. See, for example, Isoda Kōichi, *Sengoshi no kūkan* (The Space of Postwar History) (Tokyo: Shinchōsha, 1983); Eto Jun, *Sakka wa kōdō suru* (Writers Act) (Tokyo: Kadokawa Shoten, 1969), and *Seijuku to sōshitsu* (Maturity and Loss), in *Eto Jun chōsakushū*, vol. 1 (Tokyo: Kōdansha, 1973); Tomioka Koichiro, *Sengo bungaku no arukeorujii* (The Archaeology of Postwar Literature) (Tokyo: Fukuo Shoten, 1986); Matsumoto Ken'ichi, *Sengo no seishin—Sono sei to shi* (The Spirit of the Postwar Period—Its Life and Death) (Tokyo: Sakuhinsha, 1985); Hasegawa Izumi, *Sengo bungakushi* (A History of Postwar Literature) (Tokyo: Meiji Shōin, 1974).

3. *Kōda Aya zenshū,* vol. 1 (Tokyo: Chūō Kōronsha, 1959), p. 33; *KAZ* is hereafter cited in the text.

4. Miyoshi Yukio, *Nihon no kindaibungaku—Meiji Taishōki* (Modern Japanese Literature, Meiji and Taishō) (Tokyo: NHK Shimintai Jukugensho 36, 1976), p. 75.

5. Quoted in ibid., p. 75.

6. *Sengo Nihon bungakushi—Nenpyō* (A Timetable of the History of Postwar Japanese Literature), ed. Akiyama Shun, Isoda Kōichi, and Matsumoto Shin'ichi (Tokyo: Kōdansha, 1985), p. 56.

7. Brett de Bary, "Five Writers and the End of the War: Early Postwar Japanese Fiction" (Ph.D. diss., Harvard University, 1981), p. 26.

8. Ara Masahito's words. Ara's first postwar essay was called "Daini no seishun" (Second Youth). Usui Yoshimi, *Kindai bungaku ronsō* (Modern Literary Debates) (Tokyo: Chikuma Shobō, 1975), pp. 209–210.

9. Honda Shūgo, quoted in Saeki, p. 335. On Miyamoto, see Isoda Kōichi, *Bungaku—Kono kamenteki na mono* (Literature—This Masked Thing) (Tokyo: Keisō Shobō, 1969), p. 226. Hirano Ken, "Seiji to bungaku" (Politics and Literature), in Usui, p. 384.

10. Honda Shūgo, *Monogatari sengo bungakushi* (A Narrative History of Postwar Literature) (Tokyo: Shinchōsha, 1975), p. 12.

11. For a discussion of the Postwar school, see Tomioka.

12. Different people put the end of the postwar period at different times, but literary historical convention terminates it in 1956, when the Akutagawa Prize was awarded to Ishihara Shintarō's novel *Season of the Sun (Taiyō no kisetsu)*. Yoshimoto Takaaki says it ended in 1951 or 1952, with the new sense of security and the renewed discussion of a "people's literature." *Gengo ni totte wa bi to wa nani ka* (What Is Beauty in Language?) (Tokyo: Keisō Shobō, 1965), p. 312; and Yoshimoto, "Sengo bungaku wa doko e itta ka," in *Geijutsuteki teiko to zazetsu* (Artistic Resistance and Collapse) (Tokyo: Miraisha, 1972), p. 197. Sasaki Kiichi claims that ten years after the war, recovery had been accomplished. "Sengo bungaku wa genkei ka" (Is Postwar Literature Over?), in *Sengo bungaku ronsō,* vol. 2, ed. Usui Yoshimi (Tokyo: Banchō Shobō, 1972), p. 573.

The question is still discussed, and the postwar period may have ended only in 1989, with the deaths of the Shōwa emperor—Hirohito—and the popular *enka* singer and cultural icon, Misora Hibari.

13. The literature dealing with the urge to return to a lost past is vast, and worthy of a study of its own. See Miyauchi Yutaka, *Hankindai no mukō e* (Toward the Far Side of Antimodernism) (Tokyo: Ronzōsha, 1986); Hagiwara Kōtaro, "Nihon e no kaiki" (The Return to Japan), in *Hagiwara Kōtaro zenshū*, vol. 10 (Tokyo: Chikuma Shobō, 1975), pp. 485–631; Karaki Junzō, "Mukashi atte ima ushinatta mono" (That Which Was and Now Is Lost), in *Karaki Junzō zenshū*, vol. 4 (Tokyo: Chikuma Shobō, 1967); Yasuda Yojūrō, "Nihon no hashi" (Japanese Bridges), in *Yasuda Yojūrō zenshū*, vol. 4 (Tokyo: Kōdansha, 1985), pp. 9–34. Interest in the issue transcends political leanings; it is found in brazenly right-wing ideologues like Yasuda, Marxists like Nakano Shigeharu, and less overtly ideological critics like Kobayashi Hideo.

14. See Oketani Hideaki, *Yasuda Yojūrō* (Tokyo: Shinchōsha, 1983), esp. p. 72.

15. Kobayashi Hideo, "Kokyō ushinatta bungaku" (Literature of the Forgotten Home), in *Kobayashi Hideo zenshū*, vol. 3 (Tokyo: Shinchōsha, 1968), pp. 32–33.

16. Quoted in Irene Powell, *Writers and Society in Modern Japan* (London: Macmillan, 1983), p. 44. See also *Bungaku ni okeru kokyō* (The Home in Literature), ed. Sato Sōhei (Tokyo: Sasama Sensho, 1986); and Kawamoto Akira, *Kindai ni okeru "ie" no kōzō* (The Structure of the Home in Modern Times) (Tokyo: Shakai Shisōsha, 1973).

17. Isoda Kōichi, *Sengo hihyōkaron* (A Study of Postwar Criticism) (Tokyo: Kawade Shobō Shinsha, 1969), p. 140.

18. The *kokumin bungaku ronsō* (debate on a people's literature) was joined by critics across the political spectrum. Takeuchi's combination of ethnocentrism and anticolonialism most eloquently points up this convergence. He decried the notion of a cosmopolitan, free individual—which he saw as the philosophical creation of Shiga Naoya and other writers in the 1920s—both for its abstract quality and its lack of particular Japanese traits. To his mind, the universal person had a borrowed identity unconnected to native traditions. See "Kindaishugi to minzoku no mondai" (The Problem of Modernism and the People), in *Sengo bungaku ronsō*, 2: 110. The critic Ito Sei responded to Takeuchi with a vigorous defense of the "modern self," claiming that it in no way contradicted "the people." He said that native Japanese thought and Asian philosophies should be used to examine modern literature. "Dōichi no hihan kijun no kakuritsu o—Takeuchi Yoshimi e" (For Takeuchi Yoshimi: Toward the Establishment of a Single Critical Standard), in ibid., 2: 119. Takeuchi and others, such as Yamamoto Kenkichi, also called for a revival of the classics and for an infusion of modern literature with the spirit of the past. See *Sengo bungaku ronsō*, 2: 109–189. Also see Yamamoto Kenkichi, *Koten to gendai bungaku* (The Classics and Modern Literature) (Tokyo: Kōdansha, 1957); and *Kokumin bun-*

gaku to gengo (A People's Literature and the Question of Language), ed. Takeuchi Yoshimi (Tokyo: Kawade Shobō, 1955).

19. Takeuchi, "Kindaishugi," p. 82.

20. Yamamoto Kenkichi, *Koten to gendai bungaku* (Tokyo: Kōdansha, 1957), p. 3.

21. Quoted in Oketani Hideaki, "Fukazawa Shichiro kōron" (On Fukuzawa Shichiro), in *Kaien* (December 1987): 182–189. Usui Yoshimi describes the grandmother's act as joyous and revealing of great character. "*Narayama bushiko* to gendai" (The *Tale of Narayama* and the Present), in *Usui Yoshimi hyōronshū*, vol. 9 (Tokyo: Chikuma Shobō, 1966).

22. Yamamoto Kenkichi, "Kōda Aya ron," in *Shinsen gendai Nihon bungaku*, vol. 12 (Tokyo: Chikuma Shobō, 1970), pp. 456–461.

23. Tanizaki Jun'ichirō, *Tanizaki Jun'ichirō zenshū*, vol. 12 (Tokyo: Chūō Kōronsha, 1968).

24. Ishihara Shintarō, *Taiyō no kisetsu*, in *Ishihara Shintarō shū*, vol. 62 of *Shinchō Nihon bungaku* (Tokyo: Shinchōsha, 1969).

25. Eto Jun, "Atarashii sakkatachi" (New Writers), in *Eto Jun chōsakushū*, 2: 310.

26. Yasuoka Shōtarō, *Boku no Shōwashi* (My History of Shōwa) (Tokyo: Kōdansha, 1984), pp. 60, 181.

27. *Mishima Yukio zenshū* (Tokyo: Shinchōsha, 1975), p. 436.

28. *Kobayashi Hideo zenshū*, 3: 320.

Chapter 5: A World of Objects

1. *Kōda Rohan zenshū*, vol. 24 (Tokyo: Iwanami Shoten, 1949–1958), p. 152.

2. This is Hirano Ken's opinion. "Kaisetsu" (Commentary), in *Nihon bungaku*, vol. 50 (Tokyo: Chūō Kōronsha, 1966), p. 525.

3. *Kōda Aya zenshū*, vol. 6 (Tokyo: Chūō Kōronsha, 1959), p. 273. *KAZ* is hereafter cited in the text.

4. Shinoda Hajime, "Kaisetsu," in *Gendai no bungaku*, vol. 13 (Tokyo: Kawade Shobō Shinsha, 1967), p. 393.

5. Like Aya, Natsume Sōseki concentrated on the present world of material reality. According to Karatani Kōjin, Sōseki "only looked for transcendence through contact with 'things'; or, in other words, through contact with life." *Kyōfu suru ningen* (People Who Fear) (Tokyo: Trable, 1987), p. 49.

6. Mihaly Csikszentmihalyi, *The Meaning of Things: Domestic Symbols and the Self* (New York: Cambridge University Press, 1981), p. 173. For interesting examinations of objects in literary works, see Maeda Ai, *Toshi kūkan no naka no bungaku* (Literature in the Space of the City) (Tokyo: Chikuma Shobō, 1982); Mario Vargos Llosa, *The Perpetual Orgy: Flaubert and Madame Bovary*, trans. Helen Lane (New York: Farrar, Straus and Giroux, 1986), esp. pp. 126–166; William Gass, "Representation and the War for Reality," in *Habitations of the Word*, ed. Gass (New York: Simon and Schuster, 1985), esp. pp. 73–112, on the Czech novelist Danilo Kis; Lewis Hyde, *The Gift: Imagination and the Erotic*

Life of Property (New York: Random House, 1983), esp. pp. 143–282, on Whitman and Pound.

7. Rudolf Arnheim, "Art among the Objects," *Critical Inquiry* 13 (Summer 1987): 679. Martin Heidegger, *Poetry, Language, Thought,* trans. Albert Hofstadter (New York: Harper and Row, 1971), pp. 165–186; Gaston Bachelard, *The Poetics of Space,* trans. Maria Jolas (New York: Orion Press, 1964), p. 86.

8. Kōda Aya, "Kami" (Hair), in *Shinchō gendai bungaku,* vol. 34 (Tokyo: Shinchōsha, 1980), pp. 358–361. For my translation of "Hair," see the Appendix.

9. Kōda Aya, "Kansei" (Scream), in *Shinchō gendai bungaku* 34: 339.

10. See Tomioka Kōichiro, *Sengo bungaku no arukeorujii* (Tokyo: Fukuo Shoten, 1986), pp. 67–69.

11. Jay Rubin, "From Wholesomeness to Decadence: The Censorship of Literature under the Allied Occupation," *Journal of Japanese Studies,* 2, no. 1 (1978): 61–62, 78.

12. Quoted in Mark Krupnick, *Lionel Trilling and the Fate of Cultural Criticism* (Evanston, Ill.: Northwestern University Press, 1985), p. 111.

13. Judith Fryer, *Felicitous Space—The Imaginative Structures of Edith Wharton and Willa Cather* (Chapel Hill: University of North Carolina Press, 1986), p. 117, where Fryer discusses Edith Wharton. Naomi Schor describes the prejudice in Western aesthetics against material details and in favor of ideals. In this scheme "woman" is seen to be embedded in the particular and is thus devalued; the material world is associated with the feminine, and the sublime with the masculine. *Reading in Detail: Aesthetics and the Feminine* (New York: Methuen, 1987), p. 85. In a fascinating and wide-ranging study, Earl Jackson, Jr., argues that the Japanese philosophical tradition is fundamentally different from that of the West in its valorization of present material reality and in its eschewal of the sublime. "Heresies of Meaning: Immanence and Transcendence in Modern Poetry in Japan, Europe, and America" (Ph.D. diss., Princeton University, 1987). Aya's absorption in objects and details can hardly be seen as a hermeneutical attack, but it is firmly situated within the Japanese tradition. There are, however, numerous examples of Western writers confronting the transcendental through the quotidian, many of whom are women. Joyce Carol Oates writes of Emily Dickinson that "like Emerson in his terse, elliptical poems of transcendence (which Dickinson had read), the poet refines herself of the close-at-hand, the local, in order to meditate upon the universal." "Soul at the White Heat," *Critical Inquiry* (Summer 1987): 810.

14. Shimazaki Tōson, *Ie* (The House), vol. 9 of *Shimazaki Tōson zenshū* (Tokyo: Chūō Kōronsha, 1957), pp. 296, 311.

15. Natsume Sōseki, *Grass on the Wayside,* trans. Edwin McClellan (Chicago: University of Chicago Press, 1969), p. 66.

16. Ibid., p. 77.

17. See Irene Powell, *Writers and Society in Modern Japan* (London: Macmillan, 1983), for a discussion of these criticisms.

18. Eto Jun, *Sakka wa kōdō suru* (Tokyo: Kadokawa Shoten, 1969), p. 26. Eto was passionate in his criticism: "The majority of our nation's writers are like poor mothers clinging to their babies while being struck by their husbands, or like poor peasants protectively clinging to their three *tsubo* of rice paddy: they cling to their immediate circumstances and try not to part with them. What underlies such an attitude is not, of course, the devilish consciousness of the Western Aestheticists but the set attitude of people who have lost their desire for freedom because of their harsh circumstances. At bottom is a distrust of what language and action can create, which is not unrelated to the psychology of preferring one cup of rice now to one hundred *ryō* in the year to come." Ibid., p. 27. See also pp. 112–125.

19. Paul Anderer, *Other Worlds* (New York: Columbia University Press, 1984), pp. 118, 10, 13.

20. On Kafu, see Maeda Ai, *Toshi kūkan no naka no bungaku* (Tokyo: Chikuma Shobō, 1982), esp. pp. 76, 85, 139. See also Ken Ito's fascinating discussion of Kafu, in "Tanizaki's Vision of the West" (Ph.D. diss., Yale University, 1985), esp. pp. 40–91.

21. Bachelard, p. 47; Taki Kōji, *Ikirareta ie* (The Living House) (Tokyo: Seidōsha, 1984), p. 9. Taki argues that the Japanese distinguish between the material and nonmaterial worlds only vaguely and that they maintain a traditional belief that a spirit inheres in things (*mono ni kokoro aru*; p. 47). Suzanne Langer also discusses the creation of "space" out of "place" in architecture. Space is "an environment created by selfhood." *Feeling and Form* (New York: Charles Scribner's Sons, 1953), p. 100.

22. Virginia Woolf, *Orlando, a Biography* (New York: Harcourt Brace Jovanovich, 1973), p. 188.

23. The story appears in *KAZ* 7: 93–122. For my translation, see the Appendix.

24. Lewis Hyde, *The Gift—Imagination and the Erotic Life of Property* (New York: Vintage Books, 1983), p. 66.

25. Kōda Aya, *Nagareru,* in *Shinchō gendai bungaku,* 34: 151. *Flowing* is hereafter cited in the text (all citations are to vol. 34).

26. The story appears in *KAZ* 7: 125–139. For my translation, see the Appendix.

27. Mary Douglas, in *Purity and Danger: An Analysis of Concepts of Pollution and Taboo* (New York: Praeger, 1966), describes dirt as "an apt symbol of creative formlessness" (161) and disorder as a source of creativity: "Grant that disorder spoils pattern; it also provides the material of pattern. Order implies restriction; . . . so disorder by implication is unlimited, no pattern has been realized in it, but its potential for patterning is indefinite. . . . We recognize that [disorder] is destructive to existing patterns, also that it has potentiality" (94).

28. Frank Kermode, *The Art of Telling: Essays on Fiction* (Cambridge: Harvard University Press, 1983), p. 22.

29. See Yasuoka Shōtarō, "The Glass Slipper" and "The Pawnbroker's Wife," trans. Edward Seidensticker, *Japan Quarterly* 8, no. 2 (1961).

Chapter 6: Flowing

1. Kōda Aya, *Nagareru* (Flowing), in *Shinchō gendai bungaku,* vol. 34 (Tokyo: Shinchōsha, 1980), p. 64. *Flowing* is hereafter cited in the text.

2. See Nina Auerbach, *Communities of Women: An Idea in Fiction* (Cambridge: Harvard University Press, 1978), for a discussion of the creation of alternative women's communities in fiction. Annis Pratt describes a tendency among women characters in fiction by Western women to enter a world apart from the male world: "Heroes turn away from a culture hostile to their development, entering a timeless achronological world appropriate to their rejection by history, a spaceless world appropriate to rebellion against placelessness in the patriarchy." *Archetypal Patterns in Woman's Fiction* (Bloomington: University of Indiana Press, 1981), p. 169.

3. Isoda Kōichi, *Shisō to shite no Tokyo* (Tokyo as an Idea) (Tokyo: Kokubunsha, 1983), pp. 15–28. Isoda describes the shifting patterns of cultural authority in twentieth-century Japan, especially the patterns of language and literature. With the influx of country people into Tokyo in the early part of the century, Tokyo natives who resided in the shitamachi came to see themselves as the protectors of urban culture and the rest of Tokyo as peripheral. As these downtown areas became less important to the economic life of the city, passed over by modern technological advances, the sense of local cultural authority increased. The shitamachi dialect became associated with the quotidian life of native Tokyoites, while standard Japanese, spoken by new arrivals, came to be seen as a universal language, lacking the imprint of a particular culture. Standard Japanese thus became implicated with modernization, and the downtown dialect with preservation of the past. Most people seemed to turn their backs on the shitamachi dialect in favor of the standard dialect in order to assimilate and modernize. But the ones who stubbornly maintained their native speech became even more proud and arrogant in their cultural affiliation. Rohan was of this type, and so was Aya. Aya absorbed the culture of downtown Tokyo from her father—when Aya was a child, the Kōda home was in Mukōjima, near the redlight district—but she was also directly exposed to its literature. As a teenager, she read nineteenth-century demimonde fiction (*ninjōbon*), particularly the works of Tamenaga Shunsui (1790–1843), whose *Shunshoku umegoyomi* (The Plum Calendar) Rohan greatly admired. See "Ume" (Plum), in *KAZ* 4: 5–7.

4. Barbara Babcock sees the attraction to squalor as potentially positive: "Creative negations remind us of the need to reinvest the clean with the filthy, the rational with the animalistic . . . in order to maintain cultural vitality." *The Reversible World: Symbolic Inversion in Art and Society,* ed. Babcock (Ithaca: Cornell University Press, 1978), p. 32. Aya's interest in dirt and mess may have been a reaction against her father's strict sense of domestic order.

5. T. J. Clark delineates the changing economy of the demimonde and the role of

courtesans in it in fin-de-siècle Paris. *The Painting of Modern Life: Paris in the Art of Manet and His Followers* (Princeton: Princeton University Press, 1986).

6. The geisha here displays the quality of *iki,* an aesthetic term dating from the eighteenth century, used primarily in reference to women of the entertainment quarters. In the 1930s, Kuki Shōzō analyzed the concept in philosophical terms, attributing to it the characteristics of coquettishness (*bitai*), resignation (*akirame*), and resilience (*ikuji*). *Iki no kōzō* (The Structure of *Iki*) (Tokyo: Iwanami Shoten, 1977).

7. Roberta Rubenstein, in *Boundaries of the Self: Gender, Culture, Fiction* (Urbana: University of Illinois Press, 1987), sees boundaries as a threat to selfhood and as a symbol of dismemberment and marginalization: "The image of boundary suggests an inescapable identity between gynecological and existential confinement" (57). The effect of spatial constriction on women's lives is given a wider, more psychological inflection in studies of agoraphobia, which describe it as "a paradigm for the historical intimidation and oppression of women. The self-hate, self-limitation, self-abnegation, and self-punishment of agoraphobia is a caricature of centuries of childhood instructions to women" (6). Moreover, "agoraphobia is primarily a woman's strategy; one might say it is second nature to her, because being on the inside is the programming she receives as the traditional and normal female upbringing" (44). See also Robert Seidenberg and Karen DeCrow, *Women Who Marry Houses: Panic and Protest in Agoraphobia* (New York: McGraw-Hill, 1983).

8. Taturoo Uchino, *Japan's Postwar Economy, an Insider's View of Its History and Future,* trans. Mark Harbison (Tokyo: Kōdansha, 1982), p. 85.

9. For extended discussions of changes in domestic space and its rendering in fiction, see Maeda Ai, *Toshi kūkan no naka no bungaku* (Tokyo: Chikuma Shobō, 1982), p. 470; and Isoda Kōichi, *Sengoshi no kūkan* (Tokyo: Shinchōsha, 1983), pp. 200–211. "Withdrawn" writers include Furui Yoshikichi, Gōtō Eisei, Kuroi Senji, Abe Akira, and Ōgawa Kunio.

10. *Kōda Aya zenshū,* vol. 6 (Tokyo: Chūō Kōronsha, 1959), p. 304. *KAZ* is hereafter cited in the text.

11. Saeki Junko, *Yūjo no bunkashi* (A Cultural History of Courtesans) (Tokyo: Chūō Kōronsha, 1987), pp. 82–100.

12. Ibid., p. 90.

13. Tsuruta Kinya, "Mukōgawa no bungaku" (Literature of the Other Side), in *Bungaku ni okeru "mukōgawa,"* ed. Kokubungaku kenkyū shiryōkan (Tokyo: Meiji Shōin, 1985), pp. 5–36.

14. *Nagareru no oboegaki* (Memories of *Flowing*), ed. Shiotani San (Tokyo: Keizai Ōraisha, 1957), p. 49.

15. Ino Kenji, "Rohan—Mō hitotsu no kindai (Rohan—Another Modernism)," *Bungaku* (October 1970): 1041–1053. One such passage in Aya reads: "'Hai' to ōkiku, 'annai ga kiite akireru goteitaku' to chiisaku, 'soko otearai, kotchi daidokoro' to ōkiku, 'anta kitanai no heiki? Sore heiki de nai to tsutomaranai wa

yo. Hora ne, jissai kittanai daidokoro deshō. De mo atashi no sei zya nai wa, atashi kayoi da mono, daidokoro no seiwa ni wa naranai no yo. Ano Yoneko no yatsu, mattaku bussho da' to chiisai. Konsui no ii nioi ga michibiite, naruhodo uchijyū no annai wa hyosai ni inyōryōmen ni tsukusarete, nikai e dake wa nokoshita." *Nagareru,* pp. 6, 8.

16. Aya shared with writers such as Saitō Ryokū and Izumi Kyōka a dedication to a premodern and therefore not-so-accessible literary language. Saitō Ryokū (1829–1894) has become a sad but heroic figure in Japanese literary histories. He turned his back on public life in the last decades of the nineteenth century— and on the new subjects available to writers. He proudly, even arrogantly, clung to the world of premodernized Tokyo. He wrote of geisha and their melodramatic romances; he concentrated on literary style—on the beauty of the language and the complexity of literary tropes—fully aware that the number of readers who could appreciate his talent was fast dwindling. He studied with Kōda Rohan and shared his attitude toward the primacy of the surface quality of language over the expression of deeper meanings. See Miyoshi Yukio, "Hankindai no keifu" (The Lineage of Antimodernism), in *Nihon no kindai bungaku* (Tokyo: Nihon hōsō shuppan kyokai, 1976), pp. 96–98. Izumi Kyōka, too, knew that his language was increasingly perceived as opaque as more simple, unpoetic styles came to prominence. See also Takehiko Noguchi, *Kindai shōsetsu no gengo kūkan* (The Linguistic Space in the Modern Novel) (Tokyo: Fukutake Shoten, 1985).

17. Kōda Rohan, "Kangadan," in *Kōda Rohan zenshū,* vol. 4 (Tokyo: Iwanami Shoten, 1988), pp. 395–396. See also Kawamura Minato, *Oto wa maboroshi* (Sound Is a Phantom) (Tokyo: Kokubunsha, 1987), pp. 11, 15, 19.

18. It is not difficult to find similarities between Aya and early Japanese writers. Like the *Kokinshū* poets, Aya emphasizes her subjective reactions to the world and pours those reactions into her descriptions of objects, rather than trying to record an objective reality. Like Sei Shōnagon, Aya peruses a scene from a distance and seems to set out her judgments at random.

19. One critic's list of Aya's onomatopoetic and mimetic words, though in Japanese, can perhaps provide a feeling for the sounds going through Aya's mind: "giritto, dōnto, dekadeka, betabeta, butsubutsu, pikapika, chirichiri, tzukitzuki, pitaripitari, munmun, hikuhiku, bakubaku, kerakera, supon, dekun, gorotchara, noronoro, zowazowa, zuzutto, gyūtto, gatto, gikugiku, kirikiri, supetto, sayasaya, jiwajiwa, jiriri, kakirito, kippato, bisshirito, poronto, zubonto, kakitto, watawata, heguhegu." Takahashi Yoshitaka, "Kaisetsu," in *Kōda Aya shū,* vol. 59 of *Shinchō Nihon bungaku zenshū* (Tokyo: Shinchōsha, 1959), p. 417. A paragraph employing such words runs like this: "Kiraku da kara koso kaette mi ni shimijimi to se ni kakatta zawazawa dōdō to iu memagurushisa ga yoku wakatte dōjo shite iru. Moto wa hitogoto to omou yosoyososhii kokoro no ue ni naritatsu no ga jibun no dōjōshin ka to sae omou made, genzai no koto wa tashika ni shujin no uchi no shimijimi to suru toshi no se de aru. Jibun no setai no ue nara shimijimi nado to iu yoyū wa nakatta. Tada semerareru koto no os-

oroshisa de gajigaji suru no de aru" (*KAZ* 6: 122). Here is a translation: "It was precisely because she was free from worries that she was able to well understand, and deeply sympathize with, the rushing, roaring bewilderment of being caught in the current [of the years]. She even thought that her sympathy was based on a cold, distant way of looking at others and now sensed, amid the confusion of the end of the year, a depth of feeling toward her madam. If this had been her own home, she would not have had the necessary distance to feel as deeply as this. She would have been tortured by the fear of being chased [by time]."

20. Mishima Yukio, *Bunshō tokuhon* (A Reader on Style) (Tokyo: Chūō Kōronsha, 1959), pp. 12–15, 162–164.

21. Honda Shūgo, *Monogatari sengo bungakushi* (Tokyo: Shinchōsha, 1958), p. 83; Miyamoto Yuriko, *Fujin to bungaku* (Women and Literature), in *Miyamoto Yuriko zenshū*, vol. 12 (Tokyo: Shin Nihon Shuppansha, 1980), p. 431.

22. The question of "women's language" is broad, complex, and slippery. Janet S. Shibamoto, summarizing the relevant research, concludes that Japanese women's writing is syntactically loose, ambiguous, vague, diffuse, elliptical, formal, and polite compared to men's. *Japanese Women's Language* (Orlando: Harcourt Brace Jovanovich, 1987), p. 163. In the 1950s, when Aya was writing, Japanese generally seemed to characterize women's language as gentle, emotional, formal, and circumlocutional, according to one survey. *Gengo seikatsu*, vol. 2, ed. Kokuritsu Kokugo Kenkyūsho (Tokyo: Chikuma Shobō, 1955), pp. 24–27.

23. H. D. Harootunian, *Things Seen and Unseen: Discourse and Ideology in Tokugawa Nativism* (Chicago: University of Chicago Press, 1988), p. 95. Harootunian describes how the great nativist Motoori Norinaga elevated femininity to an aesthetic principle. Norinaga claimed that ancient poets perceived things as they were and reacted to them as they felt. A deep and immediate nonabstract poetry was an essentially "feminine" and "Japanese" experience, whereas, according to Harootunian, artifice, invention, and foreign modes of intellectual and abstract thought were associated with masculinity. According to Tetsuo Najita, benevolence for Ito Jinsai is "possessing the capacity to understand the authenticity of an emotive truth in a situation, person, or thing and to act empathetically without regard to personal advancement." Tetsuo Najita, *Visions of Virtue in Tokugawa Japan* (Chicago: University of Chicago Press, 1987), p. 41.

24. Yasuoka Shōtarō, *Maku ga orite kara* (After the Curtain Falls), vol. 1 of *Yasuoka Shōtarō zenshū* (Tokyo: Kōdansha, 1971), p. 181.

Chapter 7: Return to the Father

1. Kōda Aya, *Nagareru* (Flowing), vol. 34 of *Shinchō gendai bungaku* (Tokyo: Shinchōsha, 1980), p. 123. *Flowing* is hereafter cited in the text.

2. *Kōda Aya zenshū*, vol. 2 (Tokyo: Chūō Kōronsha, 1959), p. 151. *KAZ* is hereafter cited in the text.

3. This reading follows Nakamura Akira, *Meibun* (Tokyo: Chikuma Shobō, 1979), pp. 263–270.

4. Kōda Aya, *Tō* (Battle), vol. 34 of *Shinchō gendai bungaku. Battle* is hereafter cited in the text.

5. Kamo no Chōmei, "Account of My Hut," trans. and ed. Donald Keene, in *Anthology of Japanese Literature* (New York: Grove Press, 1955), p. 197.

6. Enchi Fumiko, *The Waiting Years,* trans. John Bester (Tokyo: Kodansha, 1971), p. 52.

7. Mihaly Csikszentmihalyi, *Flow: The Psychology of Optimal Experience* (New York: Harper and Row, 1990), p. 24.

Most Recent Studies of the East Asian Institute

Suicidal Narrative in Modern Japan: The Case of Dazai Osamu, by Alan Wolfe. Princeton: Princeton University Press, 1990.

Thailand and the United States: Development, Security and Foreign Aid, by Robert Muscat. New York: Columbia University Press, 1990.

China's Crisis: Dilemmas of Reform and Prospects for Democracy, by Andrew J. Nathan. Columbia University Press, 1990.

Anarchism and Chinese Political Culture, by Peter Zarrow. New York: Columbia University Press, 1991.

Race to the Swift: State and Finance in Korean Industrialization, by Jung-en Woo. New York: Columbia University Press, 1991.

Competitive Ties: Subcontracting in the Japanese Automotive Industry, by Michael Smitka. New York: Columbia University Press, 1991.

The Study of Change: Chemistry in China, 1840–1949, by James Reardon-Anderson. New York: Cambridge University Press, 1991.

Explaining Economic Policy Failure: Japan and the 1969–1971 International Monetary Crisis, by Robert Angel. New York: Columbia University Press, 1991.

Pacific Basin Industries in Distress: Structural Adjustment and Trade Policy in the Nine Industrialized Economies, edited by Hugh T. Patrick with Larry Meissner. New York: Columbia University Press, 1991.

Business Associations and the New Political Economy of Thailand: From Bureaucratic Polity to Liberal Corporatism, by Anek Laothamatas. Boulder, Colo.: Westview Press, 1991.

Constitutional Reform and the Future of the Republic of China, edited by Harvey J. Feldman. Armonk, N.Y.: M. E. Sharpe, 1991.

Asia for the Asians: Japanese Advisors, Chinese Students, and the Quest for Modernization, 1895–1905, by Paula S. Harrell. Stanford: Stanford University Press, 1992.

Schoolhouse Politicians: Locality and State during the Chinese Republic, by Helen Chauncey. Honolulu: University of Hawaii Press, 1992.

The Writings of Kōda Aya, a Japanese Literary Daughter, by Alan Tansman. New Haven: Yale University Press, 1993.

Driven by Growth: Political Change in the Asia-Pacific Region, edited by James W. Morley. Armonk, N.Y.: M. E. Sharpe, forthcoming.

Social Mobility in Contemporary Japan, by Hiroshi Ishida. Stanford: Stanford University Press, forthcoming.

Pollution, Politics and Foreign Investment in Taiwan: The Lukang Rebellion, by James Reardon-Anderson. Armonk, N.Y.: M. E. Sharpe, forthcoming.

Managing Indonesia: The Modern Political Economy, by John Bresnan. New York: Columbia University Press, forthcoming.

Tokyo's Marketplace: Custom and Trade in the Tsukiji Wholesale Fish Market, by Theodore C. Bestor. Stanford: Stanford University Press, forthcoming.

Nishiwaki Junzaburo: The Poetry and Poetics of a Modernist Master, by Josea Hirata. Princeton University Press, forthcoming.

Land Ownership under Colonial Rule: Korea's Japanese Experience, 1900–1925, by Edwin H. Gragert. Honolulu: University of Hawaii Press, forthcoming.

For a complete list of titles, write to Studies of the East Asian Institute, Columbia University, 420 West 118th St., New York, N.Y. 10027.

Index

Abe Kōbo, 78
African American literature, 5; literary transformations in, 194*n*8
Agoraphobia, in women's literature, 205*n*7
Akiyama Shun, 7, 18
Anderer, Paul, 83–84
Arishima Takeo, 9, 83–84
Arnheim, Rudolf, 73

Babcock, Barbara, 6
Bachelard, Gaston, 73
Bakhtin, Mikhail, 193*n*4
Benjamin, Walter, 16
Bloom, Harold, 31
Boundaries: in Aya's fiction, 85, 86, 105, 110–116, 137, 143–145, 193*n*4, 205*n*7; in women's fiction, 205*n*7
Browning, Elizabeth Barrett, 193*n*4

Ch'en Ch'un, 53
Chu Hsi, 53

Chūō Koron (journal), 4
Claustrophobia, in women's literature, 10, 205*n*7. *See also* Agoraphobia, in women's literature; Space
Clothes: in "The Black Hems," 89; in "The Medal," 89; transformation of, 89, 93, 94, 105–107, 108; and feminine identity, 93. *See also* Transformation
Courtesans, in Japanese literature, 117–119
Cultural authority, in the *shitamachi*, 105, 204*n*3
"Cultural performance" (Victor Turner), 11, 194*n*9

Daughters, literary, 193*n*1
Death, in Aya's imagination, 3, 59, 151
Dickinson, Emily, 4, 193*n*4, 202*n*13
Domestic service, transformation of, 57, 94–95, 193*n*4, 204*n*4. *See also* Transformation

Douglas, Mary, 203*n*27

Enchi Fumiko, 151
Eto Jun, 83–84, 203*n*18
Everyday life, in Japanese literature,
   132–133

Fathers, literary, 193*n*1
Feminine aesthetics, 2, 6, 11, 195*n*12,
   207*n*23; and authenticity, 2, 131–
   132
Feminism, and Aya, 8, 11
Fetishism, and commodities, 73
Flowing, as literary and cultural image,
   151–152
Fowler, Edward, 14
Freedom, notions of in Aya's writing,
   88, 89, 116
Futabatei Shimei, 82

Geisha: and cultural authority, 104–
   105; in *Flowing,* 105–111; and
   transformation, 108–110; in Japanese literature, 117–119; and language, 123; and concept of *iki,*
   205*n*6
Gift giving, 94

Hashimoto Shinkichi, 127
Heian literature, 6, 11, 131, 195*n*15,
   206*n*18
Heidegger, Martin, 73
Hirabayashi Taiko, 8
Hirano Ken, 60
"Hōjōki" (Kamo no Chōmei), 151
Home in literature: rejection of, 62–
   63; yearning for, 65, 118–119
Honda Shūgo, 60–61; on women's lit-
   erature, 132
Housekeeping, Rohan's attitude to,
   54–55. *See also* Domestic service,
   transformation of; Transformation
Hyde, Lewis, 94

Ihara, Saikaku, 126
I-novel, 83
Ishihara Shintarō, 66–67
Isoda Kōichi, 61, 204*n*3, 205*n*16
Ito Jinsai, 52, 133, 207*n*23
Ito Sei, 63, 200*n*18
Izumi Kyōka, 118, 206*n*16

James, Alice, 18–19
James, Henry, 16
Jewett, Sarah Orne, 10
Jewish literature, 4

Karatani Kōjin, on Natsume Sōseki,
   201*n*5
Kasai Zenzō, 63
Kawabata Yasunari, 59, 118
Kermode, Frank, 100
Ki no Tsurayuki, 195*n*15
Kitamura Tōkoku, 82
Kobayashi Hideo, 62
Kōda Aya: selfhood in, 12; conflict
   with Rohan, 17–18, 44, 138; and
   Rohan's death, 19–26, 136; critical
   opinion of, 20–22, 57–58; childhood, 29–39; Rohan's training of,
   31, 48, 50–56, 98, 145–146; marriage, 40–41; divorce, 42; reasons
   for entering geisha house, 71–72;
   uses of space, 82–88, 98; awards,
   93*n*2; literary style, 130–134,
   206*n*16. Works: *Battle* (*Tō*), 145–
   150; "The Black Hems" ("Kuroi
   suso"), 88–93; "Books" ("Hon"),
   48–49; "Connecting Things"
   ("Musubu koto"), 49–50; "Deafness" ("Tsunbo"), 123–130;
   "Dolls" ("Hina"), 96–98, 100; "Favorite Corners" ("Ki ni iri no
   sumikko"), 85–88; "Flowering
   Plants" ("Kusa no hana"), 25, 37–
   40; *Flowing* (*Nagareru*), 11–15, 71,
   76, 89, 94–95, 97, 98, 140, 145,

146; "Fragment" ("Kakera"), 25, 72; "Funeral Diary" ("Sōsō no ki"), 20, 21–25; "Garbage" ("Gomi"), 99; "Hair" ("Kami"), 73–76, 77, 88; "Kitchen Sounds" ("Daidokoro no oto"), 4–5; "Lens" ("Renzu"), 51; *Little Brother* (*Otōto*), 137–145; "The Medal" ("Kunshō"), 43–46; "Miscellaneous Notes" ("Zakki"), 46–47; "Miso Dregs" ("Misok-kasu"), 25, 26–27, 36–37; "Paper" ("Kami"), 49. *See also* Kōda Rohan

Kōda family, 18–19, 31–36, 40–42

Kōda Rohan, 16–18, 19–26; *Five-Storied Pagoda* (*Gojū no to*), 31; training of Aya, 50–56, 98, 145–146; on language, 127, 130

Kokinshū (Ki no Tsurayuki), 195*n*15, 206*n*18

Kokumin bungaku ronsō (debate on a people's literature), 200*n*18

Korean War (*1950–1953*), 61–62

Kristeva, Julia, 193*n*4

Literary inversion, 4, 5–6, 193*n*4, 194*n*8. *See also* Transformation

Maeda Ai, 82

Male criticism, of women writers, 6–8, 195*nn*12–13

Masamune Hakuchō, 17

Mason, Mary, 10

Memory, and narrative, 21, 25–29, 73, 99, 100–101, 133

Mishima Yukio, 67–68, 78, 131–132

Misora Hibari, 200*n*12

Miyamoto Yuriko, 60

Modernity: and gender, 2, 7; in *1950s*, 7–8, 63–65; and tradition, 62, 80; debate on, 62, 80, 115–116, 133, 200*n*18; and style, 204*n*3

Mori Ōgai, 131, 193*n*1

Motoori Norinaga, 7, 133, 207*n*23

Nagai Kafu, 84, 118

Natsume Sōseki: loss of home in, 63, 94; objects in, 81–82

Neo-Confucianism, 6, 52–53; and objects, 53, 79

Nishikawa Joken, 52

Nogami Yaeko, 8

Noma Hiroshi, 126

Nostalgia, 26, 98, 200*n*13; in *Flowing*, 103; and language, 122, 125, 133–134

Oates, Joyce Carol, 193*n*4, 202*n*13

Objects: in Neo-Confucianism, 53, 79; in Aya, 56, 57, 72, 76, 82, 121–122; transformation of, 57, 203*n*21; in Japanese literature, 72–73, 77, 79; in Mishima Yukio, 78; in literature, 78–79; in Sakaguchi Ango, 78–79; and modernity, 79; and gender, 79, 202*n*13; in Shimazaki Tōson, 80–81; in Ōe Kenzaburo, 126; in Natsume Sōseki, 201*n*5; in Suzanne Langer, 203*n*21; in Taki Kōji, 203*n*21;

Okuno Takeo, 7–8

Onomatopoetic language, 127, 131–132, 206*n*19

Pacific War (*1931–1945*), reactions to, 3, 58–62, 78–79, 151

Persona: creation of, 12–15, 24, 47, 116, 124–125, 135; and language of negativity, 46, 89, 98

Personal inadequacy, rhetoric of, 4, 6, 46, 89, 98, 193*n*4. *See also* Persona

Poirer, Richard, 194*n*9

Postwar economy, 105; housing in *1950s*, 115

Postwar literature, 21, 57–58, 59–62, 63, 64, 66; style, 126, 131; period-ization of, 199*n*12; and Eto Jun, 203*n*18

Ryūtei Tanehiko, 84

Saito Ryokū, 126
Sakaguchi Ango, 78–79
Sata Ineko, 10–11, 151
Sei Shōnagon, 206*n*18
Selfhood, in Aya, 12
Service, transformation of, 94, 105–
    107, 145, 148, 150. *See also* Domes-
    tic service, transformation of
Shiga Naoya, 10
Shikitei Sanba, 84
Shimao Toshio, 116
Shimazaki Tōson, 62, 94; and objects,
    80–81
Shitamachi (old downtown area of To-
    kyo), 76, 105, 203*n*3
"Social script" (Karl Joachim
    Weintraub), 194*n*7
Space: in Yasuoka Shōtarō, 67, 88; in
    Mishima Yukio, 67–68, 88, 126; in
    Japanese literature, 82–85; in Aya,
    82–88, 98, 115–116; in Nagai
    Kafu, 84; uses in literature, 84, 98,
    114, 115, 116, 150–151; and trans-
    formation, 106–109, 134; in
    Shimao Toshio, 116
Stephenson, Anne, 10
Stimpson, Catharine, 9
Style, in Japanese literature, 83–85,
    113; postwar, 126, 131
Symbolic inversion, 6, 204*n*4. *See also*
    Transformation; Women's language

Takeda Taijun, 65
Takeuchi Yoshimi, 63, 200*n*18
Taki Kōji, 84, 203*n*21
Tale of Genji, The (*Genji monogatari*;
    Murasaki Shikibu), 14–15, 39
Tale of Narayama (*Narayama bushiko*;
    Fukazawa Shichirō), 65, 66

Tamenaga Shunsui, 204*n*3
Tamura Taijirō, 78
Tanizaki Jun'ichirō, 65–66, 68
Tayama Katai, 63
Tradition: and language, 58, 125–127,
    131, 195*n*12, 206*n*16; and moder-
    nity, 62, 80, 115–116, 133. *See also*
    Cultural authority, in the *shitamachi*
Transformation: as literary strategy, 3,
    8, 16, 43, 94, 105–107, 193*n*2; of
    objects, 72–73, 80; of deprivation,
    98, 114; of war, 99; of clothing,
    108; and geisha, 108–110, 123; of
    space, 134; of feminine attributes,
    137; of service, 148, 150. *See also*
    Literary inversion
Trilling, Lionel, 79
Tsubouchi Shōyō, 6

Uemura Masahisa, 33

Walks, in Japanese literature, 120
Wharton, Edith, 10, 193*n*4
Women's community: in *Flowing,* 94;
    in literature, 204*n*2
Women's language, 123–126, 131–
    132, 195*n*12, 207*n*22; and moder-
    nity, 2; and onomatopoetic lan-
    guage, 131–132
Women's literature in Japan, 8–9, 10–
    11, 196*n*16, 197*n*22. *See also*
    Daughters, literary
Woolf, Virginia, 89
World War II. *See* Pacific War, reactions
    to

Yamamoto Kenkichi, 64
Yamazaki Ansai, 52
Yasuda Yojūrō, 62
Yasuoka Shōtarō, 67–68
Yoshida Kenko, 47, 99

Paul Schalow
May 23, 1997
New Brunswick, N.J.